BAC
ONE-ELEVEN

BAC
ONE-ELEVEN
THE WHOLE STORY

STEPHEN SKINNER

The
History
Press

Cover illustrations: *Front*: G-ASYD, BAC's multifarious test aircraft in its final guise as the 475 prototype. *(BAE Systems) Back*: PP-SDQ, a One-Eleven 520 of Sadia, later Trans-Brasil. *(BAE Systems)*

First published 2002 by Tempus Publishing Ltd
This new edition 2013

The History Press
The Mill, Brimscombe Port
Stroud, Gloucestershire, GL5 2QG
www.thehistorypress.co.uk

British Library Cataloguing in Publication Data.
A catalogue record for this book is available from the British Library.

ISBN 978 0 7524 9699 3

Typesetting and origination by The History Press
Printed in Great Britain

Contents

Acknowledgements

The idea of this book has long been in my mind and I have found it a stimulating project which has given me the enjoyable opportunity to meet and discuss the aircraft with many people who were involved with it.

I owe a debt of gratitude to a number of people not least John Prothero Thomas, former Marketing Director of BAC, who gave me access to his lecture 'Evolution of a Workhorse – the BAC One-Eleven' which I found of particular assistance in drawing together and writing the concluding chapter. Also to Chris King who, as a BAC Senior Flight Test Observer and later Chief Flight Test Engineer for BAe on the Tay One-Eleven, was a fund of information on many detailed matters of the flight testing. Chris introduced me to Bill Hurley, former Dee Howard Director of Flight Test and Certification, who provided information from the Dee Howard standpoint and lent me some of the photographs in this book. On the Tay One-Eleven I was also fortunate to make contact with Ken Goddard, author of *The Rolls-Royce Tay and the BAC One-Eleven*, with whom I had a number of helpful discussions.

My researches also drew me to the One-Eleven Test Pilots Roy Radford, John Lewis and Peter Baker, who kindly gave me their time and hospitality, the late Dave Glaser, and not forgetting Johnnie Walker (very much alive!) whom Chris King kindly introduced to my wife and I, and who regaled us with many funny stories.

I was fortunate to meet Rolando Ugolini who, as a very skilled designer, kindly drew illustrations of the aircraft, especially the unflown examples.

I would like to thank Ken Dyer, Commercial Manager of European Aviation, who generously arranged for two One-Eleven flight deck flights and gave me several hours of his time at Hurn Airport. Also Steve Costello, European Aviation's Simulator Engineer, who let me 'fly' the aircraft and just stopped me from crashing at 'Shannon'!

At the Brooklands Museum, Albert Kitchenside and Jack Fuller of the Technical Library gave me immense support, particularly on all the stillborn One-Eleven developments, as did their colleague Mike Goodall at the Museum's invaluable Photographic Archives. Heinz Vogel, former Chief Aerodynamicist on the One-Eleven, also filled in some areas which I needed to clarify with regard to the later developments during the 1970s. The team at Airbus One-Eleven Support at Filton answered questions pertaining to aircraft still in service.

Scott Harrison of the *Bournemouth Daily Echo*'s library allowed me access to their well-organised archives and photographs, which gave an interesting and significant local view on the aircraft and the Hurn factory.

Mike Phipp, author of *Bournemouth International Airport*, published by Tempus, helped me on many points as well as updating me on local One-Eleven movements.

I have been able to access a number of photographic archives which I have given credit to in the text and should like to acknowledge my gratitude to *Flight International* for allowing me to reproduce an article on 'Flying the One-Eleven' as Appendix 1.

Lastly I would like to pay tribute to all the editorial support and encouragement that my wife Jane has given throughout the writing of this book.

Preface

My enthusiasm for the BAC One-Eleven stems from the beginnings of my interest in aviation in 1963. I had the good fortune to grow up in Bournemouth not many miles from Hurn (now Bournemouth International) Airport where there was a selection of interesting aircraft movements including British United Heralds and Bristol Freighters, BEA Viscounts, Airwork Fleet Requirement Unit Seahawks and Meteors. But the most fascinating part of the airport to me was the Vickers-Armstrongs factory on the north side of the airport.

At the Vickers-Armstrongs factory (later re-badged as British Aircraft Corporation (Weybridge Division) Hurn), the last of the Viscounts were in production – to be replaced by the One-Eleven on the production line. From early August 1963, the One-Eleven prototype could be seen carrying out tests and running its engines. Then, as now, there was a very distinctive engine start noise, which I could even hear at my home some five miles distant. The weeks passed in anticipation and then, on 20 August, the maiden flight took place, which was the culmination of a very long and exciting day at Hurn. Yet only two months later the tragedy of the prototype's crash stunned the workers and executives at the manufacturers and in the locale. But the company recovered from this severe blow despite other setbacks delaying the test programme. Eventually completed, the One-Eleven was certified and entered service on 9 April 1965.

Eager to know and see more, I would visit the Hurn hangars at weekends to see the beautiful machines in production. From the drab factory, One-Elevens would emerge pristine in beautiful liveries for the airlines around the world, including Braniff, Mohawk, Aloha, American Airlines, Court Line and many others.

The remaining years of the 1960s were the main development phase of the aircraft, with the maiden flight of the stretched 500 series in 1967 followed by a rising curve of more and more deliveries and, three years later, the first flight of the 475 series – also from Hurn. Through all those years, and after, I kept notes and collected information, still visiting the factory regularly. By chance I even saw the first flight of the last production machine just prior to the Hurn factory's closure in 1984.

I had high hopes of the Tay re-engined One-Eleven and was glad to see an example demonstrated at Farnborough 1990, but was disappointed that this last chance to build on the strength of a fine British aircraft was soon to wither. One-Elevens soldiered on in diminishing numbers during the early years of the twenty-first century. Regrettably, hopes that the fiftieth anniversary of the One-Eleven's maiden flight on 20 August 1963 would be celebrated by a One-Eleven in flight failed to come to fruition as the last serviceable example, QinetiQ's ZH763 made its last flight on 26 April 2013 to the Classic Air Force Collection at Newquay.

1

The First Flight – Tuesday 20 August 1963

There was a feeling of eager anticipation in the air at Bournemouth (Hurn) Airport as crowds clustered by the roadside and around the factory waited for the first flight of the One-Eleven. It was a long wait during the warm, showery day. Shortly before 10.00 a.m., the third Viscount for Chinese Aviation (one of six of the last Viscounts built at Hurn), G-ASDS, flew to Luton to collect Hunting Aircraft executives who were to view the flight. At 10.30 a.m. the prototype, still in the flight shed, was weighed so that accurate calculations could be made for lift off and landing speeds, and two hours later she was handed over to the pilot.

For the occasion, Chief Test Pilot, BAC, Jock Bryce and Mike Lithgow, Deputy Chief Test Pilot for Vickers-Armstrongs Aircraft were to pilot it. Dick Wright and Tony Neve, Flight Test Observers, were also on board. But it was not until 2.00 p.m. that there was a slow-speed taxi run followed by a delay for the change of a brake unit. In the meantime, a Hunting Jet Provost, XR669, arrived from Luton piloted by 'Ollie' Oliver, ready to act as a chase plane during the first flight.

The dignitaries, amongst whom were Sir George Edwards and Air Marshal Sir Geoffrey Tuttle, respectively BAC Weybridge Managing Director and Vice-Chairman, Freddie Laker, Managing Director of British United Airways, the crowds and the press waited. The time was broken up by more showers and an aerobatic routine flown by Rolls-Royce's own Spitfire, G-ALGT. The afternoon had passed and still the crowds waited. Between 6.00 p.m. and 6.30 p.m. there were two high-speed taxi runs along runway 26 during which the nose was lifted and reverse thrust used for the first time. The One-Eleven then returned to the flight shed for fuelling while a snowplough drove up and down the main runway brushing off the large pools of water formed by the heavy showers.

Finally, in the early evening, the chase Jet Provost took off as the prototype G-ASHG positioned itself at runway 26. Then with that roar that was to become only too common to Hampshire's (later Dorset's) skies, Jock Bryce lifted it off into the calm, blue air and at 7.42 p.m. it was airborne after a run of approximately 3,150ft.

The first flight crew with the BAC One-Eleven prototype G-ASHG (c/n 004) at its roll out at Hurn on 28 July 1963. Left to right: Mike Lithgow, Deputy Chief Test Pilot, Vickers; Tony Neve; Dick Wright; Flight Test Observers: Jock Bryce, Chief Test Pilot, BAC. Both Mike Lithgow and Dick Wright lost their lives with the crash of the prototype on 22 October 1963. *(BAE SYSTEMS)*

The BAC plant at Hurn on 20 August 1963. The prototype BAC One-Eleven, G-ASHG (c/n 004), being towed into position prior to its maiden flight. On the left is one of the last Vickers Viscounts G-ASDS, which had made a return flight to Luton that morning to collect BAC staff from the former Hunting factory to watch the flight. *(BAE SYSTEMS)*

G-ASHG landing on runway 26 at 8.08 p.m. at Hurn Airport after a twenty-four-minute maiden flight on Tuesday 20 August 1963. Although painted in British United colours, 'SHG can be distinguished from the early BUA aircraft by the additional wording BAC on the tail and the painted registration almost hidden from view under the engine nacelles. *(BAE SYSTEMS)*

G-ASHG cruised at 220mph at 8,000ft in a westerly direction over to Yeovil with the undercarriage down, accompanied by the Jet Provost. At 8.00 p.m., as the light started to fade, it appeared in the Hurn circuit, the Jet Provost in formation on its left wing tip, and touched down at 8.08 p.m. As the sun set, the four crew disembarked by the BAC flight shed and were greeted by Sir George Edwards, waiting executives and factory workers. At the press conference Jock Bryce praised the aircraft and its ease of handling.

On that day the success of the project looked certain, with sixty orders on the books from major airlines in the United States, the UK and other parts of the world, while the only competitor, the Douglas DC-9, appeared to be lagging behind and was only in the early stages of development.

Over the next twenty-one years 235 One-Elevens were to be built in the UK and all but thirteen of them were assembled and made their first flights from Hurn. Between 1982 and 1989 nine more were assembled in Romania, making a grand total of 244.

2

The British Aircraft Corporation and the One-Eleven Project

The One-Eleven played a considerable role in the whole story of the British Aircraft Corporation itself. It was the only aircraft wholly designed and built by BAC and remained in production throughout the entire seventeen-year history of the organisation, reaching its sales peak when profits for the Corporation were at a low ebb.

The project was the first for the newly formed British Aircraft Corporation, which came into being in January 1960 when the Boards of Vickers-Armstrongs, English Electric and Bristol Aircraft agreed to set up of a joint company. BAC was to consist of their collective aircraft manufacturing companies while their non-aviation sections would remain wholly with the parent company. In May 1960, the first act of the new Corporation was to buy the aircraft interests of the Hunting Group. The reasons for the merger and acquisition were that the Government had been insistent that the large number of companies, which made up British aviation in the 1950s, could not continue and so amalgamations had to take place. As a result, by the end of 1960 there were only two major airframe manufacturers, BAC and Hawker Siddeley, and two major aero-engine manufacturers, Bristol Siddeley and Rolls-Royce.

BAC had a large number of aircraft in production and various projects under consideration. In 1960 there was uncertainty on the civil side for Viscount and Britannia production was coming to an end, while the Vanguard had been a major disappointment receiving only forty-three orders and making a loss of £17 million for Vickers-Armstrongs. The Vickers VC10, a long-haul jet, was in production but there was no new aircraft to replace the short-haul Viscount, where Vickers had established substantial market penetration and made sales of 436 aircraft.

A Long Gestation

As long ago as 1955, Hunting undertook a design study known as the P107, a four-abreast thirty-seater with two Bristol Orpheus engines, a moderately swept fin and

In 1955, Hunting undertook a design study known as the P107, a four-abreast thirty-seater with two Bristol Orpheus engines, a moderately swept fin and a cruciform tailplane. Hunting even registered the prototype as G-APOH in July 1958. *(Rolando Ugolini)*

a cruciform tailplane. The target price at £330,000 was cheaper than the Viscount 700. Hunting even registered the prototype as G-APOH in July 1958 and this was presumably forgotten about, for the registration was only cancelled in January 1964.

At the time of BAC's acquisition of Hunting, the project was appraised by the Vickers project team and believed to be a sound design. It had grown into an 80ft-long, five-abreast seater with two Bristol Siddeley BS75 engines of around 7,000lb thrust, a 500mph cruise speed, a range of 600 miles and a 'T' tail. This project was given the designation BAC107 and it was the intention for further design project work to be carried out by Hunting at Luton and by Bristol at Filton, with Vickers concentrating on the VC11 design which was a shorter-range version of the VC10. Hunting was to design and build the tail and wings, Bristol to design and build the front fuselage and also carry out final assembly. A system was set up to ensure that Vickers' civil turbine airliner experience, which because of the Viscount was by far the most relevant and extensive in the world, to be fed into the combined design efforts at Hunting and Bristol. Vickers' experience of the marketplace was used to conduct extensive surveys into the probable needs of the market, naturally concentrating on existing Viscount operators. Weybridge studies in early 1960 suggested a world market of 600 aircraft with eighty in the USA. The studies stressed the importance of maintaining a price below £500,000. The role of this small jet was seen as:

- A prestige aircraft where big jets would not operate effectively
- Able to offer increased service frequency at low cost on existing jet routes
- Operating in less developed countries where some important routes required jets, e.g. South America
- As a corporate aircraft

BAC carried out extensive surveys during late 1960 to test the market. Eighty-nine airlines were visited in all parts of the world and some sixty indicated interest in the project. Names such as Braniff, Eastern, Ozark, Aloha, Sabena, Aer Lingus, Trans-Australian Airlines and Ansett etc., were mentioned as good prospects. The feedback from these visits resulted in changes to the project which inevitably increased the weight and the All Up Weight (AUW), which went up from 48,500lb to 52,000lb. A 'double-bubble' cross section to accommodate more baggage was specified, as was a ventral door, and the early idea of a simple pneumatic system was abandoned. The BS75 engine was, however, beginning to puff rather badly and an 'overspeed' system to allow 7,550lb of thrust was being offered to maintain a reasonable airfield performance.

At this time the newly formed British United Airways (BUA) entered the field with a requirement for a jet Viscount 800 replacement capable of operating trooping runs to Malta, services to West, East and Central Africa and the burgeoning Inclusive tours market. The critical mission was Malta-Gatwick where the Viscount 833 could only carry 9,500lb of payload. Meanwhile in the USA, Braniff and Continental became immediate sales prospects and Braniff in particular required a genuine short haul 'bus stop jet' with the intention of operating extremely short sector distances with very rapid turn rounds, in contrast to the relatively long ranges required by BUA. The BUA specification led to increased design weights and the need for additional fuel, which was located in the centre section of the wing. Braniff on the other hand did not require a ventral stairway, as they would often expect to use the aircraft from a jetway, which BUA would not. So there were differing requirements that the BAC team had to satisfy.

In March 1961, the decision was made to concentrate on using the Rolls-Royce Spey and to take the engines and pods almost directly from the Trident. Testing of the Spey involved 14,000 hours on the bench plus 100 hours in a Vulcan. After the Trident flew in 1962, a flying test-bed became superfluous.

The BAC 107 was an 80ft, five-abreast seater with two Bristol Siddeley BS75 engines of around 7,000lb thrust, a 500mph cruise speed, and a range of 600 miles. Hunting was to design and build the tail and wings, Bristol to design and build the front fuselage and also carry out final assembly. *(Rolando Ugolini)*

The choice of the Spey was to be both a critical and a limiting factor in the aircraft's later development. In the 1960s, no British manufacturer would have chosen a foreign-made engine for a major project. All that was to change in years to come with the Rolls-Royce RB211 powering the Lockheed Tristar and Avco Lycomings for the BAe 146 (later RJ/RJX). Though there had been serious interest in a 'double-bubble' fuselage cross-section, BAC decided that a circular section was best.

It was on this basis that the project, as the BAC One-Eleven, was launched. This coincided with the rejection of the VC11 project by its most likely customers, and a decision in May 1961 by the BAC Board to go for the small jet. The Corporation set down an initial production batch of twenty aircraft and abandoned the more complex VC11 project. Fortunately, BAC managed to get the VC11's £9.75 million Government launch aid transferred to the new design. The design work was now centred on Vickers at Weybridge, with Hunting at Luton designing and manufacturing the wing and the tail design and manufacture being handled at Filton. The assembly line was planned for Hurn.

The Launch and the First Order

Freddie Laker and British United Airways were striving to make their mark as the largest British independent airline just as BAC was seeking customers if it was to proceed with the One-Eleven. Laker and Geoffrey Knight, then BAC's Marketing Director, were already good friends and eager to co-operate. Once the decision had been made in principle to purchase, then came a period of hard bargaining

The new order at Hurn. One of the last Viscounts, part of an order for six from China, alongside the fuselage of the first production One-Eleven for British United, G-ASJA. *(BAE SYSTEMS)*

over the performance and the price between two tough and well-seasoned businessmen. The final price was apparently agreed at Sandown races, a mere £740,000 per aircraft.

On 9 May 1961, BAC held a press conference to launch the new jet together with its first order for ten series 201s with options for five more from Freddie Laker's British United Airways. Quite a coup for a major British airliner to be launched with the announcement of an order from Britain's major independent airline, and not BEA or BOAC. The schedule was ambitious, with the first flight planned for the second quarter of 1963, certification by mid-1964 and deliveries to BUA that autumn. Sir George Edwards stated before the One-Eleven flew that BAC saw a market of 1,000 aircraft and that they would be happy with 40%, i.e. 400 similar to the Viscount's production, leaving a sizeable market to any other entrants. It is noteworthy that modern marketing methods were employed before production began; the market had been widely tested and uncovered a spectrum of requirements. The One-Eleven was not designed for a single customer, e.g. British United, unlike the manner in which the Trident and VC10 were respectively bespoke, tailored to BEA and BOAC needs. As a result this new jet had a far wider appeal from the outset.

At this point production of the smaller BAC 107 was still planned for the following year but at the end of 1961 the decision was taken to drop the project. With hindsight, this can be seen to be prudent when one considers the challenges that the One-Elevens were to present BAC.

BAC Scores an American First!

Both Ozark Airlines and Frontier Airlines placed early orders for the aircraft. However, in those days of over-regulation the US Civil Aeronautics Board (CAB) blocked the sales stating that the airlines would need Government subsidies to run jets. This appears to have been a protectionist ploy since both airlines later ordered American-built DC-9s without hindrance! No such obstacle was to stop the second customer, Braniff International of Dallas, Texas, which placed a firm order for six series 203s with options on six more on 20 October 1961, the first time a US airline had ordered a British airliner from the drawing board.

In March 1962, a mystery customer placed an order for eight, later increased to ten series 202s. In BAC publicity the order was always referred to as from an 'undisclosed customer' so it was understandable that people assumed it was an American airline anxious to avoid trouble with the CAB. But shortly after the first flight the order, which actually came from Western Airways, a Karachi-based organisation, was discreetly cancelled.

Mohawk, another American carrier, ordered four 204s on 24 July 1962 and though the CAB endeavoured to stop them, Mohawk persevered and succeeded in placing their order. Kuwait Airways ordered three and Central African Airways two on 26 September 1962. The orders were rolling in and there were no competitors. The One-Eleven owed its initial success in the American market because it was rightly seen as the first true short-haul jet. Others flying at that time, such as the Comet 4B or Caravelle, had none of the One-Eleven's quick turn-round facility. Both of these had the same narrow fuselage cross-section, a window provision that denied the flexibility of differing seating pitches, poor freight loading facilities and could not function independently of ground power.

In early 1963, Braniff firmed up its option on the second six aircraft and took out an option on two more while Aer Lingus, the Irish national airline, ordered four 208s on 3 May 1963 for delivery in 1965.

However, in April 1963 the One-Eleven no longer had the field to itself. The Americans had caught up and launched the ninety-seat DC-9-10, which was soon to pick up orders. Douglas had wisely chosen a slightly larger fuselage cross-section than BAC. A 'double-bubble' section, giving a slightly wider cabin and freight hold and two rear-mounted Pratt & Whitney JT8Ds powered the aircraft, which were heavier than the Spey but provided much more thrust. But Douglas was dismayed when the following month one of the USA's major airlines, American Airlines, made a surprising choice and selected the British product.

American Airlines and the 400 Series

Quite early in the design development history of the 200 series, American Airlines became interested in a new concept of short-haul operations. Up to this point air travel in the USA and Europe had been the preserve of the wealthy. Now, with the post-war prosperity and faster communications, transcontinental air travel was an affordable expedient and compared favourably with travelling overland.

Talks with American Airlines started at the Farnborough Show of 1960, became of serious technical interest in 1961 and virtually continuous technical/contractual negotiations then ensued until American placed an initial order for fifteen aircraft valued at more than £14 million on 17 July 1963. First delivery was scheduled for July 1965 with completion of the order by the end of that year. This was the first time one of the American 'big four' trunk operators had purchased a British aircraft, let alone off the drawing board. The *New York Times* comment was that the order assured the British aviation industry of a substantial lead in the production of short-haul jets.

Sir George Edwards put it succinctly when he said, 'American Airlines chose the British aeroplane because it does the job which they want done and because it is available at the right time. We decided to go ahead with the One-Eleven for British United Airways over two years ago because we believed in the aeroplane and its timing. Too often we have been blamed for being late. This important order has been won because we were early. The fact that we have sold 60 aircraft, 31 of them in the United States is a pretty good indication that we were right.'

Asked to comment on American's decision, a Douglas official said, 'We regret American Airlines has elected to buy an airplane built abroad and which we consider to be an inferior product to ours.'

Aeroplane magazine stated that American's decision was due to the technical merit of the One-Eleven, BAC's experience with short-haul aircraft, unrivalled outside the USA, and because the British jet would be in service two years before the Douglas DC-9. In reality much of this two-year lead was to be eroded.

The 400 Series

In May 1963, in preparation for the American Airlines order, BAC had announced two developments, the 300 and 400 series, which could carry heavier payloads over longer range. They were outwardly almost identical to the 200 series aircraft except for an additional cabin window at the front on each side, redesigned nose wheel doors and lift dumpers in addition to spoilers on the wings.

The 400 series required a very large number of changes, including higher design weights to give greater range, and were higher-powered with 11,400lb thrust Spey 25 Mk 511-14 engines instead of the 10,410lb of the 200 series. These larger Speys provided better airfield performance and the landing distance was improved by the incorporation of lift dumpers and the fitting of Hytrol anti-skid units to the brakes. These changes gave the necessary guaranteed airfield performance for the One-Eleven to be able to use La Guardia, New York's domestic airport.

The Question of Fitting Pratt & Whitney Engines

American Airlines carefully considered requesting BAC to exchange the Speys for de-rated versions of the Pratt & Whitney JT8D-5 engines as initially fitted to the DC 9-10. BAC produced two comparable specifications and contracts, one with each power unit, but American eventually decided to stay with the Rolls-Royce engines. Factors which undoubtedly affected this decision were that initial experience on the JT8 in their Boeing 727 was not encouraging, and the much heavier power plant caused significant weight increases, with the need to fit wing leading edge devices to keep the landing performance comparable.

American did, however, introduce 281 design changes into the aircraft, principally to include more sophisticated equipment, compatible with their own fleet. These improvements increased the operating weight when empty by over 2,500lb.

Interestingly, the Maximum Take Off Weight (MTOW) of the American Airlines aircraft was set at 78,000lb to give some leeway below the arbitrary '80,000lb rule' below which the Federal Aviation Administration (FAA) would certificate with two-crew at that time, because that was the MTOW of the DC4. The design was, however, capable of 87,000lb MTOW for which the FAA would have insisted on a three-pilot crew. Fortunately the FAA's 80,000lb two-crew ruling was abolished in 1966 and from that time the 300 series classification was dropped and only the 400 series classification used.

The 300 Series

As a result of the alteration in the FAA ruling and the redesignation of all higher weight aircraft as 400s, only a small number of 300s were built. Customers were Kuwait Airways (which leased them before delivery to British Eagle) and Laker Airways. The 300 series retained most of the original British ancillary items of the 200 series. The better performance, longer range and more sophisticated 400 series opened up a new market for BAC in Central America, the Philippines, Germany, Argentina and Brazil, and started the long association with Tarom of Romania.

The Planning of Production

With the go ahead in March 1961, the BAC board agreed to lay down a batch of twenty to include two non-flying test airframes.

The production was shared among four BAC factories; Hurn built the forward and mid-fuselage sections and carried out final assembly, Filton constructed the rear fuselage and tail, while Weybridge built the centre section, undercarriage and wing skins. Luton manufactured wings, ailerons and flaps but with the unfortunate closure of that site in December 1966, this work passed to Weybridge.

Hurn

Of 235 British-built One-Elevens, Hurn assembled 222 starting with the prototype G-ASHG in 1963 and ending with G-BLHD in 1984. Including Viscounts, this totals 501 turbine-engined airliners completed at Hurn. Parts were also made for the Romanian One-Elevens, of which twenty-two were to be assembled. In the event only nine ROMBAC One-Elevens were competed, with one 500 and one freight-door-equipped 475 left incomplete in 1992.

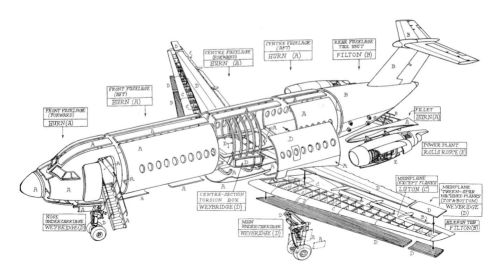

Design and production breakdown. Initially the wing mainplanes were built and assembled at Luton, but with the closure of the plant in 1966, this work passed to Weybridge. *(BAE SYSTEMS)*

The BAC factory at Hurn. First used as a temporary Flight test centre in 1951 while a runway was built at Wisley, Vickers-Armstrongs/BAC/BAe built 156 Varsities, 279 Viscounts and 222 One-Elevens and six Strikemasters at Hurn, a grand total of 663 aircraft. In the top left are the two assembly halls and in the lower left centre the Flight shed where completed aircraft were based during test flying. *(BAE SYSTEMS)*

The starting point for the Hurn factory was the need in 1951 for flight test facilities for the Valiant while a tarmac runway was laid at Wisley. Vickers took over hangars recently vacated by BOAC and based their Valiant and Viscount prototypes there briefly. Weybridge was then overloaded with work, so production of the piston-engined Varsity military-trainer was switched to Hurn where 156 were built.

Whereas prototypes and test aircraft flew from Hurn to Wisley and were based there for all experimental flight testing, production flight test was carried out from Hurn. Sometimes the period between first flight and delivery was as little as two days.

Weybridge-Built One-Elevens

Thirteen One-Elevens were assembled at Weybridge in two batches between 1966 and 1970. In early 1966 a production line was set up at Weybridge to allow Hurn to concentrate on the American Airlines' 401s and make up for the slack caused by the TSR2 cancellation. A batch of six aircraft was produced in 1966 starting with D-ABHH, an executive making its first flight in January. These machines flew from the short Weybridge runway to Wisley on their maiden flights.

G-ASHG, being rolled out of 107 hangar where it was assembled, painted in the colours of its first customer, British United Airways. It was the 277th turbine-engined airliner to be rolled out at the Hurn plant, since there had been 276 Viscounts before and there were still three more for China to come. *(BAE SYSTEMS)*

Throughout the 1960s, One-Elevens made frequent flights into Weybridge as well, especially development models for refurbishment to delivery standard. When British Eagle collapsed in late 1968, all its One-Elevens were flown into Weybridge and stayed there for some time. In 1969–1970 a second batch of seven more One-Elevens were completed there, ending with D-ANNO, a series 414, originally intended for TAE of Spain but sold before delivery to Bavaria Fluggesellschaft. On 19 December 1970 it made its first flight, which was the final first flight of an aircraft completed at this famous site. The last VC10, 5H-MOG, for East African Airways, had flown out in the previous February.

In the first years of production the plants turned out a great number of One-Elevens. Between 1965 and 1967, 100 were delivered and between 1968 and 1971 another 100. After that there was a considerable slowing in orders with only thirty-five delivered between 1972 and 1984.

The Roll Out of the Prototype

To honour British United's brave decision, the BAC-owned prototype, G-ASHG, a series 200, was painted in their blue and white colours and rolled out to great acclaim at Hurn on 28 July 1963. There was a large press presence, which praised BAC for what appeared to be a wonderful start to a programme, with sixty orders from eight airlines around the globe. This was a far better achievement than the other British civil jets then in production, the VC10 and the Trident.

3

A Technical Description of the Aircraft

The BAC One-Eleven is a twin turbine short-haul jet transport with rear-mounted engines and a 'T' tail configuration. It has a retractable tricycle undercarriage with hydraulically powered brakes and nose wheel steering. The aircraft utilises hydraulic power for flight controls, with the exception of the ailerons, which are operated by a cable and servo-tab arrangement. For the electrical system, two engine-driven generators supply power, together with an additional generator powered by the Auxiliary Power Unit (APU) mounted in the tail cone. Two Rolls-Royce Spey 512 turbofan engines power the aircraft, each rated at 10,410lb static thrust in the initial 200 series. Later series have higher-powered Speys.

Quick Turnaround

In its early days the One-Eleven was marketed as the 'bus stop jet', perhaps a throwback to the original BAC107 concept. With that in mind, BAC designed the

The first test fuselage (c/n 002) entering the water tank at Filton for pressurisation tests on 25 August 1963. This view clearly shows the freight hold doors and ventral stair apertures. *(BAE SYSTEMS)*

aircraft to be a big improvement on the successful Viscounts and Convairs in terms of turnaround time on the tarmac and to be as user-friendly as possible. To prevent delays caused by lack of ground equipment the airliner was made self-sufficient. Provision of an on-board Auxiliary Power Unit (APU) made ground power units superfluous. Airsteps, waist-high freight bays, fuelling and servicing points all located ergonomically. Refuelling would only take ten minutes.

Structure

The structure was based on the fail-safe concept. This meant that the failure of a single main structural member would not cause a collapse of the structure as a whole or reduce the strength below that required to sustain flight loads. That philosophy was applied universally to the aircraft. Flaps, fin and tailplane were conventional structures and the same was applied to the fuselage except that some machined frames were used, and two panels at the wing joint were machined from the solid.

Structural elements of the BAC One-Eleven had a proven corrosion-free track record. Wet assembly and other corrosion inhibitive techniques performed during build were comparable with standards achieved only in later years by other manufacturers, making this one of the 'cleanest' airframes among long-serving types.

During the complete BAC One-Eleven programme, for all series, no flight test data caused the primary structure to be strengthened from the original design. In fact, strain gauge and pressure plotting tests showed it to be, generally, marginally too strong. So there were regular announcements of increased operating weights resulting in improved payload and range.

Fuselage

The fuselage was fabricated using conventional semi-monocoque construction, comprising a stressed skin supported by frames and stringers. It was built in three sections; front, centre, and rear. The centre fuselage incorporated a torque box to which the wings were attached, and was sealed because of its function as a fuel tank. Entry door and window apertures, which would otherwise act as discontinuities in the fuselage structure, were reinforced using vertical posts and internal doublers. The rear fuselage, with the engine mounting frames and fin frames, was built as one unit with the fin and the tailplane mounted on the top of the fin.

Wings

The wings were of conventional torsion box design and were swept back and tapered. The wing was of triple spar configuration, having integrally machined stringers on upper and lower skin. The wing tip was fabricated from lighter gauge skin; the ribs gave the wing section its shape, and provided torsional rigidity to the structure. An integral fuel tank was formed in the wing and included a surge tank. The rear spar at the wing root provided a mounting point for the main landing gear. Further outboard, the rear spar also provided attachment points for flap track mounting brackets, spoiler hinge fittings and aileron mounting structure. Five ribs were bolted to the front spar, which formed part of the mounting arrangement for a detachable leading edge.

Static tests on a second test airframe (c/n 003) showed that structure had considerable reserves of strength. Failure of the wing occurred at 117% of the ultimate load allowing for increases in operating weights of the aircraft. The two pictures show the start of the test and just prior to failure, with the wing deflected by 6ft. *(BAE SYSTEMS)*

Systems Philosophy

The basic systems philosophy was to split each system into independent halves, each with its own power source. All systems were capable of operation from one-half system only, but in normal operation both halves were used simultaneously.

Fuel System

The integral fuel tanks were formed by sealing the main wing torsion box during manufacture. These two tanks had a capacity of 2,200 imperial gallons. The wing centre-section torsion box tank, holding 850 imperial gallons, was standard on all versions except the 200, for which it was an option. Additional tanks ranging from 350 to 1,332 imperial gallons were available, fitted in the rear of the forward freight hold.

All the fuel in the system was available to either engine or the APU. Single point fuelling was installed with an access point on the lower fuselage just below the forward section of the wing root. Most models were fitted with fuel jettison vents positioned on each wing trailing edge.

Hydraulics Systems

Hydraulic power was used to operate the landing gear, flaps, spoiler/airbrakes, tailplane trim, rudder, elevators, nose wheel steering, brakes, elevator and rudder artificial feel units, yaw damper, ventral/forward stairways and windscreen wipers.

There were two distinctly separate systems both operating with its own reservoir and should either of the engine-driven pumps fail, an auxiliary electrical pump would maintain the system. If a fault occurred there was no drill required, the crew only had to isolate the system. Items that control the airliner, e.g. elevators, rudder, etc. were independently operated by both systems. Other items were provided with adequate safeguards, for example if one hydraulics system was lost then the inboard spoilers would cease to function, but the outboard would remain in operation and vice versa. Likewise the landing gear was designed to free fall and lockdown in the event of loss of hydraulics, and the braking systems had accumulators to halt the aircraft in the most adverse conditions.

Electrical Systems

The aircraft employed a constant frequency a.c. system supplied by two generators driven by engine-mounted constant speed drive and starter units. In addition a third generator, shaft-driven by the APU and identical to the engine-driven channels, was provided for use when the aircraft was on the ground. The system was designed to give priority to the engine-driven generator. The APU generating channel and the external supply channel automatically disconnected when either one or both engine-driven generators were operating. Similarly the external supply channel disconnected when the APU generating channel was in use.

From its inception, the aim of the design was that no single fault could cause permanent loss of both generating channels. Ground a.c. power was derived either from the APU-driven generator or from an external source, through an external supply socket on the left side of the aircraft nose. The aircraft was provided with two lead-acid batteries for starting the APU and for providing stand-by power under extreme emergency conditions. A static inverter, operated from the d.c. essential bus-bar, was used to supply selected loads when no generated power was available. In the event of complete loss of a.c. power all essential services were provided for forty-five minutes.

Air-Conditioning and De-Icing Systems

There were two independent pressurisation and air-conditioning systems, one supplying the flight deck and the other the cabin. Engine warm air was used to de-ice the wings, tail and power plant intakes.

Oxygen Systems

One-Elevens were all fitted with two oxygen systems, one for the flight deck and one for the cabin. Some of the aircraft were fitted with drop down emergency passenger oxygen masks at time of manufacture and all those remaining in service in later years were modified to have them.

Landing Gear

The BAC Weybridge-designed landing gear, fabricated from ninety tons of steel, was of tricycle configuration, having a two-wheel nose gear and a pair of single axle two-wheel main gears. When retracted, the nose undercarriage was retained by a mechanical uplock. The main landing gears utilised the large inner doors for stowage retention, the doors engaging uplocks when closed. The doors were hydraulically sequenced to open and allow landing gear extension and retraction, and to close in order to aerodynamically fair the landing gear bay. Landing gear retraction time was approximately eight seconds plus a further two seconds required for the main undercarriage doors closing. A 'free fall' system allowed the landing gear to be lowered in an emergency, and provided a means of accessing the landing gear bays for servicing on the ground. One-Elevens were often seen with these doors open during servicing. Where the 200, 400 and 500 series had essentially the same 12in-wide main wheels and tyres upgraded in line with the higher weights required, the final major series of the type, the 475, had 16in-wide main wheel tyres.

Hydraulic brakes were installed on each main wheel. The braking system incorporated dual redundancy, an anti-skid system, and a parking brake facility. The aircraft was steered on the ground by means of a pair of hydraulic actuators, which could move the nose wheel seventy-eight degrees either side of neutral, when controlled by a hand wheel in the cockpit. When operated by the rudder pedals, it provided only seven degrees either side of neutral.

Flight Deck

Pilot influence was exerted by a project pilot team on the design of the One-Eleven from conception. As a result the flight deck benefited from many examples of then contemporary innovation, for instance, vision was enhanced by some of the largest windows and narrowest pillars of any airliner then flying. The One-Eleven was the first airliner whose flight deck vision was better than FAA recommendations. Simplicity of layout was combined with conventional positioning of vital instruments and systems for two-pilot operation. All controls were within easy reach of both pilots. Weather

The wing of G-ASYD, (c/n 053) showing the two spoilers on the outer part of each wing and the inboard lift dumpers fitted to all but the 200 series. The spoilers operated differentially with the ailerons to assist in roll control and together to brake the aircraft during landing. The lift dumpers acted only on landing. This photo shows the later, longer flap track fairings as fitted to the 475 and 500 series and the fuel jettison pipe. The black cheat line and chequer board were to assist in camera focussing during performance tests. *(BAE SYSTEMS)*

radar presentation and nose wheel steering control were provided for each pilot. Vital systems were on the centre panel, subsidiary systems being in the roof panel. Blind flying panels were built around the Collins Flight System in an uncluttered 'T' layout. Above each panel were master warning lights. As usual, engine instruments were centrally placed with space on either side for hydraulic, fuel and pressurisation systems. A neat pedestal embodied throttles, h.p. cocks, speed brakes, flaps and conventional trimmers with autopilot and radio controls operable by either pilot. So at no stage in flight should either pilot be required to leave his seat to deal with an emergency.

The split-system philosophy considerably reduced the number and complexity of emergency drills to be carried out by making automatic use of the full performance of the remaining systems. In addition, the number of controls and indicators on the flight deck was significantly reduced compared with then contemporary aircraft. There was no requirement for a third flight crew member as on the Trident and Boeing 727, and design was not compromised in order to omit a third crew member.

Colour styling was extended from the passenger cabin to the flight deck which, as a result, was attractive as well as workmanlike. Stowage was provided for hats, coats, flight bags and airways charts. A lockable folding door separated the flight deck from the passenger cabin. The British Air Registration Board (now CAA) and the US Federal Aviation Administration approved the flight deck.

Flying Controls

Primary flight controls on the BAC One-Eleven consisted of servo-tab-operated ailerons, a hydraulically powered rudder, and a pair of hydraulically powered elevators. Secondary controls included a variable incidence tailplane, spoilers, lift dumpers (on all but the 200 series), and trailing edge flaps. Built-in redundancy ensured that control was retained in the event of a failure, and the hydraulically powered rudder and elevator systems were operated via mechanical linkages should hydraulic pressure be lost. The flight control system was provided with stall warning and protection, and incorporated artificial feel in the pitch and yaw axes.

Passenger Cabin

The passenger accommodation was designed for genuine flexibility in operation, so precise furnishing scheme layouts, position of galleys and associated matters varied from airline to airline. Consequently, should a customer wish to alter the cabin arrangements to suit a particular form of operation, or to impose an individual airline 'personality' on the interior, the job could be done relatively simply. Toilets, galley units and other amenities were located at either end of the parallel-sided passenger cabin, in which seats and passenger service units and a divider bulkhead could be adjusted fore and aft.

The standard aircraft initially provided accommodation for sixty-five passengers, sixteen first class, four-abreast, and forty-nine tourist class five-abreast, the movable bulkhead dividing the tourist and first class compartments. Fixed fittings and furnishings permit maximum versatility and convertibility of interior layouts from the standard version. The structural design of the floor allows seat pitch to be reduced to as low as 29in and customers often required the short fuselage 200/400/475 series to be flown in all tourist eighty-four to eighty-nine seat layouts and the longer 500s in 109 or even 119 passenger arrangements. Seat attachment rails in 15ft lengths were provided throughout the passenger compartment for easy and rapid installation of seat units, which were capable of a wide range fore-and-aft adjustment in 1in increments.

The covering and trimming of the interior of the cabin made use of acrylic painted surfaces, plastic and upholstery fabrics and plastic formings. Below the level

A typical five-abreast passenger cabin layout is illustrated here. Cabins were initially fitted with luggage racks but in 1977 'wide-body look' interiors with lockers were introduced for new build aircraft and as retro-fit on existing fleets. *(BAE SYSTEMS)*

of the hat rack, cabin interior trim was made up of plastic mouldings which were replaceable and extremely easy to clean.

There were twenty-four elliptical windows on each side of the fuselage of the early 200 series; later 200/300/400/475 series all had an additional window forward. The 500 series machines had thirty-three windows. Each window was 14in high by 9in wide. The window pitch was 20in. All passenger windows had three panes. Either of the two outer structural panes could carry the full pressure differential but normally only the outer one carried the load. The third pane was for scratch protection inside the cabin and, if damaged, could be easily and quickly changed, independently of the window itself. Variable-position blinds were fitted to each window.

Flush-mounted passenger service units, which incorporated individual reading lamps, cold air outlets and cabin attendant call buttons, were fitted to the underside of the overhead hat racks, convenient to each passenger. These units could be moved fore and aft to suit the individual seat layout. In later years of service a 'wide-body look' cabin ceiling and lockers with openable doors replaced these.

Two pressurised freight compartments were located under the cabin with doors on the right of the aircraft, each easily accessible by waist-high doors. Unusually these doors open outwards on a hinged carrier and swung down outside the fuselage with the carrier forming a loading lop. On the longer fuselage 500 series the freight compartments were larger but means of access remained the same.

Luggage being loaded into the rear cargo bay. The cargo door swung down to the outside relatively unusual in aircraft design. Note the stub wing fitting for the Rolls-Royce Spey engine. *(BAE SYSTEMS)*

Ventral stairs were fitted to almost all versions of the One-Eleven. These retracted into the space upwards with the bottom-most two steps rotating onto the body of the stairs during retraction. *(BAE SYSTEMS)*

Airsteps and Doors

There were two passenger doors on the aircraft; one forward of the passenger cabin on the left side, the other was in the rear pressure bulkhead and approached through a ventral entry with built-in hydraulically operated airsteps which were fitted to most aircraft, though not, for instance, Braniff's 203s. Airsteps were also fitted to the forward passenger entrance and installed in all models except BUA's 201s and BEA's 510s. The forward airsteps were supported at the doorway by rollers fitted to the aircraft structure which acted as the fulcrum upon which the steps were lowered and raised and which also supported the steps as they moved in and out. The handrails and stanchions folded flat on the outer side of the step side beams when the steps were retracted. The steps were retracted hydraulically and lowered mechanically into a sealed sheath beneath the cabin floor and did not obstruct the use of jetways and other airport installations. The galley service door was on the right-hand-side of the fuselage and opposite the forward passenger entrance. The front passenger entrance and galley door opposite, which were openable from

G-ASHG in flight during its short test flying career from 20 August to 22 October 1963. *(BAE SYSTEMS)*

inside and out, were a plug fit (i.e. pressurisation loads were carried by the doorframe pressing on to the fuselage structure and not by a series of bolts). The forward doors opened outwards on a parallel linkage and were fitted with an automatic lock to prevent them blowing in the wind. The rear cabin door opened into a recess so that it did not obstruct the passageway from the ventral stairway to the cabin when open.

All short-fuselage versions, except for two of the 408s built for Channel Airways, had one emergency overwing exit on each side of the cabin over the wing. These two 408s and all 500 series were fitted with two overwing emergency exits per side. Flight crew could escape by using ropes through the openable windows on the flight deck. Most of the 475 and 500 series were fitted with inflatable slides, as were some of the 400s. Other types had only non-inflatable slides on delivery.

Engines

The lower-powered Mk 505-14 engine was used on 'SHG and initially on 'SJA and on 'SJB. Later the Spey Mk 506-14AW was fitted and used for all the flight testing. Essentially the Spey Mk 506-14AW was an uprated 505-14 and ran hotter than subsequent marks of Spey; the 'A' denoted a small turbine and 'W' denoted water injection. It went into service on the BUA and Helmut Horten's executive aircraft only.

The remaining 200 series aircraft all had the Spey Mk 506-14 of 10,410lb nominal sea level static thrust, each with the larger turbine, and those fitted with water injection were designated as the Mk 506-14W. The engine and pod installation was generally similar to the side pod installation of the Trident and therefore came to the One-Eleven with a good background of flight experience. The Spey 25 Mark 511-14 engine in the One-Eleven 300 and 400 models (and the Zambia Airways 207s and RAAF 217s) was more powerful at 11,400lb. Even more power was needed for BEA's heavier 510s which were powered by 12,000lb thrust Speys, while the later 500s and 475s had Spey 25 Mark 512-14DWs of 12,550lb.

Specific fuel consumption was 0.783lb/hour/lb payload at Mach 0.78 at 25,000ft. Response to slam acceleration was good, power being obtained in two seconds from the approach conditions. Engine accessories were grouped on the underside of the engine for accessibility. Starting was by a low-pressure air starter supplied by the APU or external supply.

Speys in some 200s, 400s and all 475s and 500s were fitted with Water Injection, whereby de-mineralised water was sprayed into the combustion chambers during take-off at hot or high airfields. This enabled the maximum take-off power to be maintained by increasing the engine rpm but keeping within turbine temperature limits. Use of this system ceased during the later years of operation.

Thrust reversers, which were fitted to all versions, had internal clamshell doors which when selected swung into the engine sealing the jet pipe, deflecting the flow through exhaust cascades above and below the engines. In the event of fire there was a two shot extinguisher system.

A close up of the Rolls-Royce Spey engine nacelle and APU exhaust in the extreme tail of D-ALAS (c/n 208) for Paninternational. The provision of the APU gave the One-Eleven independence from ground power units previously needed to provide power for systems when the engines are not running. *(Author)*

Spey Hush Kit

Hush kits were fitted as standard to all aircraft built from 1976 onwards and the greater majority of the earlier machines had them fitted. This was designed to enable all series of the aircraft to meet the Stage 2 noise regulations.

These alterations comprised a new reworked lining fitted to the nose cowling to reduce forward compressor noise, a new jet pipe to reduce rearward compressor noise in an extended 6ft rear nacelle cowling, a six-chute silencer nozzle to reduce tailpipe noise, and complementary modifications affecting the stub wing.

There was an appreciable performance penalty for 400/475/500 (200s in brackets):

- Increased empty weight by 295lb (329lb)
- Cruise fuel consumption increase 1.7%
- Static take-off thrust loss 0.25% (0.5%)
- CG affected by 2% SMC (Standard Mean Chord)

In 1976, BAC and Rolls-Royce charged £103,725 for the fitting of hush kits to each aircraft.

Auxiliary Power Unit

An Auxiliary Power Unit provided air for conditioning for the cabin, and engine starting and power for systems. This APU built by Garrett AiResearch was a small on-board gas turbine easily started by a press-button on the flight deck. The APU was tested in a rig at Weybridge using the rear fuselage of the scrapped prototype Viscount 700, G-AMAV. When on the ground One-Elevens were almost always found with the APU running providing power, so ground power equipment was unusual. This is a common feature on all commercial aircraft now – but the British jet was the innovator.

Maintenance

Accessibility of systems and airframe equipment and ease of maintenance were given particular attention in the engineering of the One-Eleven. The guiding principles were that no maintenance task should take more than eight hours, that it must be possible to remove one system without disconnecting another, and that it must not be necessary to remove one component to gain access to another.

Tasks were facilitated by having the systems equipment based in separate bays. Much of the work could be achieved without platforms or steps. Using the engineering mock up at Hurn, a special exercise was made to evaluate removal and refit times for equipment.

Ground Testing

BAC's worldwide operating experience via the Viscount, Vanguard, VC10 and Britannia (something Hunting had been rather short of) enabled it to lay down a realistic test programme for the new aircraft. These tests were driven by Sir George Edwards' comment that he had often heard that an aircraft was delayed because of some faulty, minor, inexpensive piece of equipment.

As a short-haul jet, the average flight time of the One-Eleven might be no more than forty-five minutes, which meant that the structure had to be designed for a minimum crack-free life of at least 30,000 hours of 40,000 cycles. The comprehensive test programme went well beyond that figure and the structure was tested to 100,000

A full-scale hydraulic and flying control rig was constructed at Weybridge to assess the operating of the systems. For example, on the left 'wing' the spoilers can be seen extended and the right main 'undercarriage' is also visible. *(BAE SYSTEMS)*

flights or 85,000 flying hours. The second fuselage to be built was used for structural testing and was transferred to Filton from Hurn on 1 February 1963. After pressure tests, wings were added and underwent static strength tests covering all major design cases, followed by tests to demonstrate fail-safe features. The remainder of this airframe, comprising the tail fuselage, engine mountings and fin, were tested separately in a similar manner. Wing bending loads were applied to the centre section simultaneously with the application of fuselage pressure loads. Failure of the wing occurred at 117% of ultimate load.

To complement this series of tests, a further complete fuselage and wing centre section (the sixth airframe built) was used for fatigue testing at Filton, during which flight loads were simulated while the fuselage was pressurised in a water tank. The first phase, equivalent to 30,000 flights or cycles, was completed prior to the prototype first flight and, with the addition of wings in October 1964, a further 70,000 cycles were completed. BAC's initial aim was that the primary structure should be free of any major defect for at least 40,000 flights. Later the structure was cleared to 85,000 hours on the 200, 400 and 500 series while the 475 was only ever cleared to 50,000 hours. The highest time an aircraft reached at May 2002 was almost 80,000 cycles (i.e. take-offs and landings).

Large bird impact tests were also inflicted on the tail unit and a main wheel burst inside the wheel bay. Both tests proved the survivability of the airframe to such extreme incidents. Exhaustive tests took place on the landing gear to represent 240,000 flights, including retraction, extension, landing and taxiing loads.

An equally comprehensive programme of system tests matched the sequence of tests to prove structural integrity. A full-scale hydraulic and flying control rig was constructed at Weybridge to assess the operating of the systems. Hurn produced a complete wooden engineering mock-up to check the fit of all the parts together, plus a complete electrical loom. There were systems mock-ups at each appropriate site and Weybridge accommodated the customer mock-up. So BAC were making absolutely sure that when in service nothing would fault the One-Eleven!

4

The Challenging Flight Test Programme

After successfully making her maiden flight, G-ASHG made just four more from Hurn before positioning to the BAC Flight Test Centre at Wisley, Surrey, in August 1963. Situated just three miles from Vickers' main production site at Brooklands in Weybridge, Wisley had space for a decent runway of 6,700ft, almost twice the Brooklands' runway length. As a result, Weybridge-built aircraft made the first flights to Wisley and their production test flying was flown from there.

Wisley's main function was experimental flight testing and from the end of the Second World War the test programmes of the main Vickers types had all been flown

The first One-Eleven, G-ASHG at the Wisley Flight Test Centre. G-ARVF, the sixth VC10 for BOAC is taxiing out to take off and the tail of the last Vanguard, CF-TKW, for Trans-Canada Airlines is protruding from the hangar. *(BAE SYSTEMS)*

The tragic scene at Cratt Hill, Chicklade, in Wiltshire, where the prototype One-Eleven G-ASHG crashed on 22 October 1963 killing all seven crew after entering a deep stall from which recovery was not possible. It had descended at 10,000ft per minute in a flat attitude and on impact only moved forward 70ft. *(The Times)*

from there: the Viking, Valetta, Varsity, Viscount, Valiant, Scimitar, Vanguard, VC10 and Super VC10, an impressive list of antecedents for the One-Eleven. Sad to say, the One-Eleven programme was the last to be flown from Wisley as the site closed on 14 April 1972 and the hangers were demolished. In the late 1960s and early 1970s, the majority of the flight test team had relocated to Fairford, Gloucestershire, for the complex and lengthy Concorde programme. However, the runway and apron are still very much in existence and serve as a reminder of its former importance to the UK civil and military aircraft industry.

The Initial Flight Test Programme

Over the next two months (September–October 1963) the bulk of the flying was handled by Jock Bryce and Mike Lithgow, who made a preliminary assessment of the One-Eleven. The test programme set off at a cracking pace with G-ASHG making fifty-three flights of eighty-one hours in sixty-three days. The first phase of the flight programme had been devoted to a preliminary assessment of the systems and general engineering, measurements of performance together with handling characteristics. 'SHG also flew to Luton on a special demonstration flight to Hunting Aircraft employees who had played such a part in the original concept and were manufacturing the wings.

22 October 1963

On 22 October 1963, G-ASHG took off from Wisley at 10.17 a.m. on that fateful morning, crewed by Mike Lithgow, Dick Rymer (co-pilot), R. Wright, G. Poulter, D. Clark, (flight test observers) B. Prior, (Assistant Chief Aerodynamicist), and C. Webb (Assistant Chief Designer). But just twenty-three minutes later at 10.40 a.m. it crashed and exploded at Cratt Hill, Chicklade in Wiltshire, killing all seven crew. Very shortly afterwards the news broke at Wisley. Brian Trubshaw, Jock Bryce and Mike Crisp, Flight Test Manager, and others immediately set out to inform the families of those killed before flying to Boscombe Down and then on to the crash site.

The Prototype's Final Flight

The British Civil Airworthiness Requirements demands that any aircraft must pitch down at the stall and easily recover normal flying altitude without too great a loss of height. The One-Eleven had entered a stall from which it was unable to recover.

G-ASHG had previously carried out a number of stalls, the first on flight 47. On flight 53, the final flight, it had already executed four stalls before entering a fifth at 15,000 to 16,000ft, which resulted in the crash. Information extracted from the two flight recorders (called 'black boxes' by the press) showed that at the stall, the loss of lift was large and abrupt, causing downward acceleration and a rapid increase in incidence (i.e. the angle of attack of the aircraft to the airflow).

A condition rapidly developed in which it would be impossible for a pilot of even Lithgow's calibre to appreciate the situation sufficiently quickly and therefore prevent further build up in incidence. As the incidence increased owing to downward acceleration, the elevator started to trail up. Lithgow arrested this and partial down elevator was applied some three seconds after the stall, but the aircraft response was too slow to stop the angle of incidence increasing. The result was that the elevator power was then insufficient to manoeuvre the aircraft nose downwards and out of the stall.

Ultimately, the effectiveness of the tailplane and elevator was reduced to a fraction of the normal value. At this incidence the elevator servo-tab power was insufficient to stop the elevator trailing up. As the One-Eleven descended at 10,000ft per minute the pilots maintained a massive 100lb push force on the elevators, but to no avail.

Another photo of the wreckage of G-ASHG at Cratt Hill, Chicklade, Wiltshire. Nearest to the camera is the front passenger door; behind it is the tail and the left Spey engine. *(via Mike Phipp)*

Lithgow tried banking the aircraft into a sideslip and increased power but G-ASHG was in a stable stall from which recovery was not possible.

The prototype did have two customised emergency exits, one in place of the rear ventral stairs, and one in place of the forward freight door (see Appendix 9). The latter door was held in place by explosive bolts which, when fired, would fall away and a chute would slip down to cabin floor level jutting out into the slipstream below the aircraft, allowing the crew to escape. As the prototype neared the ground, at probably only a few hundred feet from it, a sharp explosion was heard by the onlookers, indicating that some late attempt was made to escape. Tragically no one managed to escape and all seven crew were killed by ground impact. In fact, the forward freight door escape hatch was found inverted and out of place in the wreckage, which indicates an attempt was made. After impact with the ground, the One-Eleven slid forward only 70ft along the ground and then exploded and caught fire almost immediately. The conflagration was so severe that most of the aircraft was burnt out except for the tail and the extremes of the wings.

The Causes of the Crash

Why had this happened? The AAIB (Aircraft Accident Investigation Branch) Report into the accident concludes that a weakness of the design was the functioning of the

The forward escape hatch fitted to the prototype, some early test aircraft and the BAC development aircraft G-ASYD, provided an exit through the forward freight hold. This view of G-ASYD shows the explosive bolts around the forward freight door surround which could be detonated to jettison the door and allow a blast shield to slide down into the slipstream to facilitate escape. *(Author)*

elevators, which were aerodynamically operated by servo-tabs. This meant that if the pilot wanted the machine to nose down he would push the control column forward, which would activate the servo-tab upwards, the aerodynamic effect of which would move the elevator down. This servo-tab operation had proved insufficient in the stall to rotate the aircraft down and out of the stall.

The report also expressed that:

- BAC had experience of the stalling problems of T-tail aircraft and had adopted a more gradual process for the VC10 stalling programme.
- There was no anti-spin parachute fitted, which might have saved it (and which the Ministry of Defence insisted on for military aircraft testing).
- The pilots had been given insufficient information on the stalling characteristics of the One-Eleven. They believed that an increase in incidence would be preceded by a visible pitch-up warning them. In fact there was no pitch-up in this configuration, incidence increased until the point where the aircraft was locked into a stall and the elevators were useless.

- The incidence meter specially fitted on the flight deck only read to twenty-five degrees and it would have been prudent to fit one that registered higher incidences.
- Emergency escape procedures were not laid down or practised.

The BAC Remedy

In their statement about the crash on 4 November 1963, BAC stated that there would be 'alterations to the wing leading edge to improve the nose-down pitching characteristics and modification to the elevator linkage to permit a more direct mechanical linkage between the pilot's control and the elevator'. For the next nine months the only stalls tested were in the wind tunnels, with 1/10th scale free-flight replicas dropped from helicopters at 3,000ft, with computers or in a flight simulator.

In an attempt to restore confidence, BAC stated that the next four aircraft would now be used in the test programme. In an upbeat note, the Corporation said that it was still confident of deliveries taking place to British United Airways and Braniff Airways in the last quarter of 1964.

One of the stalling test models. For nine months after the crash of G-ASHG the only stalls carried out were on models or in the simulator. *(Author)*

Re-starting the Test Programme

With the loss of G-ASHG and the shock to all those involved, the test programme came to a temporary halt since there were no One-Elevens in the air. After much debate at the highest level about fitting a tail parachute, the decision was made to resume the testing as soon as possible, so no major modifications were made to the second aircraft on the production line. The alterations would come later.

There was a two-month gap before the first production aircraft, G-ASJA, fitted with escape hatches like the prototype, took to the air from Hurn on 19 December 1963. It was a freezing cold, beautiful, bright day with only a few onlookers, as BAC had invited the press to hospitality at a local public house, the New Queen Inn at Avon. In fact BAC had laid on such lavish hospitality that only three of the journalists accepted the offer of transport to Hurn to watch the flight. So concerned were the BAC Public Relations Department that they even refused to name the crew. So when the unnamed crew, actually BAC Chief Test Pilot Jock Bryce, accompanied by Dave Glaser, Hurn's Chief Production Test Pilot, took it down runway 08 for one slow taxi, a fast nose-raising taxi run and then a powerful take-off, there were few watching. The programme was back on! G-ASJA landed back at Hurn and left for Wisley in January.

First production aircraft, G-ASJA (c/n 005) taking off from runway 10 at Wisley in January 1964. Just visible is the initial tail parachute fitting below the APU in the tail. *(BAE SYSTEMS)*

G-ASJA was tasked with systems development and in early January 1964 was fitted with an anti-spin parachute in a small fairing under the APU (Auxiliary Power Unit) in the tail as designed for the prototype but not fitted. On flight 5 (16 January) the parachute was streamed on landing as part of the Flight Test commissioning process for the aircraft. Since 'SJA did not do any stall development or certification testing this was the only occasion it used a tail parachute. Then on 14 February, G-ASJB, the second production aircraft, made its first flight, joining 'SJA at Wisley. G-ASJB was scheduled to undertake performance and crew training and did not have the emergency escape hatch fitted through the freight hold owing to the low-risk nature of testing, but did have an escape hatch instead of the rear stairs. Two weeks later, 'SJB flew with a trial installation of the new wing leading edge, designed to give a more pronounced nose down pitch at the stall. The wing fences and all other features remained unchanged. Both aircraft were fitted with tail parachutes at this time but these were deemed insufficient for stalling trials protection and were there only as a stopgap. In fact after a short time these

A close up of the tail parachute fitting on G-ASJA. This was soon removed after it was realised that this parachute might become entangled with the tail if deployed so a larger parachute on a longer lead was needed. Note the emergency escape hatch fitted into the ventral stairs panel. Above the registration is the APU intake. *(BAE SYSTEMS)*

were removed because if deployed in flight there was a risk they might become entangled with the tailplane.

To complicate aspects of emergency protection, on 31 December 1963 G-ARTA, the prototype VC10, was flying on stall tests piloted by Brian Trubshaw when one of the elevator brackets broke causing serious flutter and a very dangerous situation. So, Trubshaw jettisoned the escape hatch. However, after the freight door had been jettisoned, the chute just fell away rather than staying in position to allow slipstream protection for the crew as they bailed out. As the One-Eleven chute followed the same pattern it was clear it had to be redesigned and trialled. (See Appendix 9).

Roland Beamont's and other Pilots' Assessments of the Aircraft's Handling

With the loss of Mike Lithgow and Dick Rymer, and with Jock Bryce failing his medical for flying, BAC was temporarily short of test pilots. So Roland Beamont, Chief Test Pilot of English Electric and Deputy Chief Test Pilot of BAC, decided to

Left to right, first production Standard VC10, G-ARVA, first and second production One-Elevens, G-ASJA and G-ASJB (c/n 006) at Wisley. The short-lived 'SJB was fitted with the revised wooden leading edge glued to the original metal version. *(BAE SYSTEMS)*

visit Wisley to see how the One-Eleven testing was progressing. He was concerned with what he defined as 'controllability problems' and on 6 March 1964 he flew G-ASJB with Brian Trubshaw, who had just been put in charge of the One-Eleven programme. Beamont had been very impressed with the VC10 but had a very different view of the One-Eleven, complaining that the pitch and speed control left much to be desired, to the extent that he thought there might be another accident. Other pilots agreed with him.

In an interview with the author, Dave Glaser, former Chief Production Test Pilot at Hurn, said how unpleasant he found flying the One-Eleven with its original elevator control. He flew G-ASHG on flight 5 with Bryce and Lithgow and like Beamont found control very difficult on approach – he bounced it badly on landing. Likewise in his autobiography Brian Trubshaw was critical of the handling of original elevator control. Roy Radford remarked that only shortly after being recruited onto the flight test team at Wisley he was asked to land one of the early aircraft with the servo-tab elevator and also found it difficult owing to the amount of lag between control input and response. Johnnie Walker, another experienced test pilot, commented on the half-second lag with the servo-tab arrangement, which made for difficult landings in turbulence or wind shear conditions. This problem was not alleviated by the initial tendency for the main wheels to shimmy, temporarily fixed by adding 60lb weights to each main wheel and eventually solved by reversal of the wheel assembly.

G-ASJB's Heavy Landing

On 18 March 1964, at 10.46 a.m., G-ASJB took off on a performance check and pilot conversion flight. It was its twentieth flight, with a crew of five piloted by 'Dinty' Moores and Staff Harris. Some two and a half hours later, Staff Harris moved into the left-hand seat to carry out a landing. On approach the aircraft descended a little below the normal approach path, the touchdown was earlier than the pilot had anticipated, and it bounced 20ft which was followed by a second heavier touchdown, nose wheel first, after which it bounced to about 50ft. The aircraft then struck the runway very heavily in a nose-down attitude and the landing gear collapsed, the nose and right undercarriage breaking away from the aircraft. The damaged aircraft, with only the left main undercarriage in place, then slid more than 1,000ft along the Wisley runway in a westerly direction, turning through little short of 180°, and came to a halt with the rear fuselage severely damaged and the left engine almost severed from the fuselage. Fortunately there was no fire and only minor injuries. A BAC internal report stated that there might have been serious injuries if any crew had been in the rear of the machine.

BAC tried to minimise the negative press coverage by stating there had been a crosswind blowing which had caused the accident. Freddie Laker of British United,

A previously unpublished photograph taken on 18 March 1963, of G-ASJB seriously damaged on the Wisley runway. Though it was announced that it would be rebuilt, the aircraft was dismantled and later scrapped. *(Brooklands Museum)*

who was to have received G-ASJB as part of his order, also backed up this story in the press. The aircraft was dismantled and the fuselage was taken to Hurn where the author saw the seriously damaged fuselage in the west end of the flight shed, well hidden from public view. BAC announced that the aircraft would be repaired as a demonstrator for the company, registered as G-ASVT, and that a new model 201, registered G-ASTJ, would be built for British United. In fact, the wreck was soon dismantled. Part of one of the wings was used for fuel flow tests at Weybridge and was on display at the time of writing in the Brooklands Museum. The nose lingered at Hurn for some years and was later scrapped after being used for bird impact tests on the windscreen. There is a story, which may be apocryphal, that during these tests they ran out of fresh plucked birds and obtained some frozen ones which, when fired from the gun, smashed the windscreen. The ability of the landing gear to 'wipe off' in the event of a crash landing without puncturing the wing tanks was rightly

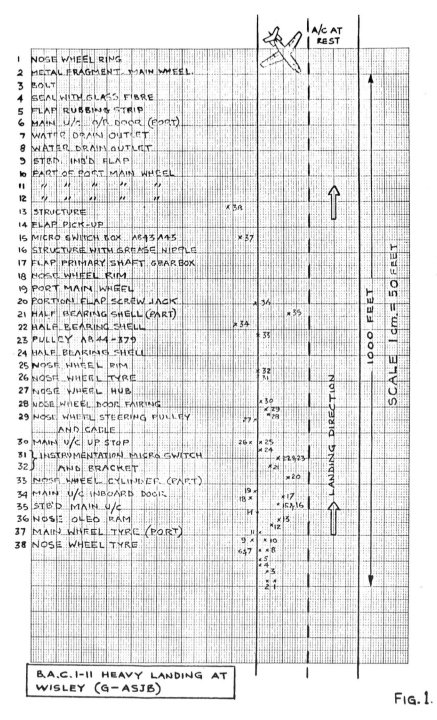

1 NOSE WHEEL RING
2 METAL FRAGMENT, MAIN WHEEL
3 BOLT
4 SEAL WITH GLASS FIBRE
5 FLAP RUBBING STRIP
6 MAIN U/C O/B DOOR (PORT)
7 WATER DRAIN OUTLET
8 WATER DRAIN OUTLET
9 STBD. IND'D FLAP
10 PART OF PORT MAIN WHEEL
11   "   "   "   "   "
12   "   "   "   "   "
13 STRUCTURE
14 FLAP PICK-UP
15 MICRO SWITCH BOX AB43A43
16 STRUCTURE WITH GREASE NIPPLE
17 FLAP PRIMARY SHAFT GEAR BOX
18 NOSE WHEEL RIM
19 PORT MAIN WHEEL
20 PORTION FLAP SCREW JACK
21 HALF BEARING SHELL (PART)
22 HALF BEARING SHELL
23 PULLEY AB44-379
24 HALF BEARING SHELL
25 NOSE WHEEL RIM
26 NOSE WHEEL TYRE
27 NOSE WHEEL HUB
28 NOSE WHEEL DOOR FAIRING
29 NOSE WHEEL STEERING PULLEY
         AND CABLE
30 MAIN U/C UP STOP
31 ⎱ INSTRUMENTATION MICRO SWITCH
32 ⎰   AND BRACKET
33 NOSE WHEEL CYLINDER (PART)
34 MAIN U/C INBOARD DOOR
35 STB'D MAIN U/C
36 NOSE OLEO RAM
37 MAIN WHEEL TYRE (PORT)
38 NOSE WHEEL TYRE

A/C AT REST

1000 FEET

SCALE 1cm. = 50 FEET

LANDING DIRECTION

B.A.C. 1-11 HEAVY LANDING AT
WISLEY (G-ASJB)

FIG. 1.

Diagram of the G-ASJB crash indicating the wreckage on the runway and how the aircraft had turned almost through 180° before coming to rest. *(Brooklands Museum)*

regarded as an excellent safety feature. An expensive, inadvertent but extremely real test of this feature was made as a result of 'SJB's crash.

It had been intended to use G-ASJB for Airworthiness Performance work at Torrejon, near Madrid, during the summer of 1964. This was to be followed by Operational Performance measurements in the UK and, after Christmas, to take 'SJB to Johannesburg for hot and high Airworthiness Performance. However the accident, which can be at least partly attributed to the poor manual elevator control, curtailed all that planning.

As can be imagined, BAC was very concerned what effect another accident would have on sales and customer confidence. Chris King, then a Senior Flight Test Observer, was with 'SJA on a demonstration flight in Rome and the team came back quickly because there was fear that her special category licence to fly might be revoked. Ian Muir, one of Chris's colleagues who witnessed the crash of 'SJB, said it had sounded like a fork-lift truck hitting a series of massive dustbins.

On With the Flying

The third production machine for BUA, G-ASJC, flew on 1 April 1964 straight from Hurn's runway 08 to Wisley. A month later on 6 May, out of sequence, the fifth production aircraft, G-ASJE, took to the air, since the fourth production machine G-ASJD was held back on the production line to be fitted out with special equipment in order to re-start the low-speed handling trials.

G-ASJC had a single hydraulic system elevator control, an interim standard for test purposes, which enabled certain Flight Testing to proceed. The system had representative structural stiffness, enabling the flutter clearance work to be done. It also provided a representative elevator control system, permitting aircraft handling trials. 'SJE, fully furnished, was used for system testing, including radio and cabin air-conditioning and customer demonstrations. It flew a ten-day demonstration tour of the Middle-East in August and made the type's first appearance at the Farnborough Airshow in September 1964 along with G-ASGA, the first Super VC10. On the final day of the show the first BUA VC10, G-ASIW, was demonstrated in place of the Super VC10, creating a beautiful publicity shot for the airline as the One-Eleven overflew the VC10, both in British United's colours.

The sixth example to fly was the first to appear in another colour scheme. And what a colour scheme! Registered N1541 it was the first of fourteen for Braniff International. It too joined the others at Wisley. The fourteen aircraft for Braniff were different from most models in that they had no ventral stairs in order to save weight. N1541 was soon re-registered as G-ASUF for demonstration flights and made the first visit of the type to Heathrow on 6 July 1964.

Some of the test fleet at Wisley in June 1964, N1541, G-ASJA, 'SJC (c/n 007), 'SJE (c/n 009) at Wisley. N1541 (c/n 015) which was later temporarily re-registered G-ASUF. All the aircraft still had the original rounded nose and tail bumper but G-ASJC had the revised wing leading edge. *(BAE SYSTEMS)*

Up to mid-August 1964 test flying with the six aircraft used in the test programme, 'SJA, 'JC, 'JE, N1541, 'JD, 'JF (their order of first flight) had totalled 620 hours. Development of aircraft systems was rapid and trouble free, and work on the air, fuel, electrical, hydraulic, oxygen radio and APU was virtually complete. Work on interior noise levels had proceeded to a point where a flat noise curve was obtained for the whole cabin. Performance testing had taken place in Madrid and stall testing was about to resume.

G-ASJD Re-Starts the Stalling Tests

This aircraft was delayed on the production line and flew after G-ASJE and N1541 because she was to take on the low-speed handling trials, which had ceased with the crash of G-ASHG in October 1963. It was fitted with the new leading edge and larger inboard wing fences (both in trial wooden fittings) to give a better nose-down pitching moment and in place of the servo-tab elevator a powered elevator in a trial installation.

It had the following special fit for the trials:

- a nose probe
- a large amount of internal instrumentation
- cameras to observe wool-tufted wings which would indicate the air flow
- two escape hatches (as had 'SJA and 'SJC)
- a very large anti-spin parachute fitted well aft of the aircraft so that it would not foul the tail in a spin or stall
- a special alteration to the reverse thrust cascades whereby selection of reverse would provide upward thrust

Peter Baker, who had become One-Eleven Project Pilot in December 1963, made its first flight. He had joined BAC from Handley Page in July 1963. A very experienced test pilot, at Handley Page he had mainly flown Victors, and on one occasion after an uncontrollable pitch-up he had had to deploy a tail parachute to recover the machine, hereupon the Victor went into an almost vertical dive, hanging as it was from the parachute. So he knew about stalling problems.

G-ASJD's Forced Landing

On 20 August 1964, a year to the day since the first flight of the ill-fated prototype, Peter Baker accompanied by Staff Harris and a crew of two took off from Wisley to carry out stalling tests at 20,000ft over Wiltshire. While holding a target incidence there were some oscillations, so Baker pushed forward on the control column, but he then had the impression that the aircraft was not responding correctly and that it might be in a stable stall. As a result the tail parachute was streamed and upward and full thrust was used, without apparent effect, which increased his conviction that G-ASJD was in a stable stall. Two 'Mayday' calls were transmitted – Boscombe Down responded with a compass course to steer. At a height of 5,000ft, with a descent of 6,000ft per minute, and judging that it was already too late to ask the crew to escape, Baker considered making a forced landing. By using full flap and full power he found, to his surprise, that the rate of descent was reduced to 1,000ft per minute. An area of grassland on the Tilshead army ranges was selected and the One-Eleven made a wheels-up landing, sliding some 400 yards and severely damaging the flaps and bottom of the fuselage. Other than this, the damage was superficial.

Helicopters arrived from Boscombe Down and took the crew there for a medical examination while fire tenders from Salisbury, Devizes, Amesbury and a crash unit

G-ASJD (c/n 008) at Hurn fitted for stalling trials with a nose probe, wooden test installation leading edge, wing fences newly positioned inboard of the original position, fully powered elevators and large rear parachute fitted sufficiently far out not to tangle with the tail if deployed. *(BAE SYSTEMS)*

from Boscombe Down arrived at the scene, but they were not needed. The spot was only about ten miles across the downs from where prototype G-ASHG had crashed the previous October.

One can imagine the reaction at BAC's headquarters when they heard the news that another One-Eleven was down. Initially BAC informed the press that until they had questioned the crew and scrutinised the aircraft instruments they would not comment on the cause of the incident nor the tests on which it was engaged. Later, in the evening, BAC told *The Times* journalists that the forced landing appeared to have nothing to do with the tests it was undertaking.

Brian Trubshaw was holidaying in Scotland at the time and was hauled back to Wisley, arriving in the early hours of the following morning. The BAC Flight Test team had analysed the flight recorder results and already knew that the aircraft was fine. Peter Baker arrived at Wisley and admitted his fault to Trubshaw and Sir George Edwards. Trubshaw insisted that he stay on – even though others wanted him to resign. Peter Baker went on to fly One-Elevens and Concordes and became the Civil Aviation Authority's Chief Test Pilot.

Close up of the substantial parachute installation on the tail of G-ASJD. *(BAE SYSTEMS)*

Test firing of the parachute at Hurn. The parachute cover is in the air and on the end of the line is the bolt that is fired to eject the parachute. Because there is no airflow in a stationary test, the parachute will not open out. *(BAE SYSTEMS)*

During stalling tests on 20 August 1964, the pilot mistakenly believed that G-ASJD was in a deep stall and deployed the parachute, which was not jettisoned resulting in a forced landing at Tilshead on Salisbury Plain. The parachute can be seen in the foreground. *(Bournemouth Daily Echo)*

Close up of G-ASJD being lifted to enable the undercarriage to be extended. The surface of the wing is covered with wool tufts, which were filmed from camera ports fitted instead of the cabin windows to indicate the airflow. *(Crown copyright A&AEE Boscombe Down)*

What had gone wrong this time? Baker had had the mistaken impression that the aircraft was in a stable stall and he had expected that deploying the parachute would give a pronounced downward pitch as it had so demonstrably done in his Victor experience. But since the aircraft was not in a stall the deployment of the parachute did not result in this downward pitch, reinforcing Baker's view that the machine was in a stable stall and not responding. If he had jettisoned the parachute the aircraft would have just flown on.

Lifting bags were used to raise G-ASJD whose undercarriage was then extended by free fall. There were some stories that she was so little damaged that she might be flown off from a nearby dirt airstrip to Boscombe Down – but this may just have been BAC spin. In fact, 'SJD was dismantled on site and returned to the Hurn production line, making a *second* first flight some nine months later on 13 June 1965. It was delivered to British United on 5 August and is the oldest One-Eleven still flying at the time of writing, operated by the Defence Research Agency based at Boscombe Down.

It was fortunate that Peter Baker crash-landed the aircraft – imagine the result if the crew had baled out, it had then crashed and the flight-recorder information had been difficult to extricate from the wreckage. Notwithstanding the evidence disproving any flaw, there were some who remained to be convinced and a few staff who even felt the aircraft was jinxed. The sales staff went through a miserable time having to constantly brief customers as to the causes of one crash and then another and another. John Prothero Thomas and others had to tour the world to explain

The fuselage of G-ASJD, showing some signs of damage, crossing the River Avon at the village of Avon near Hurn, returning to the factory for repair. *(Bournemouth Daily Echo)*

the accidents and some airlines were very difficult to satisfy. Existing customers wanted to know about their delivery dates and BAC had such problems that they were unable to give these with any reliability because of the need to incorporate modifications on aircraft already built or being built.

The publicity of the crashes deterred potential customers and helped the competition – apparently Alitalia was on the point of purchasing One-Elevens but then changed its mind and bought DC-9s, thirty-two in total. Roy Radford was in Madrid demonstrating the One-Eleven to Iberia when news of G-ASJD came through and Iberia then decided against purchasing them and also bought DC-9s. And who else?

Through to Certification

After all that drama and expense the remainder of the test programme was less troubled but still took longer than expected, G-ASJF and 'SJH having flown in July and September respectively. 'SJF was used for demonstrations and 'SJH flew straight to Filton, as did N1542 for Braniff, where they were put into storage for preparation to final delivery standard. By October 1964, the *Bournemouth Evening Echo* reported that 1,000 hours had been flown and first deliveries and services might be possible by December that year – but the reality was more prolonged.

Chris King, Senior Flight Test Observer, describes the way in which BAC finished the low-speed handling trials:

> G-ASJC had embarked upon Flight Resonance testing in August and the programme, plus the associated brief appraisal of high speed handling, was completed in some 18 flights on September 3. With the loss of 'SJD in August, instead of reverting back to performance, it was decided that 'SJC would become the aircraft used for stall development and certification plus the associated low-speed handling.
>
> SJC then embarked on a grounding, which took the best part of 4 weeks, to fit and commission the tail parachute and stall protection systems. It flew again on September 29th, captained by Brian Trubshaw with Ollie Oliver as co-pilot. These two shared all the stalling development and certification flying, in conjunction with Dave Davies of ARB, while Ollie, Peter Baker and Roy Radford conducted the associated low speed handling and tail load development flying plus development of the undercarriage shimmy fix.
>
> We thought the stalling programme went pretty well even though testing was approached cautiously, as one would expect having lost 2 aircraft and a crew on previous trials. Most of the stalls were done around 15,000ft and there was no noticeable difference in aircraft handling between doing them with power on or

with engines at idle; i.e. as one would expect there was no propeller slipstream effect! To save time, therefore, it was decided that stalls at 30,000ft would only be done at idle power. Dynamic stalls sometimes caused a rather rapid wing drop, of perhaps 50 to 60° that was always in the sense of rolling out of the turn. Higher Mach number at the stall, when this occurred, was originally thought to cause the phenomenon. However, being unsure of the line the ARB would take with regard to the wing drop, Dave Davies was invited to conduct a preliminary assessment on Jan 16, 1965, flight 186. He didn't like the wing drop at all; Murphy's Law gave him one that dropped into the turn and he reached around 100° of bank. He was also subjected to the first engine surge experienced by a One-Eleven, which required the engine to be throttled to avoid exceeding Turbine Gas Temperature (TGT) limitations – a situation that was unacceptable to the ARB. That resulted from performing turning stalls at 30,000ft with power on! Back to the drawing board; particularly when BAC were investigating the problem further, a surge occurred that necessitated the engine being shut down!

By then it was suspected the cause of the wing drop was some sort of discontinuity between the balsa and metal leading edge resulting in airflow separation that only occurred when pulling 'g'. Rolls-Royce believed fitting a fuel dip unit could automatically control the engine surge; similar to devices fitted to control engine surge during gun firing on military aircraft. The 2½% leading edge was engineered by gluing balsa wood to the original, prototype standard, metal leading edge; meaning aircraft to that standard, 'SJA to 'SJD, could not use wing anti-icing. The first Braniff aircraft, N1541 also registered as G-ASUF, always flew with the original leading edge until it was refurbished because it was not used for aerodynamic testing. Its main purpose was to test radio, weather radar, autopilot, interior cabin noise and cabin comfort measurements.

So 'SJC went to Hurn on January 31, 1965, flight 196, to have production standard, new metal leading edges and fuel dippers fitted. The aircraft flew again on February 8, 1965 and performed turning stalls en route to Wisley. All went well from then onwards. BAC conducted 7 flights exhaustively checking for wing dropping. The problem was fixed. Dave Davies flew 4 flights, between February 13 and 17 for his handling assessment, and they were satisfactory.

The fuel dipper was developed over the next 15 flights and Dave checked it out on March 8, 1965, flight 223. He finalised other ARB testing on 'JC on March 25 and 31, 1965. With the completion of these trials 'JC was ferried to Filton on April 4, flight 248, to undergo its refurbishment programme prior to delivery to BUA.

As you will now appreciate, testing associated with stalling continued almost up until the ARB certificate was issued and until well after the delivery of crew training aircraft to Braniff.

G-ASJA, piloted by Roy Radford and Chuck Thrower with a crew of thirty-three on board, flew to Dakar in North Africa via Madrid on 16–17 October for four weeks of performance trials. At Dakar it made nineteen flights and at Torrejon Air Force Base near Madrid, a further thirty flights finishing on 13 November. The data gathered during these trials completed all that was necessary for the certification of the take-off, climb and landing performance of the type. The purpose of the tests was to measure the performance when operating at maximum weights at hot and high airfields. These tests permitted its initial certification for operation at airfields up to 5,000ft. The limits were raised still further when additional trials were made at Johannesburg early in January–February 1965. While in Madrid the opportunity was taken to demonstrate the aircraft to Aviaco, the Spanish domestic airline, and though negotiations over a sale continued for some time they were never finalised.

G-ASJG, the seventh for British United, flew on 31 October 1964 and was assigned as the Certificate of Airworthiness acceptance aircraft. Altogether six aircraft were used for certification flying, more that 1,900 hours were flown and over 2,000 landings made.

A significant factor about the flight testing was that systems testing was completed in half the time allotted – fortunate when one thinks how much time had to be spent

An example of the instrumentation typically found inside a test One-Eleven. *(BAE SYSTEMS)*

on the low-speed handling. All static strength tests were completed in July 1964 – the wing ultimately failing at 117% design payload, which led to a 20% increase in design weights. Progressively higher weights were certified as tests and experience was gained.

Fuselage fatigue tests on a test airframe at Filton had reached 30,000 'flights' by this date, and testing went on to reach 100,000 'flights' in late 1967. This thoroughness in the testing phase bore fruit subsequently; many One-Elevens went on to achieve more than 40,000 flying hours and a handful even achieved 50,000 hours, and some made more than 70,000 landings. Though the test programme had proved rather fraught, which had taken the normal fun out of the proceedings, there were lighter moments. For instance, Johnnie Walker was flying the first aircraft for Braniff, temporarily registered G-ASUF, from Wisley on runaway autopilot trials, and he had tried to start engines but could not. At that time the Speys were fitted with troublesome Constant Speed drives which would jam and could only be freed by hitting them with a rubber mallet. So he switched off in order to allow maintenance to sort it out. Then the Flight Engineer reported that a boy was on board, but as the doors were opened the boy ran off. BAC was embarrassed by the lax security since Wisley was expected to be one of the centres for the most important British military aircraft – TSR2. It was obviously not very secure. The newspapers got hold of the

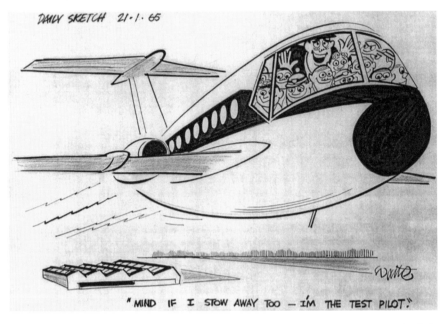

" MIND IF I STOW AWAY TOO – I'M THE TEST PILOT."

The *Daily Sketch* published this cartoon in January 1965 after a stowaway was found on G-ASUF, piloted by Johnnie Walker at Wisley. *(Johnnie Walker)*

story and a few days later, on 21 January 1965, a cartoon appeared in the *Daily Sketch* humorously depicting the situation.

Getting to certification still continued to present challenges. A stick pusher system was fitted (as on the VC10 and Trident) – since without this, the aircraft did not fulfil the certification requirements which demanded a nose-down attitude at the stall. On approaching a stall, the aircraft had a stick-shaker that vibrated the control column to draw the attention of the crew to the likelihood of a stall – if they did nothing, seconds later the stick-pusher would push the aircraft's nose down. These two devices are activated by two vanes on either side of the front of the fuselage, just below the window line. As an additional precaution all One-Elevens on initial flight test carried angle of attack indicators, activated by a vane fitted through a special orange window in place of the third window on both sides of the fuselage on early 200s. (It was the fourth window on later production 200s, 300s, 400s, 475s and the ninth window on the 500s). The information from these vanes was then shown on a temporary flight deck display, which was removed on completion of flight testing prior to delivery.

G-ASJG flew with all the modifications which had appeared variously on others:

1. Nose radome elongated 1ft – a better radar/aerodynamic shape – improved the look of the aircraft, too.
2. New profile wing leading edge and bigger wing fences moved inboard.
3. Stick-shaker and stick-pusher system activated by Airflow sensors, (Gianninni Vanes).
4. Production version of the power-controlled elevator with tandem elevator jacks which gave a much more definite control than the original servo-tab arrangement.
5. Small extractor cowl fitted to the APU exhaust to facilitate airborne re-lighting.

Publication of the Crash Reports

In March 1965 the crash reports on the prototype and 'SJD were published – they had both been held up by the Ministry of Aviation to help BAC. (There was never a full report on G-ASJB, only a paragraph in a digest of accidents). To be reminded of such unhappy events at a time when there were further delays in completing certification, and when BUA were rewarded for their enterprise by having to suffer the embarrassment of a third postponement of inaugural service date, seemed singularly ill-timed. Many believe that publication was delayed so that they would appear *after* the aircraft had gone into service, but that the delays threw this scheme out of gear.

Conclusion

Chris King, Senior Flight Test Observer (writing to the author) wrote, 'The manner in which the BAC Flight Test Department sorted matters out demonstrates the large degree of flexibility and effort required on everyone's part to alleviate the effects of the three accidents.'

5

The 200 Series in Service

Freddie Laker, Managing Director of British United Airways, saw off the ninth aircraft for BUA, G-ASJI, from Gatwick on 25 January 1965, on the first stage of an intensive 200-hour four-week route-proving programme. Most of BUA's European destinations were visited during the trials. During a typical day's flying G-ASJI made four return stages to Genoa, Jersey, Malaga and Majorca, giving a total daily mileage of approximately 7,500 miles and an elapsed time of fourteen hours. Typical turnarounds were just sixty minutes to simulate the type of high-intensity operation for which the aircraft was designed.

A full Certificate of Airworthiness was awarded on 5 April 1965 and the first service was flown from Gatwick to Genoa on 9 April by the tenth aircraft owned by British United, G-ASJJ. Among those on board were Geoffrey Knight, Managing Director of BAC, Weybridge Division, and Freddie Laker, who had shown initial confidence in the project by ordering ten One-Elevens straight off the drawing board in May 1961. A few days later, the new jet was introduced on the services to Rotterdam and Amsterdam.

However, BAC's deliveries were a long way behind schedule. BUA only received three aircraft in April ('SJH, 'SJI, 'SJJ), one in May ('SJF), two in July ('SJE, 'SJG), one in August ('SJD), the first production machine 'SJA in October, and 'SJC and the replacement for 'SJB, registered G-ASTJ, in November 1965. Laker had originally expected to start services in late 1964 and have all his fleet before the summer of 1965. Notwithstanding when all their fleet was delivered, British United expanded their use by introducing the first domestic jet services in the UK between Gatwick and Edinburgh, Glasgow and Belfast. The company also flew to a large number of destinations in Europe and West Africa and on many inclusive tour routes to holiday destinations in the Mediterranean. BUA soon found that the self-contained nature of their new equipment meant that they were able to schedule quick turnarounds and achieve a very high utilisation with their new machines. The One-Elevens had passenger appeal, which was demonstrated by the constant requests made to the airline from passengers wishing to fly on the new jets. This was partly because of the very generous seating pitch since each aircraft was only fitted out with sixty-nine to

The One-Eleven's first service; G-ASJJ (c/n 014) at Gatwick about to fly to Genoa on 9 April 1965. Third and fifth from the left: Freddie Laker and Geoffrey Knight, Managing Directors of BUA and BAC respectively. *(Brooklands Museum)*

G-ASJJ (c/n 014) for British United flying low over BAC's test airfield at Wisley, Surrey. It crashed on take-off from Milan-Linate in January 1969, all passengers and crew surviving. *(BAE SYSTEMS)*

seventy-four seats. However, later operators squeezed in another two or even three rows and Channel Airways even fitted ninety-nine seats! But even with their more generous seating layout BUA was pleased to report total seat/mile costs as 2.05d (=0.0085p at 1965 prices) and utilisation as 7.1 hours per day.

With the merger of BUA and Caledonian to form British Caledonian in 1970 the 201s were retained, except for 'SJA which was converted to executive use by Marshall's of Cambridge and sold to Barwick Industries in the USA. The remaining eight 201s ('SJJ crashed in 1969 – see Chapter 13) together with the 501s and 509s ordered in 1968 became a major part of the merged fleet. A further disposal was made in 1971 when 'SJD was sold to the Ministry of Defence and registered XX105. She returned to Hurn for the substantial modifications needed for her new role (see Chapter 14).

Across the Pond – The Douglas DC-9

Before the British aircraft entered service the DC-9-10, approximately the same size as the One-Eleven, made its maiden voyage on 25 February 1965 and gained certification on 23 November 1965. Whereas the One-Eleven took almost twenty months from first flight to first service, the Douglas product was in service only eight months after its first flight. The competition had almost caught up with the innovators; not an untypical story where British industry is concerned.

Douglas had orders from a wide spectrum of airlines including Air Canada, Bonanza, Delta, Eastern Hawaiian, KLM, Swissair, and TWA, many of which had been courted by BAC and some of which had come near to ordering the British aircraft. The order from Eastern was very significant because it was then the largest airline in the world. BAC had virtually bagged the order, but Douglas had the sense to offer the short-term lease of DC-9-10s and develop the stretched DC-9-30 for later delivery to Eastern. This early stretch of their basic design was to give them the edge in getting orders over the One-Eleven, for BAC were unable to offer a stretched aircraft at that time. Douglas also took full advantage of the wider 'double-bubble' cross-section of their fuselage in the battle for sales and, by placing the cabin floor comparatively lower than in the British jet, could provide more room at shoulder height without reducing freight capacity.

Initial versions of the DC-9 were powered by de-rated 12,000lb thrust Pratt & Whitney JT8D-5 turbofans. By comparison with competing BAC One-Elevens, their operating cost per seat/mile was higher, emphasising the urgent need for Douglas to develop a higher-capacity version. It had been intended to develop stretched versions from the earliest design stage, so the evolution of a higher capacity cabin was not long delayed. It was achieved by the insertion of a 14ft fuselage plug to give maximum seating for 119. Other changes included an increase of 4ft in wing span, the introduction of full-span wing leading-edge slats, and the installation of 14,000lb

The first Douglas DC-9, N9DC, at Douglas' plant at Long Beach. It first flew on 25 February 1965. Following the crash of the first One-Eleven a substantial redesign of the DC-9's tail and wing took place to improve its stalling performance. The speedy development of the aircraft meant that many potential One-Eleven operators purchased them. Production of the DC-9 and its developments continued until 2006 and almost 2,500 were produced. *(Author's collection)*

thrust JT8D-7 turbofans as standard. Designated as the Series 30, the first of these was flown on 1 August 1966, and initial services were operated by Eastern Airlines on 1 February 1967.

The One-Eleven's Order Book

In April 1965, when the One-Eleven's first commercial service began, the order book totalled seventy-four aircraft from eleven operators. Fourteen aircraft had been completed and major components for the fiftieth were in production. The production rate was two per month, rising to four per month in 1966. On the two production lines at Hurn were examples for Braniff, Mohawk and American Airlines of North America, Aer Lingus, Central African Airways and the two 400 series development aircraft.

Into Service in the United States with Braniff

The third Braniff One-Eleven, N1543, was delivered to New York (Newark) on 13 March 1965 prior to the granting of FAA certification. Piloted by BAC's Peter Marsh, Johnnie Walker and Braniff's George Cheetham with a Navigator and Flight Engineer, she was delivered just as 178 Viscounts before her on the same 4,300-mile route. The flight began from Hurn then to Prestwick for Customs clearance. Then it headed north to Keflavik in Iceland to take on fuel. N1543 then flew over the Denmark Strait to Sondrestrom Fiord in Greenland and the longest leg of 1,010 miles to Goose Bay for a second refuelling. On then to Montreal where the ferry equipment of H/F radio and Loran radio navigation system was removed. The last leg was the 430 miles to Newark, New Jersey. (In all a total of sixty-nine newly built One-Eleven 200s and 400s were to follow this same delivery route to US airlines and corporate users between 1965 and 1969.)

On arrival, N1543 embarked on intensive crew training and was joined by N1544 on 6 April. Braniff needed early delivery so that sufficient crews were available for airline service to commence immediately upon receipt of the FAA full type certificate. That meant these aircraft were not at the final certification standard when crew training commenced; bearing in mind the certification activity was still continuing in England in parallel with crew training.

Chris King became the BAC expert for setting stall-warning systems and was seconded to Braniff in April 1965 to ensure that on the first two delivered, N1543 and N1544, the stall systems were set to final certification standard. The hardware modifications comprised time delays to obviate nuisance stick shaker operation during heavy turbulence and refinement to protect against the severe dynamic stall techniques that ARB and FAA pilots were adopting.

His task was to supervise Braniff's installation of the new equipment, check the rigging of the airflow sensors, the Giannini Vanes, set up the revised system and check it functioned correctly. A successful check flight on 14 April, flown by Johnnie Walker, ensured the system operated at the expected speeds and angles of attack. All worked out fine and Braniff crews were cleared to include stalling in their syllabus from then onwards. Meanwhile, British Certification had been granted on 9 April and the FAA granted their approval following these modifications to the Braniff aircraft on 16 April.

All this hard work was leavened by a couple of amusing events. Celebrating after completing the stalling system work, the team ordered champagne. The waitress apologised to Chris King and Johnnie Walker that there was no local champagne so offered them 'foreign stuff' at the same price of $4 a bottle. It was Moët & Chandon! During the training flights there was an interesting example of the differences between American and English aviation. The Controller queried Peter's request to do an overshoot. Peter insisted he did. The Controller said, 'This will be interesting'.

N1543 (c/n 017), first delivery to Braniff from Hurn on 16 March 1965. From second left, Johnnie Walker, Test Pilot, unknown, Peter Marsh, Test Pilot, Capt. George Cheetham of Braniff, others unknown. Below the first and third windows are the Gianninni vanes for stick shaker and stick pusher systems fitted to all aircraft and introduced as a result of the aircraft's stalling problems. *(BAE SYSTEMS via Mike Phipp)*

In American Aviation English pilots say 'Go Around' because 'overshoot' means going off the end of the runway.

First Services

Prince Phillip visited Braniff's Dallas base on 25 April 1965 to inaugurate the aircraft at a special dedication ceremony. The first service in the USA was flown on the same day, from Corpus Christi, Texas, to Minneapolis, Minnesota. Braniff branded them as 'Fastback' jets, fitted with twenty-four first-class and thirty-nine coach-class seats. The Dallas/Fort Worth-based line received two more One-Elevens in April, one in May, one in June, two in July including the first built, N1541, which had carried the British registration, G-ASUF; the remainder were delivered by December 1965. The airline stated they had never introduced a new airliner which had received such public approval. By the middle of the following year Braniff's aircraft were serving twenty-eight places over sectors as short as 67 miles and as long as 1,189 miles between Dallas and Washington, DC. Braniff was achieving an average utilisation of nine hours forty-six minutes daily over fourteen sectors.

Braniff operated a spider's web of services mainly radiating from Dallas and the skein of services reaching down to South America. The airline flew the One-Elevens mainly on multi-stage routes – with perhaps four or six intermediate stops – which gave an average sector length of 272 miles. Mohawk in contrast had an average sector of 171 miles, with Aloha of Hawaii having even shorter sectors of typically 127 miles whereas American Airline's was nearer 300 miles.

The user-friendly convenience of the One-Eleven was proving itself to the airlines which had chosen the machine over its rivals. The combination of airstairs, auxiliary power unit, waist-high baggage holds and single-point pressure refuelling meant the operators were able to set new standards of short-haul productivity. In the first year of operations the seven delivered (five to Braniff and two to Mohawk) averaged 3,960 landings each and Braniff's aircraft were averaging a daily flying utilisation of nine hours twenty-six minutes over fourteen route segments. The true working day was nineteen hours and its reliability the best ever for a new type.

Whereas the first few Braniff machines were painted in the sweeping red, white and blue of N1541, this livery gave way to a very different and varied scheme with aircraft painted a solid colour which could be beige, green, yellow, orange, ochre, dark or light blue with black titling.

By February 1964, Braniff had placed firm orders for fourteen aircraft with options for twelve more. The additional orders would have replaced the last of the prop-powered Electra and Convair equipment, making the airline all jet-powered by 1966. Braniff did not take up the options on the additional aircraft and subsequently phased-out all of its One-Elevens in favour of the Boeing 727 except for N1543, which remained in use as a corporate aircraft with the airline until 1977.

Aer Lingus

Aer Lingus's first Hurn-jet, EI-ANE, a series 208 configured for seventy-four passengers, made a two hour forty-five minute first flight piloted by Dinty Moores and Dave Glaser on 28 April 1965. Less than a month later, on 27 May, it started a six-day shakedown tour to a dozen European cities. Aer Lingus's first public service was Dublin – Cork – Paris on 3 June 1965. The introduction of the jets caused the Irish airlines load factors to grow substantially but the Irish line was later to grow impatient with BAC's inability to stretch the aircraft. The airline switched loyalties and ordered Boeing 737s and never expanded their One-Eleven fleet beyond the initial four. These doughty machines remained in service until 1991 as more and more larger 737s were delivered. After twenty-five years of sterling service and the longest continuous use of the 200 series by an airline, they were withdrawn at the beginning of 1991. All were sold to Hold Trade Air in Nigeria, but 5N-HTC, the former EI-ANE returned to Southend and was scrapped at Stock, Essex, in 2001.

Mohawk

Mohawk was the largest regional carrier in the States and the first regional airline to order jets so was determined to celebrate its first jet, N2111J, in some style. A brass band was laid on for the roll-out ceremony at Hurn on Saturday 27 March 1965, and the first flight piloted by Dave Glaser on 5 May was filmed from one of the BAC de Havilland Herons for broadcast on American television. The Mohawk series 204s all included 11 or 111 in their registrations, e.g., N1112J, N1113J, etc. N2111J was delivered on 15 May, named *New York* by Mrs Rockefeller, and the first service was operated on 27 June. All the Mohawk aircraft were given names of American states

Ceremonial roll out of N2111J (c/n 030) first for Mohawk at Hurn on Saturday 27 March 1965. *(BAE SYSTEMS)*

One of Mohawk's order, N1124J (c/n 134) was temporarily registered G-AWDF for braking trials at Torrejon in Spain in March 1968. Only partly painted in the Mohawk colours, the gold lining, titling and tail motif were only applied on her return to Hurn from the trials and prior to delivery. *(Author)*

and though the original order was only for four, Mohawk continued ordering the jets until they owned a total of eighteen machines.

The delivery of the jet airliners guaranteed Mohawk immediate impact. For the first time the company found itself competing on an equal footing with American Airlines. Not only did it improve the competitive position with regard to passengers but also towards the crew – which was also a first. The cabin layout was unusual with alternative rows of four and five abreast seating which gave an air of spaciousness that competitors did not offer. Cabin staff found it easy to move around and work in the body of the aircraft; there were fewer mishaps and greater productivity from cabin personnel.

Mohawk had always achieved quick turnarounds but the special features of the British short-haul jet had ideal design features for them; APU, powered airstairs at the front and rear, single-point refuelling and waist-high freight-bay sills. The airline estimated that these features saved them $35,000 (at 1965 prices) plus one employee per aircraft. After only eighteen months of use Mohawk found they could achieve through stops of six minutes and terminal stops of ten minutes. For example, at a through stop, sixty-four disembarked and forty-seven boarded in an amazing six minutes. The net result was that Mohawk calculated it was able to schedule three One-Eleven flights for every flight by the piston-engined Convairs that the jets had replaced.

Aloha of Hawaii

Another operator of the 200 series in the United States was Aloha of Hawaii. It ordered two 215s in 1965 and a further aircraft in the following year which was demonstrated at the Paris Air Show prior to the long delivery flight to Hawaii. For Aloha the One-Eleven was their first jet and its introduction was a considerable undertaking for a small operator. However, its introduction proved to be relatively easy and like their American counterparts they were soon delighted to discover that the type clocked up an impressive utilisation. However, like Aer Lingus, Aloha needed greater capacity so bought 737s. The One-Eleven fleet was sold to Mohawk, which was itself taken over by Allegheny Airlines in 1972. Allegheny standardised on One-Elevens and DC-9s, purchasing eight One-Elevens from Braniff, giving a total fleet of thirty-one. In later years Allegheny had the ventral stairs removed from the former Mohawk and Aloha machines to save weight and to standardise them with the former Braniff 203s which were not built with them. This large fleet put in an impressive utilisation with many of them clocking up very high hours and landings. The last services were flown in 1989 and some were scrapped (some even returning to their birthplace at Hurn for this ignominy) while others were sold to Nigeria.

N1128J (c/n 181). After a hectic life, first owned by Mohawk and then US Air pictured here at Hurn in 1990 waiting to be stripped of parts and then broken up. 200 series aircraft can easily be distinguished from the later 400 series by the nosewheel door arrangement. *(Author)*

N11183 (c/n 185) third and final 215 for Aloha landing on runway 26 at Hurn. On its delivery flight to Hawaii it was demonstrated at the Paris Air Show hence the number 284 was painted on its nose. *(BAE SYSTEMS)*

Central African Airways non-delivery and British Eagle

Two 207s were ordered by Central African Airways in September 1962, and both of them, VP-YXA and 'YXB, were ready for delivery in April 1966. Unusually these 207s (like the two 217s for the Royal Australian Air Force) had the higher-powered Spey 511s with water injection of the 400 series which provided better performance, especially necessary where high temperatures reduce engine thrust.

Central African Airways was jointly operated by Rhodesia, Malawi and Zambia but, as a result of Rhodesia's Unilateral Declaration of Independence, Britain's Labour Government imposed a trade embargo. Both aircraft made their maiden flights at Hurn in February and April 1966 respectively, in the airline's livery but without titling. After some delay, the One-Elevens were bought by the fledgling Zambia

Originally built for Central African Airways as VP-YXB, this 207 is seen here taking off from runway 28 at Wisley repainted as 9J-RCI (c/n 040) for Zambia Airways. It made a tour of Zambia and was then leased to British Eagle as G-ATVH. *(BAE SYSTEMS)*

Ordered originally by Kuwait Airways, this 301, G-ATPL (c/n 035) was leased to British Eagle from new. It later flew with Dan-Air and then Ladeco in Chile. *(Brooklands Museum)*

Airways which was unable to operate them at that time and who leased them to a then important independent British airline, British Eagle. Whereas the first became G-ATTP straight away, the second was painted in Zambia colours as 9J-RCI and demonstrated in Zambia, becoming G-ATVH on return to the UK. The two aircraft then inaugurated British Eagle's domestic jet services, though during 1967 'TVH was leased to Swissair, which was short of capacity because of a late delivery of DC-9s. At the end of 1967 both aircraft were delivered to Zambia Airways, serving there until 1975 when they returned to the British register and joined Dan-Air. On the demise of Dan-Air in 1992 they were flown to Chile and served with Ladeco until withdrawn from service three years later, where they remain stored at the time of writing.

Besides the leased Zambia Airways 207s, this once important British independent also operated 300 series One-Elevens. Kuwait Airways had ordered 301s in 1962 but they were leased to British Eagle before delivery, so together with two 304s of its own this gave British Eagle a fleet of five 300s and the two 207s. The fleet was used for its scheduled European services but with Eagle's bankruptcy in 1968 all seven were sold on.

6

The 400 Series Development, World Tours and in Service

The First One-Eleven 400 – G-ASYD

Piloted by Peter Baker with Brian Trubshaw as co-pilot, Chris King, Senior Flight Test Observer and others, the first 400 series development aircraft G-ASYD (c/n 053) took to the air on 13 July 1965 painted in a rather unprepossessing minimalist colour scheme. There was red titling 'British Aircraft Corporation' on both sides of the front fuselage, but little else to attract the eye. Like its sister, G-ASYE, it was in bare polished metal with two grey painted areas, the rudder and a section of fuselage over the wing. This aircraft was, however, to carry many other colour schemes through its immensely varied twenty-nine year life and metamorphoses with BAC and then British Aerospace.

That first flight from Hurn Airport lasted two hours twenty-five minutes and, three days later on flight 5, it was flown to BAC's Flight Test Airfield at Wisley in Surrey. By the end of July, only eighteen days since leaving the production line, thirty-eight flights and over seventy hours had been logged. When 'SYD first flew it was with Spey Mk 510-14, an interim standard. These were exchanged for the Spey 511-14, which she first flew with on 8 September just before the performance trials at Torrejon, near Madrid, starting on 11 September 1965.

It was based there until late October undergoing FAA certification. While there the flight test engineers found a difficulty in complying with landing distances – so in order to achieve this it was decided to push the aircraft onto the ground during flare, which proved successful. The FAA representatives watching had expected that this might push the undercarriage through the wings. But no, the manoeuvre proved successful and another section of the certification could be signed off.

This was especially pertinent when it is taken into account that some major structural components in 'SYD's centre section were manufactured to the 200 series, as opposed to the standard 400 series. The reason was for expediency, not

The crew disembarking at Hurn on 13 July 1965, after the first flight of the 400 series prototype, G-ASYD (c/n 053). From the left Chris King, Senior Flight Test Observer, Mike Crisp, Flight Test Manager, Brian Trubshaw, Chief Test Pilot and Peter Baker, who captained its maiden flight, others unknown. *(BAE SYSTEMS)*

programme slippage resulting from the Flight Test accidents. 'SYD's position in the production line was necessary to meet programme requirements for completing deliveries to American Airlines on time. Because the aircraft was built around the centre fuselage/wing centre section, the assembly of those parts had to be laid down relatively early. Consequently, there was insufficient time to design and manufacture some 400 series components for 'SYD. Moreover, 'SYD needed to complete its Flight Test programme well in advance of the first American Airlines delivery. The consequences of this substandard strength were insignificant in relation to flight-testing. 'SYD's chief limitations as a 400 series were rate of descent at touchdown limited to 9ft/sec while production aircraft are limited to 10ft/sec.

By 'SYD's first birthday it had clocked up 370 flights, 613 hours and 1,046 landings. An impressive debut indeed. The 400 series was granted full FAA certification on 22 November 1965.

World Tours with G-ASYE – The Most Travelled Civil Demonstrator

On 16 September 1965, in the same uninspiring colour scheme G-ASYD's sister, G-ASYE (c/n 054), made her maiden flight from Hurn. After shakedown trials it was delivered to Marshall's of Cambridge in November for the fitting of an executive interior in the front cabin and airline seating in the back ready for the World Sales Tours.

Now painted in the much more becoming red, white and blue BAC livery, G-ASYE set off from Wisley on the first of its tours on 17 November 1965 with Tour Manager Jock Bryce and flown by BAC's Peter Marsh and BUA's Captain Arthur Rusk. The tour was strenuous by any standards, covering 25,000 miles in the USA and Central America, and making a total of sixty-eight flights in seventeen days. The team did not miss a single appointment with the twenty-two organisations and seven airlines to which it was demonstrated. An impressive record. G-ASYE returned to Wisley on 8 January 1966 after a period of use by American Airlines for crew-training.

At the end of the first part of the World tour in December 1965 G-ASYE (c/n 054) was used by Page Airways in the USA for demonstrations to potential business customers. It displayed the logos of all the One-Eleven customers: British United, Braniff, Mohawk, Kuwait Airways, Central African Airways, Aer Lingus, American Airlines, Philippines Airlines, Aloha, British Eagle, British Midland and TACA. (BAE SYSTEMS)

At the end of 1965, having delivered thirty-four aircraft to five airlines and flown 35,000 hours, the One-Eleven's troubles were now well and truly of the past and production really began to accelerate as orders came in.

Meanwhile G-ASYE, back in the UK for a mere thirteen days, was soon off on its travels again piloted by 'Ollie' Oliver and Roy Radford. This second tour was even more extensive than the first, with 70,000 miles covering South East Asia and Australasia with 130 demonstrations during the forty-seven day tour. BAC made substantial efforts to sell the aircraft to New Zealand National Airways Corporation which operated Viscounts, and proposed a special, extra high-powered 300 series aircraft with Spey 25 512s as later used in BEA's 510s to meet the New Zealanders' challenging payload needs. BAC also played on local and patriotic connections by arranging for a message to be taken from the Mayor of Christchurch, very near Hurn Airport, to the Mayor of Christchurch, New Zealand. But for all these efforts, in mid-1967 the New Zealand airline plumped for Boeing 737s saying that they would have preferred the One-Elevens but the 737s were larger and cheaper.

G-ASYE pictured on 21 January 1966 just about to set out on the second part of its World Tour from a cold and miserable Wisley, piloted by (from the left) BAC Test Pilots 'Ollie' Oliver and Roy Radford with Capt. Vyvyan-Robinson of British Eagle. This second tour covered South East Asia and Australasia with 130 demonstrations during the forty-seven day tour. *(BAE SYSTEMS)*

A major port of call during the second part of the tour was the Philippines. The right side of the aircraft was partly repainted in PAL's colours for her visit to several cities including Bacolod where it received a warm welcome. *(Brooklands Museum)*

Still showing some signs of PAL branding on the right engine nacelle, G-ASYE is seen at Taipei. *(BAE SYSTEMS)*

On 5 April 1966 there was yet another tour, this time of South America, which continued until 1 May of that year. Yankee Echo flew the usual delivery route via Iceland and Greenland, which had already been used by twenty-eight One-Elevens destined for US customers. 'SYE began its demonstrations in Bermuda and then went on to the Bahamas, Trinidad, Brazil, Paraguay, Uruguay, Argentina, Chile, Peru, Ecuador, Columbia and Venezuela. At Asuncion in Paraguay the President watched a demonstration while 'SYE flew past with most of the Paraguayan Cabinet on board. The One-Eleven made a striking impression on local aviation in South America by making the first-ever jet landings at many airfields because of its excellent performance and lack of need for specialised ground equipment.

In this hectic six-month period from November 1965 to May 1966, G-ASYE travelled 160,000 miles with 334 separate flights, on average two flights a day and visits to nearly seventy airlines and forty business corporations hosting 4,600 guests and all at a comparatively low cost of £250,000. The work of the BAC team responsible is apparent. As a result of the widespread publicity and the demonstrable effectiveness of the new jet tours there were orders valued at £10 million for six aircraft from TACA of El Salvador, LACSA of Costa Rica, LANICA of Nicaragua, Aerocondor (later cancelled) and Victor Comptometers.

Soon after returning home in May 1966, G-ASYE's registration was cancelled. It was reconfigured as a 410 series executive jet for Victor Comptometers and delivered as N3939V in September.

The One-Eleven 400 Series in Service with American Airlines and Around the Globe

In late August 1965 the *Bournemouth Evening Echo* reported that Hurn would be concentrating on delivering the American Airlines' 401s and in order to help this flow, six aircraft were assembled at Weybridge. As stated in Chapter 2, the development of the 400 series was very much predicated on the American order. It was the third American operator to introduce the One-Eleven but was the first to inaugurate the 400 series into service.

Branded as the '400 Astrojet' the American aircraft had the distinctive finish of the airline's fleet. One-Elevens were normally produced in yellow primer and then finished in the various airlines' liveries with grey painted undersides. But like G-ASYD and 'SYE the American aircraft were finished in bare polished metal and those areas fabricated from the solid, that is the rudder and the cabin over the wing were initially primed in grey and later painted silver to match the colour scheme. Below the window line there was a red cheat line with red titling over the windows.

The first 401, registered N5015, flew on 4 November 1965 and was delivered just before Christmas. All the other twenty-nine aircraft followed at close intervals with

Channel Airways' G-AWKJ (c/n 128) and BEA's G-AVMU (c/n 134) on the Hurn flight test apron in early 1969. *(Author)*

N5019 (c/n 059) for American Airlines showing the front airstairs which retracted neatly under the floor. Photographed outside the Flight Shed at Hurn, N5019 was the 200th turbine-powered aircraft built by BAC for a North American customer. *(BAE SYSTEMS)*

the final delivery in December 1966 averaging one every twelve days. One aircraft N5032, briefly carried the registration G-ATVU for a demonstration to SAS in Sweden and BAC was optimistic of an order but sadly SAS decided on DC-9s. That same machine later returned to the British register and flew for BA.

The first service was flown on 6 March 1966 on the New York–Toronto route and then services were gradually expanded until they covered an extensive network in northeast and central United States. On many routes the jets were in competition with Lockheed Electras or piston types. Not surprisingly American Airlines now had an appreciable competitive advantage. Mechanical reliability was so excellent that the type was easy to schedule and the Spey proved unequalled in its service record. The average stage length was 230 miles and the British type accounted for 17% of American services. But, as so often with the One-Eleven story, while American praised the aircraft in operation, before long passenger demand was such that the

The first of thirty One-Elevens for American Airlines, N5015 (c/n 055). Like many American One-Elevens it later became an executive aircraft. *(BAE SYSTEMS)*

airline needed a larger type and replaced their machines with Boeing 727s after only six years. Had the 500 series been available earlier American Airlines might not have made that decision. And what of the One-Eleven fleet, pensioned off well before its time? Twenty-one of the thirty-strong fleet became executive aircraft; the others went to various airlines. Two (c/n 059 and c/n 076) were later re-engined as Tay One-Elevens (see Chapter 12).

Philippines Airlines

The BAC sales team notched up another success when Philippines Airlines placed an order for two 402s in November 1964. During G-ASYE's World Tour in February 1966 she visited the Philippines and the airline's colours briefly appeared on one side of the aircraft to celebrate PAL's 20th anniversary. In April 1966 the first of PAL's many aircraft was delivered. Like Mohawk, this airline continued to order steadily over the years, so many more 400s and 500s were delivered. Philippines Airlines flew

The second aircraft for Laker Airways, G-AVBY (c/n 113) a series 320 was leased to Air Congo from 1967–1968. *(BAE SYSTEMS)*

Five One-Elevens at Luton. Autair of Luton operated a total of five 400 series aircraft before rebranding as Court Line and the purchase of the larger 500 series machines. Four 400s are seen here on the Luton tarmac including G-AVGP (c/n 114) and G-AWKJ (c/n 128). On the extreme left is a Dan-Air One-Eleven. *(BAE SYSTEMS)*

One of the two large final assembly hangars at Weybridge in January 1970. Three Hurn-built aircraft are in for refurbishment: Cambrian One-Eleven G-AVOE, former Autair One-Eleven G-AWXJ and Uruguayan flag carrier PLUNA's Viscount 745 CX-BHA. At the far end of the hangar is the final VC10, 5H-MOG, a Super VC10 for East African Airways. *(BAE SYSTEMS)*

the type on both domestic and international routes for a total of twenty-six years until 1992, with some of them having the most chequered of careers (see Chapter 13).

With UK Airlines

Besides British Eagle there was also another British One-Eleven 300 series airline, for after his departure from BUA at the end of 1965, the irrepressible Freddie Laker decided to start his own airline, Laker Airways. Freddie was soon in conversation with his old friend, Geoffrey Knight of BAC and on 8 February 1966 ordered three One-Eleven 320Ls for delivery in the following year – soon increased to four aircraft. BAC even provided a loan to Laker to help him start the airline, not a service they normally extended to customers. Another 300 series machine, formerly with British Eagle, was added to the fleet in 1971. Laker was only ever in business to operate IT (inclusive tours) and charter flights and with the demise of the airline in 1982 the four aircraft were sold.

Channel Airways, a British mainly inclusive tour and charter operator based at Southend, ordered four 408s in 1966 but only ever operated two at any one time. Two of the aircraft were specially built with an additional window exit over the wing,

TACA of El Salvador ordered two One-Elevens after the World Tour. The Second, registered YS-18C (c/n 106) made its maiden flight and was delivered in February 1967. *(Author)*

LACSA of Costa Rica ordered a series 409, TI-1056C (c/n 108) in January 1966, also as a result of G-ASYD's World Tour. The Airline later received a second 400 and graduated to the 500 series. *(Author)*

like in the 500 series, which enabled Channel to pack up to ninety-nine people into the aircraft. Never the most secure of operators, in 1972 the airline went bankrupt.

Yet another British airline, Autair of Luton, joined the queue to buy the BAC twin jet in late 1967 and received three 416s in time for the busy 1968 summer period. Like most other British independent airlines its main market was charters, but it also operated some British domestic services from Luton to UK destinations and Holland. Autair was later to become Court Line and a major, if somewhat short-lived, colourful 500 series user (see Chapter 8).

In Latin America

The One-Eleven 400 was quite a hit in Latin America and had an initial near-monopoly of the market. It sold widely, if in very small numbers, being operated by Austral of Argentina, TACA of El Salvador, LACSA of Costa Rica, LANICA of Nicaragua and the Brazilian line, VASP. Austral and LACSA later graduated to the 500 series, as did many others. Austral, the first South American One-Eleven operator, bought four 420s for its domestic and international routes to be flown from the capital, Buenos

Aires, using them until 1988, but continued services with a fleet of 521series until 1994. LACSA had two 409s which were replaced by three 531s and a single 515 (see Chapter 8).

Europe

In March 1967 Bavaria Fluggesellschaft, became the first German One-Eleven operator by leasing a 402 originally built for PAL and later ordered two 414s. Bavaria used its eighty-four-seat aircraft on routes from Munich to holiday destinations in Italy, Spain, France and Yugoslavia, also serving medium-range destinations such as Athens, Brussels, Istanbul, Malta and Tunis. Additional 400s joined the fleet in subsequent years as traffic grew and were superseded by 500s.

BAC had tried to hard sell One-Elevens in Spain, first to Iberia and then came very near to making a deal with Aviaco. But there was only ever a single One-Eleven on the Spanish register and that was a 402 originally ordered by PAL and delivered to

Three Weybridge assembled aircraft at the Wisley Test Centre in February 1970. EC-BQF (c/n 161) one of thirteen One-Elevens completed at Weybridge, just after repossession from the Spanish operator TAE. It is sharing the tarmac with the last VC10, 5H-MOG destined for East African Airways and Aer Lingus Viscount, EI-AOI. *(BAE SYSTEMS)*

G-AXBB (c/n 162) had a chequered career serving with LACSA of Costa Rica, Quebecair, and Germanair before joining Gulf Air. Subsequently it flew with British Island Airways and then Okada of Nigeria. *(BAE SYSTEMS)*

TAE of Bilbao as EC-BQF in March 1969. Flown on inclusive tours into Spain it was repossessed by BAC early in 1970 and finally sold on to TAROM as YR-BCH.

In what was a precedent for an Eastern Bloc country, Tarom, the state airline of Romania ordered six 424s in 1968, which eventually led to more orders and licence production (see Chapter 11).

Elsewhere the One-Eleven spread its wings wide including, for example, in the Arabian Gulf, when Gulf Air of Bahrain became the first operator in the Middle East, receiving a series 432, G-AXOX, in 1969. Additional One-Elevens were bought and leased and used on routes throughout the Gulf and to India and Pakistan until operations ceased in 1977.

The One-Eleven's entry into service was a great success, with many airlines reporting large increases in passenger load factors and a high utilisation. Additionally the world tour had allowed many potential customers to see the aircraft at first hand and be convinced of its versatility and sturdiness as a short-haul workhorse. However these would-be customers were also being courted by Douglas with the DC-9 and Boeing with the 737. And since the American aircraft could carry more passengers and as air traffic trends indicated substantial increases, BAC came under pressure to produce a larger version. Since there was still some stretch left in the Spey engine, the BAC project team set to work to produce the 500 series.

7

At last, the Stretched One-Eleven – the 500 Series

When BAC saw the specification for the Boeing 737 in early 1965 it was immediately apparent that it was a bigger machine – with the typical six-abreast Boeing cross-section, with longer range and bigger payload; a threat to both the One-Eleven and the DC-9.

Boeing had decided to go ahead with its 737-100 on 19 February 1965 and three days later Lufthansa ordered twenty-one machines. The 737 used the same fuselage dimensions of the 707 and 727 with scaled-down 727 wings. The engines, like the DC-9s, were Pratt & Whitney JT8Ds at 14,000lb thrust. Note that this was almost 3,000lb more thrust available than Spey-engined One-Eleven 500. Before the first flight on 9 April 1967, Boeing, like Douglas, introduced an extended capacity version, the 737-200 (with a maximum capacity of 124 seats) and quickly won an order for forty from United Airlines.

By Christmas 1965, Sir George Edwards and John Prothero Thomas of BAC presented a special ninety-two-passenger-capacity 400 series to the Britannia Airways Board in an attempt to equal some of the Boeing 737-200's specification. The battle for the order was a two-cornered contest between Boeing and BAC because Douglas did not press the case for their short-haul jet. What BAC so evidently needed to do was to stretch the One-Eleven to meet the Britannia Airlines' requirements and capture a very lucrative order. The glaring problem was that the company had neither the financial reserves nor the substantial orders for an extended version, to make that viable at the time.

In order to boost sales of the home product, Tony Crosland, the Labour Government's President of the Board of Trade, ordered Britannia Airways to buy the BAC product. In defiance Britannia refused to knuckle under and ordered three 737-200s. The Government grudgingly stood aside and allowed them to do so, but insisted on Britannia paying 14% import duty on the purchase. Blithely ignoring the financial penalty, Britannia went on to order twenty-four more Boeings 737-200s in the years that followed and now operates the latest 737-800s.

By the late 1960s the lack of a larger version of the One-Eleven was a critical obstacle to further sales. BAC endeavoured to sell a version of the One-Eleven 400 series to Britannia Airways, but the airline purchased Boeing 737-200s (G-AVRN shown here) and operated many more. The 737 has been an immensely successful programme and is the best-selling airliner in the world. *(Author's collection)*

British European Airways (BEA) also demonstrated patriotic fervour by expressing an interest in Boeing 727s and 737s in June 1966. Ironic to reflect how BEA now seemed keen to replace the Trident that had been designed exactly to their specification and had entered service only two years earlier. However, the Labour Government told BEA to think again and look at domestically produced aircraft which meant, as an equal to the 737, a larger version of the One-Eleven. Having pronounced this 'Buy British' edict the Government prevaricated for a year in its support for the One-Eleven 500 which was tied up with compensation payments for the cancelled TSR2 and the Government's political agenda of nationalisation. As a result of this delay Aer Lingus, which would have waited for the stretched One-Eleven, went ahead and ordered Boeing 737s. Eventually the Labour Government had to provide development costs of £9 million, which were to be repaid by a levy on sales. So BAC set to work on the stretched version, which eventually achieved eighty-six Hurn-built sales and nine Romanian assembled aircraft, amply repaying the Government's investment through export earnings and frustrated imports.

The early BAC market surveys in 1961 had shown that airlines were principally interested in a cheap aircraft/mile cost machine, reflecting both the continuing decrease in traffic growth rates of the 1950s, and the cost and capacity problems they had encountered with the new big jets, the Boeing 707 and Douglas DC-8. The jet stimulus was only just commencing in the early 1960s and BAC realised by the mid-1960s that demands for a stretched version were now going to intensify. However, with no growth version of the Spey in sight, many orders – notable among them that of Swissair – were undoubtedly lost because no clear stretch capability was on offer.

During the initial project and market phase of the One-Eleven, BEA had shown relatively little interest in the aircraft since the airline believed that Trident and turbo-prop aircraft would meet their needs for the foreseeable future. However, the worldwide success of the One-Eleven and BEA's own changing perception of its needs wakened an interest, which BAC was quick to exploit.

It had been clear for some considerable time that a larger version of the aircraft was needed, but up to that point no further power increases of the Spey-25 were available. BAC had put great efforts into trying to market a version of the 400 series for BEA in 1966, essentially for its internal German services, but the seating capacity was too low and seat/mile costs too high to attract an order. BEA's Viscounts were facing major competition on the internal German services from PanAm's 727s between Berlin-Tempelhof and the major West German cities.

The Launch of the Spey 512

As a result, after prolonged negotiations with Rolls-Royce, the Spey 512 was launched, providing an increase in power, which allowed the basic airframe to be stretched. The initial BEA requirement was for a relatively short-range aircraft and thus only a modest rise in Maximum Take Off Weight (MTOW) to 91,000lb from the 87,000lb of the 400 series was required. BEA was by then very wedded to the three-crew cockpit concept used on the Trident, but in recognition of the excellent worldwide acceptance of the two-crew BAC aircraft, agreed to the One-Eleven cockpit layout, albeit with some special modifications.

Almost two years behind stretched versions of the competition, the 500 series was launched on 27 January 1967 with an order for eighteen series 510s from BEA which would be used mainly on services in West Germany. BEA insisted on compensation from the Government for having to order aircraft which were not its first choice. And the Government meekly agreed. This was a great weapon for salesmen from Boeing and Douglas who would point out to airlines contemplating purchasing One-Elevens that one of Britain's two major carriers had to be subsidised to use the aircraft.

The new version had the fuselage extended by 13ft 6in in two sections, one forward of the wing of 8ft 4in, and one aft of the wing of 5ft 2in. This allowed for four extra seat rows increasing normal capacity from seventy-nine to ninety-nine, though 500s sometimes carried as many as 119 passengers. The wings had small extensions of

Stretching in progress at Hurn. G-ASYD (c/n 053) previously the 400 series development aircraft, being cut into three and extended to become the 500 series prototype. The forward part of the fuselage has already been opened up and moved forward while the section aft of the wing awaits a similar process. *(BAE SYSTEMS)*

2ft 6in each. Overwing exits were doubled to two either side, underfloor hold volume was increased and the structure was strengthened. The APU was increased in power and Spey 25 engines with 12,000lb thrust were installed.

Stretching G-ASYD to a 500

On 4 February 1967, G-ASYD flew Wisley-Hurn on flight 476 in order to be versioned as the aerodynamic prototype of the 500 series. Sixteen days later it was cut into three and a 100in extension fitted fore with a 62in extension fitted aft of the wing together with the extended wing tips. Structurally complete on 28 April, systems checks and the installation of test instrumentation were carried out during May followed by engine runs on 22 June, leading to a first flight six weeks ahead of schedule on 30 June 1967.

Piloted by Brian Trubshaw, with Roy Radford as co-pilot and two test observers, Ian Muir and Chris King, 'SYD took off on its 'second' first flight from runway 26 at Hurn at just about 12:30 p.m. and landed seventy-four minutes later. Take-off weight was

Crowds of BAC workers gather in the sunshine on 30 June, 1967 to watch the first flight of G-ASYD. Piloted by Brian Trubshaw, with Roy Radford as co-pilot and two test observers, Ian Muir and Chris King, 'SYD took off on its 'second' first flight from runway 26 at Hurn at 12.30 p.m. and landed seventy-four minutes later. *(BAE SYSTEMS)*

77,000lb, including 12,000lb of comprehensive test equipment able to measure and record approximately 800 parameters continuously. BAC Flight Test used automatic cameras, multi-channel trace recorders and magnetic tape recorders to record the information. Initially powered by Spey Mk 511, 'SYD was transferred to Wisley on 3 July to begin the business of flight testing. This included general handling, position error (PE) runs, stick jerks, tail loads, trim curves, Dutch rolls, stalls, measured landings and a trip to Bedford for minimum take-off speed trials. After the fitting of the more powerful 12,000lb thrust Spey 512s in January, it flew to Torrejon near Madrid for a month in February 1968 for runway trials, accelerated stops and noise tests; the flight testing was incessant. 'SYD was used for the bulk of the certification and performance schedules, flutter testing and autopilot development.

'SYD's Water Ingestion Incident

Chris King related an interesting incident during 'SYD's test programme:

All passenger category civil aircraft undertake water ingestion testing to ensure they can safely operate from partially flooded runways. For the One-Eleven, the requirement was to ensure the spray plume from the main and nose wheels did not cause serious engine malfunction. To prove this, the aircraft was accelerated/decelerated at various speeds in take off and landing regimes through a water trough with an average water depth of 1 inch. Cine cameras were positioned on the ground to the side of the runway beside the water trough. A helicopter was used to film from above and in front of the aircraft and a camera was mounted on the outboard left hand flap track fairing so the spray patterns could be recorded from various angles.

The trough was constructed on a fairly level bit of runway at RAE Bedford, by gluing 'T' sectioned rubber to the runway surface to retain the water. To accommodate the slight runway slope, cross dams were glued so water levels were maintained at the mandatory 1 inch. The airfield's fire tenders supplied water for the troughs.

The 500 series trials were conducted with 'SYD and on August 21, 1967 Peter Baker had had a successful day and we had one final run to do. But the wheels had destroyed one of the cross dams and as a result the water depth varied from 2 inches at trough entry to zero at the exit, what did we think? Peter and I had a quick conflab and decided that we would give it a go. After all the average depth was 1 inch wasn't it? On entering the water, there was an almighty bang, every Master Warning, except Fire, came up on number 1 engine and its associated systems. The engine stopped instantly. After taxiing back to dispersal, a quick visual inspection of the compressor face from the ground revealed nothing was apparently wrong with it.

We went back to Wisley by road where there were a lot of serious faces at the debriefing because this could be a significant problem for certification. All we knew at the time was the engine had unexpectedly stopped. The next morning, when the films had been developed, we found about 5 frames on the high-speed camera where something appeared to come out of number 1 intake through a solid plume of water and then go back in. A few days later, Frank Taylor, one of the Rolls-Royce service reps at Wisley told me the engine had stopped from take-off rpm in ¾ of a revolution. Why had it happened and how did he know that? Well, what we saw on the film coming out the intake, had been a first stage compressor blade that had broken off. He retrieved it, very mangled, when the engine was stripped.

The surfeit of water, which was far more than the certification requirements, had proved too much for the engine and it had suffered from indigestion!

From mid-1968 through to the end of the following year 'SYD was engaged in performance improvement testing for the developed 500 series with modified flap tracks fairings, leading edge and brakes. In September 1968, 'SYD emerged from the Wisley hangars looking resplendent in the new blue and sand colours of British

Now a 500, 'SYD pictured at Wisley in September 1968, painted on one side in the new BUA colour scheme for a publicity film together with a VC10. The other side remained in the BAC house livery. *(BAE SYSTEMS)*

United Airways or the more sober BAC red, white and blue depending on which side she was viewed. The port side was BUA, the starboard BAC. The liveries were a 'quick spray job' so that some aerial filming could be carried out for BAC/BUA/Rolls-Royce film being made, starring the One-Eleven and the VC10.

More testing was carried out at Wisley until April 1969 when 'SYD flew into the 'birthplace' of British aviation at Brooklands at Weybridge. This was the only time SYD visited Brooklands until her retirement twenty-five years later. Here an inspection was carried out and on the 13 November 1969 she took off from Brooklands and returned to Wisley.

G-AVMH – The First Production 510

In the meantime, on 7 February 1968, G-AVMH, the first BEA 510, made its maiden flight crewed by Roy Radford and Dave Glaser with James Munro of BEA and two observers. There had been concern at Hurn that 'VMH would miss the flight date because of the late delivery of the higher-powered Speys for 500 series but Rolls did eventually deliver them in time to meet the schedule.

On the day following 'VMH's maiden flight, it was positioned to Wisley to begin the test programme. This aircraft was used to confirm the performance and fly at maximum weights which 'SYD could not do because it was a conversion and not built to full 500 structural strengths. From August to November 1968, 'VMH tested all the specific BEA changes to the 510 series aircraft which Trubshaw claimed were equivalent to the cost of another aircraft! These changes included a different flight deck layout with a moving map display and the surprising decision not to incorporate the forward airstairs. In later years these alterations led to crew-rostering difficulties for BEA/British Airways with the emergence of two distinct groups of pilots; one group flying the 510s and another group piloting all the other 500 series.

Subsequently 'VMH was principally engaged in automatic approach and landing system development to the Category 2 standard required by BEA. Category 2 allowed the aircraft to operate where the weather minima were G mile runway visual range and where the pilot could fly the aircraft down to a decision height of 100ft to see if the ground was visible. If the pilot could not see the runway from this height,

BEA's first two 510s, G-AVMI (c/n 137) and G-AVMH (c/n 136) either side of G-ASYD on the Wisley tarmac in May 1968. G-AVMH was used to confirm the performance and maximum weights which 'SYD was unable to do because she was a conversion and not built to full 500 structural strengths. *(BAE SYSTEMS)*

the aircraft would overshoot and return for a second attempt. If the ground were visible, the pilot would land.

Sometime later, 'VMH's duties were taken on by G-AVMR, which spent eighteen months based at Wisley in autoland development and so was the last of the order to be delivered, on 5 May 1970.

G-AVMI was handed over to BEA on 8 July 1968 for crew training and on 15 August the 500 series was certified. The total number of hours involved in these trials was 387 by 'SYD and 394 by the first three production 510s, 'VMH, 'VMI and 'VMJ. The 510s met or handsomely exceeded the entire range of its contractual performance, for example, take-off and landing distance were better than stipulated and payload 3,800lb greater. A very thorough testing phase was now over but, across the pond, the equivalent Douglas DC-9-30 had entered service eighteen months earlier, in February 1967.

Super One-Eleven – What's in a Name?

In November 1967, BEA ran a competition to name their 500s and, from 898 entries received, alighted on the apt if somewhat unimaginative 'Super One-Eleven'. The winner was Brian Madge, BEA Moscow manager, whose suggestion won him a fortnight's holiday for two in Cyprus. The decision naturally provoked a certain amount of criticism from BEA employees, who claimed the name was neither imaginative nor original, since it was already in use by British Eagle.

500 Series Developments

Whilst the BEA stretched version of the aircraft did not attract any other buyers, it laid the foundation for the much more significant 500D series, aimed specifically at the European inclusive tour (IT) industry. The IT market had grown rapidly, from 13% of all passengers carried on international flights by UK carriers in 1963, to more than double (31%) by 1968. This market was one that independent carriers could easily enter in those heavily regulated times and some airlines, for example BUA, had introduced One-Elevens as early as 1965, followed by others such as British Eagle in 1966.

However, when Britannia ordered the Boeing 737, it was clear that BAC would have to work fast to preserve a healthy share of the UK market and this led to the rapid improvements of the 500 which became the 500D version. By now, BAC had enough real service and structural test experience under its belt to be extremely confident of the BAC One-Eleven structural performance limits. This allowed significant increases in all the design weights, with the MTOW rising to over 98,000lb and then to 104,500lb, with very small weight penalties and alterations. The name of the game at that time was to maximise seating with precious little regard for comfort, and seat pitches down to twenty-nine inches were not uncommon. This, together with fiendish devices such as seat-back catering where the meals were fitted into a seat back compartment, allowed the IT airlines to operate with 114 or more passengers at ranges which satisfied 95% of the IT demand at the end of the 1960s. These increased operations clearly required additional payload performance and that was achieved by introducing water-injection for the Spey 512-14DWs with 12,550lb thrust. The first pair of these was tested on 'SYD in July 1968. When BAC offered the developed 500 later that year they now had a product which was in a stronger position to compete with Douglas and Boeing. But the latter's much more powerful engines were to continue to give it the edge over the British aircraft.

In making a concerted effort to win sales from Boeing, BAC also introduced some exciting changes to the specification. There was a great deal of very sophisticated aerodynamic and performance work on the profiling of leading edges, flapjack fairings, etc., and the tuning and careful flight test measurement of stalling speeds, braking performance, etc. The thoroughness of this investment, in time and quality,

The 150th One-Eleven delivery. G-AVMX (c/n 151) branded 'Super One-Eleven' pictured outside the Flight Shed at Hurn in June 1969. BEA aircraft were painted in an understated version of the airline's livery because of the shared services operated with Air France in Germany. *(Brooklands Museum)*

paid off well, since the 500D was bought by BUA, Caledonian, Court Line and British Midland Airways (BMA) in the UK, in addition to several German charter companies. Over time it became Europe's most widely used IT jet with over half the 3 million UK passengers travelling to short-haul destinations flying on BAC One-Elevens. The additional performance range and lower seat/mile costs of this aircraft also gained sales in Central and South America, the Bahamas and the Philippines.

To exemplify the performance improvements the early 510s built for BEA could only carry a full payload of 23,000lb over 800 miles where the 500D was able to carry a slightly greater payload over 1,500 miles. In fact, the 500D could transport a 20,000lb payload for 2,000 miles – double the range of the 510.

The Market Situation in 1970

After five years in service, the One-Eleven was Europe's most successful airliner programme ever, and Britain's largest dollar earner. Ordered or re-ordered sixty-five times, it was in operation in a long list of countries from Argentina to Zambia, with twenty-seven airlines, four corporate users and two governments. For example, Mohawk had placed seven re-orders for the aircraft since its original contract in 1962. There were ninety-two flying in the Americas and ninety-six in the rest of the world. But sales were still hard fought, with competition on most sales from McDonnell Douglas and Boeing. Whereas the One-Eleven relied on exports for 64% of its sales, for the American competition the position was reversed, with only 40% of sales for export. The very large home market in the USA, with the increasing demand for short-haul flights across and within the North America, was of course the reason for this difference.

BAC carried out market surveys at six-monthly intervals for the five years ahead and their latest projection, in early 1970, was for a further 139 sales over that period of which thirty-eight might be satisfied by the second-hand market, generating a possible 101 new sales. This would take the total sold to 299 by 1975. Sadly, these projections were not realised and BAC's two major competitors were to dominate the market to such an extent that derivatives of each are still in production at the time of writing. Over the years ahead the DC-9 was stretched again and again, becoming the McDonnell Douglas MD-80 series in the 1980s and further revamped as the MD-90 series in the 1990s. After the take-over of McDonnell Douglas, Boeing decided to keep the 106-seater MD-95 in production re-branded as the Boeing 717. The 737 has been so developed that there are versions able to accommodate a wide range of differing requirements, with the largest able to accommodate as many passengers as its forebear, the Boeing 707.

The Thrust Barrier

Throughout its head-to-head competition with US aircraft, first the DC-9 and later the Boeing 737, the BAC One-Eleven always had to face the problem of significantly less power available from the Spey than the rival's JT8s could provide.

Initially, competition with the DC 9-10, whose Pratt & Whitney engine was de-rated and did not provide a particularly efficient solution, was not very fierce. Statistics over the first year of operation in the US showed fuel consumption was much better on the BAC One-Eleven, and the Rolls-Royce engine was soon able to establish a high level of reliability and smooth running. However, a resurgence of traffic growth in the early 1960s convinced many airlines that they would need an aircraft of approximately 100 seats, and here the Pratt & Whitney was ideally suited to provide a perfect power plant for the DC 9-30 and later the Boeing 737-200.

In 1967, Sir George Edwards told Harold Wilson that he forecast sales of 200 if there was no further Spey development and of 400 if there was. Sir George was quite accurate.

If American Airlines had opted for the Pratt & Whitney version of the BAC One-Eleven in 1963 the story might have been very different, and in retrospect BAC should almost certainly have offered the Pratt & Whitney as an alternative power plant to the market at this stage. However, for various political and financial reasons BAC failed to take this step and hence it fell to the BAC engineers to try to produce by refinement what their American counterparts could achieve by power. The range of power increase of the Spey showed a growth of 20% in thrust over six years, which compared quite well to that of the JT8. It bears repeating, however, that the American engine had started at 14,500lb compared to the 10,400lb for the Spey and this made it a fundamentally better-sized engine for the class of aircraft it was to power.

With BAC's insistence on the conservative structural design, it was obviously unlikely that the BAC One-Eleven would achieve significantly lighter structure than its counterparts, although its efficiency in these terms was very competitive. It was therefore only aerodynamic efficiency which could be used to try to redress the balance, and here the BAC engineers and flight test team produced remarkable results in matching the improvements of the US competitors, by a combination of careful wing design improvements and flight test measurement techniques.

This meant that in some circumstances the One-Eleven, with a take-off thrust of 12,500lb per engine, could carry the same number of passengers a lot further out of a critical airfield than an aircraft with 15,000lb of thrust per engine available. Unfortunately, these particular circumstances did not occur often enough to swing the balance and win sales.

8

The 500 Series in Service

BEA and British Airways

BEA's aircraft first entered service on an ad hoc basis on 1 September 1968 on the Berlin–Hamburg and Berlin–Bremen routes with full scheduled services commencing on 17 November that year. BEA and BAC held the 'Super One-Eleven' fleet-naming ceremony at Farnborough on 18 September, and 'VML took part in the flying demonstration during the week. Seven 510s were delivered by the end of that year and the remainder, except for 'VMR which was held back at Wisley for autoland trials until May 1970, were delivered during 1969. The handing over of G-AVMX to BEA on 28 June 1969 was a notable achievement for BAC as it was the 150th One-Eleven delivery. The 510s were delivered in a ninety-seven seat, single class configuration and gradually took on all the German services. BEA received a dramatic 35% increase on introduction of the type to the German schedules. In 1971, One-Eleven services were expanded and a division was set up in Manchester where they were maintained and flew all BEA flights from there to European destinations.

As a hangover from the war and the division of Europe, only aircraft of the Allied powers could operate domestic flights in West Germany. Consequently it was PanAm, Air France and BEA that flew these routes. Because of jet competition from PanAm's Boeing 727s, Air France and BEA agreed to jointly run their flights with the new One-Elevens. However, since this was a shared operation it was deemed necessary to tone down the BEA-ness of the livery. But how to achieve this? There followed a period of indecision during which the aircraft flew in incomplete schemes before someone hit on the idea of reducing the size of the BEA logo on the fuselage and removing the fin flash entirely, merely painting 'Super One-Eleven' on the fin, thus emphasising the aircraft not the airline.

On merger with BOAC to form British Airways on 1 April 1974, BEA brought twenty-five One-Elevens to the combined operation; its original order plus four Cambrian 400s and three 400s that BEA had purchased for services out of Birmingham just prior to the merger. In 1978, BA indicated its intention of purchasing 737s and though

BAC contested this strongly, instead offering a 600 series aircraft (See Chapter 10), the order was eventually placed for nineteen Boeing 737s. One commentator has written that BA never seriously considered BAC's One-Eleven 600 proposal and British Airways operated well over 100 examples of the American twin-jet. When placing the Boeing order in 1978, presumably to placate the British manufacturer, BA also ordered three One-Eleven 539s from BAe and traded in two 400s. These 539s were built to the standard specification; (i.e. without the special non-standard and costly BEA fit of the 510s) and were delivered in mid-1980. G-BGKE, the first of the three 539s was the first One-Eleven to have a tail assembled in Romania as part of the licence agreement signed in 1979.

Though withdrawn from the German services in 1986, two years later BA inherited thirteen more 500 series with the takeover of British Caledonian. These thirteen machines were used on Birmingham and Manchester Domestic and European services from autumn 1988. The One-Eleven proved ideal for operation from these important regional hubs. Even though services with the airline proper finished

Manchester 1970: a BEA 510, British United's G-AWYS (c/n 175) on lease to Swissair, a Laker 320 and another British United 501. Note that all except the BEA aircraft have the convenience of forward integral airstairs that BEA eschewed. *(BAE SYSTEMS)*

Four BEA aircraft: G-AVMO (c/n 143), another BEA One-Eleven 510, G-AVMX (c/n 151) and G-AVMT (c/n 147) at Berlin Tempelhof in the 1970s. G-AVMO is now preserved at the National Museum of Scotland at East Fortune. *(BAE SYSTEMS)*

in 1993, it was not until five years later that One-Elevens ceased operating with franchise partners, such as Maersk, and so ceased to appear in BA colours. The last service was flown on 4 August 1998 by G-AWYS, just one month short of the thirtieth anniversary, which would have fallen on 1 September that year.

BEA's initial reluctance to adopt the One-Eleven proved to be misplaced, for the airline used a total of forty-four series 400s and 500s for varying periods over virtually thirty years between September 1968 and August 1998, when it was part of the BEA or BA fleet.

The Disposal of the BA Fleet

Between late 1991 and early 1993 the whole fleet was ferried to Hurn for storage. In 1992, two were donated by BA to museums, 'VMO to Cosford and 'VMU to Duxford, both of which are regularly open to the public. The remaining sixteen were bought by European Aviation in 1993 (see Chapter 15). Some of the other 500s went to Africa and European also purchased others. The 400s were sold to Okada Air, Nigeria and to Nationwide Air Services in South Africa. Two of the 539s also went to Okada and the remaining 539 to DERA (now QinetiQ) at Boscombe Down.

British Independent Operators – BUA

In early 1968 British United Airways (BUA) announced an order for four 501s which were delivered in the following year and three more joined their fleet in 1970. Only a few days after the BUA order, Caledonian joined them by ordering three 509s. But unlike BUA, Caledonian was a somewhat unenthusiastic purchaser of the 500 series since its management actually wanted 737s and only bought the Hurn-built airliner because the Department of Trade and Industry struck a deal with them to make them purchase the One-Eleven. Adam Thomson, former Head of Caledonian, states in his autobiography that Caledonian also wanted to buy Boeing 707s for long-haul services and that the Board of Trade waived duty on those on the condition that Caledonian bought One-Eleven 500s and gave no publicity to the deal. With this insight, Adam Thomson's words when announcing the order, now read in a somewhat different light: 'I am pleased to say that the BAC One-Eleven 500 emerged as the aircraft most suited to the needs and demands of our particular market. We are impressed with its performance and believe that our One-Eleven 500 fleet will give us exceptional reliability with economy of operation … I wish to stress that all of us at Caledonian are delighted to be buying British aircraft.' (*The Bournemouth Echo*).

British Caledonian Airways

At the end of 1970 British United and Caledonian merged to form British Caledonian Airways giving it a large fleet of short and long fuselage One-Elevens. At the time of the merger the combined fleet was eight 201s and twelve 500s of differing types.

The first of BUA's 501s, G-AWYR (c/n 174) on the disused runway at Hurn in April 1969. After service with BUA, British Caledonian and Ryanair it was sold to Executive Airline Services of Nigeria as 5N-ESB in 1998. *(BAE SYSTEMS)*

British Caledonian's G-AWYR (c/n 174) also flew with Ryanair and British Airways before sale to EAS in Nigeria, where it was grounded in 2002. *(BAE SYSTEMS)*

G-AXLL (c/n 193) a series 523 for British Midland at Hurn in December 1969. After serving with many operators it flew for European Aviation which sold it to Savannah Airlines of Nigeria. In the background is 'white tail' G-16-11 (c/n 197) which went on to serve with Germanair and finally with Austral. *(Author)*

Eighteen years later British Caledonian Airways was itself taken over by British Airways. By then the early 201s had all been disposed of, 'SJJ had crashed, 'SJA was in executive use, SJD was sold to the Ministry of Defence and the remaining seven were purchased by Pacific Express of California. There were thirteen 500s, nine of which had been delivered new to the airline and four bought second-hand.

British Midland Airways

Having originally ordered two 303s and then cancelled them, British Midland Airways became an operator of three 119-seater 523s in early 1970. They were used on scheduled services from East Midlands Airport and on holiday charters. Finding themselves frequently unable to compete on price with larger operators in the inclusive tour market, British Midland withdrew from this arena in 1972 to concentrate on its scheduled services and, by the end of 1974, the One-Elevens had been sold to Transbrasil.

Court Line: Halcyon One-Elevens

Whereas the short period of One-Eleven operation by British Midland does not seem to have left much impression, the metamorphosis of Autair into Court Line, the multi-coloured operator of the 500 series, is much better remembered.

Though Court Line's period of operating the One-Eleven was comparatively short, it made an indelible mark because the airline decided to rename itself and, in contemporary marketing speak, totally overhaul its brand. When Court Line emerged

Court Line aircraft at Luton in 1970. In the foreground G-AWBL (c/n 132) the only Autair 416 to serve with the renamed carrier and two 518s G-AXMK (c/n 205) and G-AXML (c/n 206) in the background. *(BAE SYSTEMS)*

This One-Eleven first operated with Bahamas Airways, then Court as G-AZEB (c/n 188) and finally with Phillipines Air Lines until it was retired in 1995. *(BAE SYSTEMS)*

After Court Line's collapse, G-BCCV (c/n 198) was returned to BAC at Hurn. It is seen here in Court livery with the titling blanked out. It went on to serve with Monarch and Dan-Air. *(Author's collection)*

on 1 January 1970, it chose to use the strength of its parent company's name, a shipping line. Between December 1969 and April 1970 the newly named carrier took delivery of seven 518s while only one of its previous four 400s was retained. The airline ended its scheduled services and branded itself as Britain's premier holiday airline. So with new aircraft, a new name, a new livery and new uniforms designed by Peter Murdoch of the Royal College of Art, it was poised to seize a large slice of the newly affluent holiday market at affordable prices.

Each of the seven One-Elevens was finished in a pastel colour, either pink, orange or turquoise, with a silver logo and white wings. Quite a change for the generally staid British liveries of the time. The one 416 series remaining, G-AWBL, was repainted in the turquoise scheme. The cabin staff uniforms were designed to represent the exterior colours of the aircraft and all other items such as tickets, timetables, check-in points were designed in the same colours to reinforce the brand message. Each aircraft was given a Halcyon fleet name, for example, *Halcyon Sun*, *Halcyon Breeze*, *Halcyon Sky*, etc. (Halcyon is Greek for peaceful and happy.)

Halcyon Cabin Style

In order to maximise revenues the 518s were laid out in a very high density seating arrangement with 119 seats, a layout used by some other operators and the most ever fitted in a 500 series. Savings were made in other areas and, in order to speed up catering and reduce costs, the airline hit upon the idea of having two airtight food trays fitted in the headrest of the seat in front: one tray for the outbound journey and the other for the return. This avoided the need to upload food at the outbound destination. It also enabled the passengers to open the tray and eat when they wanted. Though these trays were fitted with locks, some 'devious' passengers found the means to open both trays and so ate the food intended for the return flight, leading to many complaints. As a result this shrewd idea had to be discontinued and the airline reverted to the normal arrangement of food served from trolleys.

The boom in mass tourism in the early 1970s brought swift success to the company and Court bought more One-Elevens, two more 518s from BAC and three 517s from Bahamas Airways. They even leased in additional 500s and also leased them out to Aviateca, Lanica, Cyprus Airways, Germanair and to Leeward Islands Air Transport, which was partly owned by Court Line. By 1974 the world economic downturn fuelled by the swingeing oil price rise put paid to Court, which ceased operations on 15 August 1974. The BAC jets were repossessed by the manufacturer and other creditors, and were swiftly passed on to other airlines.

Caribbean and Latin American 500s

Just as the shorter-bodied 400 series had made its mark in the Caribbean and in Latin America, the 500 soon followed in its wake. After leasing two 400s from BAC, Bahamas Airways bought two 517s, VP-BCN and 'BCO, and a 301 series, VP-BCP, in 1969/1970. All three were delivered in their resplendent colour scheme and briefly flew services from Nassau to the United States until the airline ceased trading. BAC repossessed the 517s, stored them at Wisley and then sold them to Court Line, while the 301 was sold to Laker Airways.

Aviateca of Guatemala chose the 500 in November 1970 and started operations only one week later with a leased Court Line 518, G-AXMK, registered as TG-ARA. Their own TG-AZA was delivered on 25 March 1971 and was later supported by leased 500s from BAC, which served until the end of the decade. The Aviateca routes spread out from Guatemala City to the Southern USA and other Central American cities.

A Germanair aircraft on test flight from Hurn. This can be deduced by the incidence vane fitted in place of the ninth cabin window. This photo also gives a good view of the 500's extended wing tips and the longer flap track fairing introduced on the developed 500 to reduce drag and only later fitted to BEA's 510s. *(BAE SYSTEMS)*

Having started One-Eleven operations with a 409 in 1967, LACSA of Costa Rica received another two years later. Delighted with their One-Eleven experience they soon decided on the larger 500 series and ordered three 531s, which were delivered at yearly intervals from 1971. Later, in 1973, these were joined by a 515 formerly operated by Paninternational and British Caledonian and the fleet continued in use on scheduled routes throughout the Caribbean until 1982.

Austral of Argentina was, like Philippines Airlines, an early adopter and loyal customer of the British short-haul jet. Operations began in 1967 with the delivery of LV-IZR, the first of four 420s. These were followed by three larger 521s two years later. Needing more aircraft for their extensive domestic network serving twenty cities, Austral bought seven various second-hand 500s and also leased more One-Elevens. But by the early 1990s, Austral sought a replacement for the type and replaced them with McDonnell Douglas MD-80s, a super-stretched DC-9 development. All the 500s were broken up in Argentina except two 500s which European Aviation bought and they escaped back to Hurn. European's plan was to hush-kit the pair to comply with the Stage 3 regulations but that programme was not viable, they never flew again and were scrapped there in early 2001 (see Chapter 15).

German Charter Operators

The One-Eleven 500s made quite an impression on the German charter market with Paninternational buying two in 1969 and Germanair and Bavaria Fluggesellschaft, which was already using 400s, following suit with orders. The latter two airlines merged in 1977 to form Bavaria Germanair, with a fleet of seven 500s and two 400s of various marks, and further merged to become Hapag-Lloyd two years later, which operated the aircraft until 1979. They were all sold on to other operators, namely Philippines Airlines, Austral, British Caledonian and Air Malawi.

500 Series Demonstration Tours

Tireless in its quest for new customers for the One-Eleven, the Corporation organised a series of demonstration flights in late 1969 and early in the following year. As there was no dedicated 500 series demonstrator, a number of production 500 series were enlisted for the task. The first of these was a demonstration in Amsterdam on 15 October 1969 with an Austral series 521. This aircraft had made its first flight as G-16-9 and was temporarily registered as G-AXPH for the visit. On return to Hurn it soon received an Argentinean registration and was delivered to Austral on 18 November 1969.

Another One-Eleven for the German tour market with Panair, D-ALAT (c/n 187) factory fresh at Hurn. It later flew with Germanair, Hapag-Lloyd and Austral. *(BAE SYSTEMS)*

Roy Radford flew another 500, temporarily registered as G-AXSY, on a tour of Canada, the United States and the Caribbean from 30 November to 12 December 1969. To indicate the intensity of demonstration tours the crew actually made nine flights on one day alone, 5 December, in the Caribbean. Destined for Germanair as D-AMUR, G-AXSY was soon back at Hurn and delivered to Germany.

American Certification

In the early 1960s, with all the orders for the One-Eleven from various American carriers, BAC had decided to simultaneously obtain American (FAA) and British certification for the 200 and 400 series. With the 500 (and 475 later) there was no such impetus to receive an FAA type certificate because there were no orders from airlines in the USA. This was not an obstacle to foreign operators flying into the States, but any indigenous US airline would have required this. This lack of certification was to cause problems later with the Dee Howard Tay re-engining programme.

African Tour

For another series of demonstrations of the 500 series BAC used an aircraft originally destined for Paninternational but which was not delivered to them. It made its first flight on 9 December 1969 as G-16-11 and for a tour of Africa was painted in a BAC livery and registered G-AXVO.

On 20 February 1970, the *Bournemouth Daily Echo* reported the tour as follows:

Recently a BAC One-Eleven 500 carried out a tour of East and North Africa to demonstrate to the airlines there the ability of its latest version of the One-Eleven to perform efficiently and economically under the exacting climatic conditions.

On an extremely tight schedule, the team, led by Sir Geoffrey Tuttle, vice-chairman of BAC Weybridge Division, visited nine countries and carried out seven demonstration flights in seven days.

First port of call on the African continent was Cairo in Egypt, where officials of United Arab Airlines joined the aircraft for a demonstration flight, during which the One-Eleven became the first commercial jet ever to land at Alexandria Airport.

On the following day at Khartoum, senior personnel of Sudan Airways and members of the British diplomatic service visited the aircraft before the BAC team departed again for the next stop on the tour, Entebbe, in Uganda.

After a one-hour flight from Entebbe, which afforded the East African Airways guests magnificent views of the world-famous Murchison Falls and the nearby game reserves, the One-Eleven flew on to Mombassa, where the stay coincided with the arrival of President Makarios of Cyprus on a State visit to Kenya.

President Kenyatta of Kenya inspected the One-Eleven demonstrator before meeting President Makarios, who arrived from Lusaka in a Zambia Airways One-Eleven 200. Next port of call was Kenya's capital Nairobi where more officials of Super VC10 operator East African Airways were BAC's guests for a flight over the Central Highlands.

During the following day's demonstration from Lusaka BAC's Assistant Chief Test Pilot (One-Eleven) Roy Radford who headed the flight crew for the tour, banked the aircraft low over the Zambesi River to give the Zambia Airways guests a fine view of the Kariba Dam development. After returning that night to Nairobi the team was off again early in the morning for Malta, where officials of Malta Airways were shown over the One-Eleven 500 on the ground at Luqa Airport.

The final demonstration flight of the tour was made from Algiers on the following morning, and the aircraft arrived back at Hurn in the evening, having carried out a total of 22 flights in under seven days.

Roy Radford added that on the flight from Entebbe, Idi Amin, who became President of Uganda one year later, was one of the passengers and asked Roy if the ventral exit could be used for dropping paratroops. Roy replied that it could not. Idi Amin also asked him to fly in very low circles over Amin's home region of Uganda and if he might address his people. Rather bemused, Roy flattered his ego and let him 'speak' to the people using the aircraft's public address system, but of course, the crowds could not have heard him through a system designed purely for internal communication.

Delivery Record and Double Centuries

In March 1970, shortly after the African tour, BAC's Hurn factory made a production record, never to be repeated, by delivering ten 500s to six customers in one month. The aircraft delivered were two each to British United, British Midland, Court Line and Paninternational, and one each to Caledonian and Germanair.

Just five months after making this delivery record, BAC announced on 6 August 1970 that orders had now reached 200 with the placing of orders for four 500s from Philippines Airlines, two more for Court and an additional machine for Paninternational.

The 3 November 1971 saw the two hundredth One-Eleven delivery as BAC's test pilots Lou Roberts and Fred Clarkson left Hurn with PI-C1181, PAL's third 527. The value of sales and spares had now reached over £300 million, two-thirds of which had been for export.

One for Switzerland

There were only ever two Swiss-registered One-Elevens, a 500 used by Phoenix, a Swiss independent charter operator and a 400 for which the contract was never finalised. There were also three aircraft variously leased by Swissair but these were never given Swiss registrations and stayed on the British register. However, Phoenix, which bought a 529 registered HB-ITL in 1971, flew it on a wide range of inclusive tours to the Mediterranean and North Africa from its base in Basle until 1974. Then Phoenix went out of business and the One-Eleven transited to warmer climes in Argentina and joined the Austral fleet.

PAL's Twenty-Six One-Eleven Years

Philippines Airlines started with 402s in 1966 and gradually replaced them with 104-seater 500s in the 1970s. Three 527s were delivered in late 1971 followed by two more received in 1974. With the takeover of two local operators PAL became the

HB-ITL (c/n 212) which flew for the Swiss tour operator, Phoenix, from 1971 to 1974 seen at Gatwick. It had first flown as G-16-13 in 1970 and after the collapse of Phoenix was sold to Austral but crashed south of Buenos Aires in March 1981. *(BAE SYSTEMS)*

sole national airline, and, with more capacity needed, eight second-hand 500s were gradually added to the fleet, with the last arriving in 1980. The fleet was used mainly for domestic services, which were expanded considerably in the 1970s when new local airports were built. The last of the British jets was retired in 1992 and replaced by 737s. The nine survivors were put into store and bought by European Aviation. Seven were broken up for spares and two flew halfway round the world back to their birthplace at Hurn with Bermudan registrations as VR-BEA and VR-BEB. They were never used and so never flew again. The first was broken up but at the time of writing the second is still intact on the Hurn fire dump.

Transbrasil of Brazil, which had operated as Sadia, operated a large fleet of 500s on domestic Brazilian services commencing in the latter part of 1970 and continuing until early 1978. The first three bought new from BAC were 520s, registered PP-SDQ, 'SDR, 'SDS, followed by three 523s which had first been operated by British Midland and became PP-SDT, 'SDU, 'SDV.

Stranded in Nicosia

In May 1974, Cyprus Airways started One-Eleven operations with a BAC-leased 518, G-AXLM, only to have it stranded for eighteen months with other airliners at Nicosia Airport because of the Turkish invasion of the island. Two more were leased from BAC and flew Cyprus Airway's routes throughout the Mediterranean and to the Middle East. In late 1977 and early 1978 the airline finally took delivery of three new 537s, 5B-DAG, 'H, 'J and operated them right through until 1995 when they emigrated south to start operations with Nationwide Air Charter of South Africa.

Transbrasil's PP-SDU (c/n 211) at Hurn in October 1973 still carrying its British registration, G-AXLN. *(BAE SYSTEMS)*

Cyprus Airways G-BCWG (c/n 204) first served with Court, then Monarch, which leased it to Cyprus Airways and then BAC sold it to PAL, where it ended its days in 1996. *(BAE SYSTEMS)*

The Second-Hand Market

Airlines function in a dynamic market where mergers, take-overs, bankruptcies and changes of equipment often take place. The whirligig of operators and ownership throws up some interesting combinations, for instance, Pacific Express of the United States bought seven British Caledonian 201s and nine former Braniff aircraft plus three American 401s only to be itself taken over by Braniff in 1988. So Braniff was once more operating the British airliner, including some of its original purchases, after a gap of eleven years. However, these operations were short-lived, for in the following year Braniff ceased operations.

In contrast, Dan-Air, a major figure on the British scene, never owned any brand-new One-Elevens but used almost all the major types, 200s, 300s, 400s and 500s plus a Romanian-built 561. In the 1970s and early 1980s Dan-Air purchased various versions from a variety of operators and BAC. The airline flew a substantial set of scheduled services in Europe but was taken over by British Airways in November

After sixteen years with BUA and British Caledonian, here G-ASJC (c/n 007), the third production One-Eleven, is about to leave Gatwick for the United States, where she became N101EX with Pacific Express. This airliner later merged with Braniff and, registered as EI-BWI, it returned to Southend and was broken up in 1996. *(BAE SYSTEMS)*

Dan-Air never owned any brand-new One-Elevens but used almost all the major types. This 500, G-BDAE (c/n 203), was previously with Court Line and after service with Dan-Air was bought by British World which registered her G-OBWD; it was broken up at Southend in 2006. *(BAE SYSTEMS)*

1992 in a deal which did not include the One-Elevens. Whereas the short-body versions had already been sold, the eleven 500s were purchased by British Air Ferries which put five into service.

Arkia, the Israeli independent airline, provides a simpler example. In 1977–78 BAC sold two 500s formerly owned by Transbrasil to Arkia. They mainly flew on charter operations to Europe but ceased operations in 1979, when the manufacturer again sold them on. One went to PAL and the other to Dan-Air.

Though there were a number of important first-time buyers of the type in North America, there were also carriers which had significant used fleets such as Pacific Express, mentioned above, and Florida Express, which purchased Pacific Express's 201s in 1986 having earlier bought nine 203s from US Air. Though the diaspora of the American Airlines primarily benefited the executive market, some of their 401s were also added to this large fleet which ran services based in Orlando in Florida through the south-east of the United States. In the States there were many users of small fleets for limited periods, including Atlantic Gulf Airlines, Britt Airways, Cascade Airways, Challenge International Airlines, Classic Air and International Air Tours.

Trans Canada Airlines (TCA), later Air Canada, operated large fleets of both Vickers Viscounts and Vanguards and had been a prospective launch customer for the stillborn VC11, so BAC had hoped for a definite sale of the One-Eleven to them. But it was not to be and TCA became a major user of the DC-9, which it continued to use in large numbers until 2002. But there was some compensation for BAC when two of the bankrupt British Eagle's 304s were sold to Quebecair of Canada in 1969 and were followed by three other 400s in the following years. Quebecair used the British jets for a total of sixteen years when their fleet was sold to Nigerian and British users.

There were many other airlines that bought used the One-Elevens for varying periods but there was also an important lease market, which placed aircraft in liveries of airlines, which the manufacturer would like to have had in their order book.

Leased One-Elevens

As the number of aircraft delivered grew, so did their temporary usage by other airlines, as owners sought to maximise the income from their investment by leasing out aircraft when they were not needed to carriers which were short of capacity.

The Israeli airline Arkia leased two aircraft from BAC, the first of these was temporarily G-16-22 but on delivery took Israeli marks as 4X-BAR (c/n 230). *(Brooklands Museum)*

After its tour of Zambia, 9J-RCI was leased as G-ATVH to British Eagle in 1966. The following year it was subleased to Swissair for six months and it is seen here at Zurich-Kloten Airport. *(BAE SYSTEMS)*

The manufacturers also engaged in this activity, providing spare aircraft to assist an airline often with the expectation that a lease could result in a later sale. On other occasions where BAC could not provide early delivery of new aircraft, they leased an aircraft until the new machine was delivered.

As a result there are a large number of airlines that have operated the One-Eleven yet never bought them. Airlines such as KLM, Lufthansa, SAS and Swissair, for example, used them in the late 1960s and, through the continuing years of the century, so did many, many other airlines, large or small, well-known or long-forgotten. A very well-known lessor of the Hurn jets, itself based at Hurn, was European Aviation about which more is written below (pp. 197–202).

9

The Hot Rod – the One-Eleven 475 and 670

Unable to stretch upwards because of thrust limitations, BAC reviewed the characteristics of the One-Eleven and decided that with the new aerodynamic and structural improvements, a very high performance smaller aircraft could be of major interest in the Third World countries. The solution to this specification often used in both aircraft and automotive engineering is a mix and match arrangement. From this concept came the 475 series, using the body of the 200/400 but retaining the extended wing, leading edge and powerplant of the 500 series. This provided an aircraft of eighty-seat capacity, able to operate from 4,000ft strips and ideal for hot and high operations. Announced in January 1970, the 475 series was promoted with the following features most of which, but not all, were introduced on the aircraft:

- 200/300/400 series length fuselage
- Spey 512-14DW of 12,550lb thrust – as used on the 500 series
- extended wings like the 500 series
- larger main wheel undercarriage – to give rough field performance. The main wheels now measured 44in in diameter and 16in in width, i.e. 4in taller and 4in wider than the normal One-Eleven size; besides being at a lower pressure to provide a bigger 'footprint'. The pressure of the tyres was 80lbs per sq. in. (psi) at MTOW, half that of the 500 series. These larger wheels required the re-design of main gear bay, doors and underbelly. Optionally a rough-field kit could be fitted which included glass fibre coating of the undersides, wings and flaps. Deflectors were fitted between the main wheels to stop debris being thrown into the engine intakes.

These capabilities allowed the aircraft to be considered for an entirely new market segment, mainly in remote locations in Third World countries, where many of the airfields were of poor quality, perhaps unpaved dirt strips. The requirement, to be able to operate from unimproved strips, led to design and flight test work which

BAC was optimistic of the sales potential of the 475, as can be seen by these models painted in the liveries of Finnair, Fiji Airways, East-West, TAA and Qantas. However, none of these airlines purchased any. *(BAE SYSTEMS)*

resulted in a fully approved rough runway kit, far simpler but just as effective as anything produced by the Americans. The performance and engineering trials, both in the UK and overseas, were very comprehensive and resulted in a jet aircraft which could go anywhere where a DC-3 could operate. This variant sold to Peru, in the Pacific Islands, in Central Africa and the Middle East but, sadly, the 1973 oil crisis had an adverse effect on traffic prospects in the Third World more than anywhere else and curtailed interest in an aircraft of this size and capability for many years.

The Conversion of G-ASYD to the 475 Series Prototype

April 1970 was a busy month for 'SYD and it began with its 1,000th flight. That flight involved wet runway tests when the Wisley fire engines sprayed 67,000 gallons of water over the runway. A week later, in preparation for the 475, there were gravel

The One-Eleven 475 was designed for operation from unprepared strips so before 'downsizing' as the 475 prototype, 'SYD (c/n 053) carried out gravel runway trials at Wisley as a suitably protected 500 prototype. Note the cameras fitted below the nose and on the top of the wing. *(BAE SYSTEMS)*

runway tests with 'SYD carrying out a number of trials pertinent to its future role while still a 500. A 300ft long by 6ft wide strip of limestone chunks were laid on the Wisley runway and the aircraft was protected with a layer of balsa on the underbelly and fitted with protection cages on the air intakes. Some twelve runs were made through the gravel with various flap settings to simulate the effects of landing and take-off from unmade runways.

Both these trials proved successful so a few days later, on 8 May 1970, 'SYD flew into Hurn for conversion. This involved removal of the fuselage plugs inserted when it was extended to the 500 series length. The main wheel bay was reconfigured to accommodate bigger wheels and tyres, giving a noticeable bulge. The job of cutting open a fuselage into three pieces and the subsequent join up was no mean task – especially on a development machine, where the interior was not merely seating but sensitive and expensive flight test equipment with all its sensors and additional cabling. So it was not only normal systems wiring that had to be shortened and reconnected but also all the test instrumentation that accompanied it.

All tribute was due to the BAC engineers who completed the task one month ahead of schedule and, on 27 August 1970, Roy Radford took 'SYD into the air from Hurn's runway 26 for a 'third' first flight but on this occasion as the 475 series prototype. Dave Glaser accompanied him as co-pilot with two flight test observers on board. Immediately after take-off Roy brought the prototype back along the Hurn runway at 300ft to allow for publicity shots. The 475 then climbed to the west to carry out tests, returning fifty-five minutes later. On landing, the nattily dressed Roy Radford

G-ASYD being 'shrunk' at Hurn to become the 475 prototype, with the two plugs fitted when it was lengthened to a 500 already removed, though the aft fuselage has not yet been joined up. *(BAE SYSTEMS)*

The first production 475, destined for Faucett of Peru but initially registered as G-AYUW (c/n 239). This view shows the bulged main undercarriage bay that was fitted to this series in order to accommodate the larger wheeled main undercarriage. *(BAE SYSTEMS)*

(as described by the *Bournemouth Echo* and witnessed by the author) gave a press conference and television interviews. A few weeks later, 'SYD was demonstrated at Farnborough Air Show. But despite the abundant evidence of the aircraft's abilities there were few orders for the 475 – at that time only two for Faucett of Peru.

The Rough Field Trials at Waterbeach

While G-ASYD was undergoing flight trials, a survey team led by Dr Robert Graham was inspecting undeveloped runways and landing strips in locations as far apart as Alaska, Brazil, Peru and Labrador in order to build up a composite picture of the sort of conditions the 475 series would confront in service. BAC took samples from these runways and constructed a 1,500ft test strip on a disused runway at Waterbeach in Cambridgeshire. The strip consisted of a 9in-thick limestone sub-base, topped with a further 9in of gravel and sand. This mixture was the average profile for surface conditions that the survey results had thrown up.

In the meantime the aeroplane was being prepared for the trials. Abrasion resistant paint covered the underside of 'SYD and the inner flaps had glass cloth protection. Gravel deflectors between the pairs of main and nose wheels gave protection to the landing gear and hydraulic pipes. Aerials and beacons protruding from the underside of the fuselage were also protected. Rubber deflectors were fitted between the pairs of wheels to prevent stones bouncing at random after hitting the inside of the tyres. Finally, large, low-pressure tyres were fitted. These precautions became known as the 'Protection Kit' and could be fitted as standard items on 475 production aircraft. As with the 500 series trials at Wisley, matt black paint was used

In May–June 1971 G-ASYD flew a series of trials on a specially prepared rough runway at Waterbeach which resulted in certification for the 475 for operation from unmade airstrips. *(BAE SYSTEMS)*

The five One-Elevens completed at Hurn in December 1967. The RAAF's A12-125 and A12-124, Bavaria Flug's D-ANDY, VASP's PP-SRT and PP-SRU. (c/n 124, 125, 127, 119, 126). *(BAE SYSTEMS)*

G-ASJA (c/n 005) making a sprightly take-off from the Brooklands runway after refurbishment to production standard following almost two years test flying. Because of the restricted length of the runway, aircraft had to be airborne at the yellow hatched markings. *(BAE SYSTEMS)*

EI-ANE (c/n 049) St Mel, the first aircraft for Aer Lingus sold to Hold Trade Air of Nigeria in 1991, broken up ten years later. *(BAE SYSTEMS)*

A fine underside shot of American Airlines' first aircraft, N5015 (c/n 055), showing how their machines were uniquely finished in a polished metal finish which was the base of the airline's livery. *(BAE SYSTEMS)*

Laker's G-AVBY (c/n 113) and a new RAF VC10, XV107, at Brooklands. Owing to the restricted length of the runway and poor approach, One-Elevens only occasionally flew into Brooklands. *(BAE SYSTEMS)*

Engelhard Industries N270E (c/n 120) photographed at Heathrow. It was fitted with a twenty-five-seat executive interior and 1,000 gallon auxiliary fuel tanks. *(BAE SYSTEMS)*

A beautiful shot of PAL's PI-C1171 (c/n 215). After twenty-five busy years with this carrier it was broken up in 1996. *(BAE SYSTEMS)*

Taking off from Hurn's runway 26 is Austral's first 521 which was delivered in November 1969. It initially flew with the British 'B' registration G-16-7 but soon became LV-JNR (c/n 192). *(BAE SYSTEMS)*

Hurn trio, the nose of Court's G-AXMH (c/n 202), G-AXMI (c/n 203) and the tail of British Midland's G-AXLM (c/n 211). *(Author)*

A view of one of the two Hurn production lines at the beginning of 1970. In the foreground is G-AXMJ (c/n 204) for Court Line and behind are Caledonian's G-AXYD (c/n 210), BUA's G-AXJM (c/n 214) and another Court, G-AXMK (c/n 205). In a seven-week period between 17 February and 7 April all made their maiden flights. *(BAE SYSTEMS)*

Halcyon Sun, Court Line's G-AXMH (c/n 202) showing off one of the tremendous colour schemes the aircraft were painted in. *(BAE SYSTEMS)*

The second production 475 G-AZUK (c/n 241) landing at the Farnborough Air Show in September 1972. It also flew on demonstrations in the South American and was delivered to Faucett as OB-R-1080 in July 1974. *(BAE SYSTEMS)*

Air Malawi's 7Q-YKF (c/n 243) entered service in 1972 and was sold to GAS Airlines of Nigeria in 1993. *(BAE SYSTEMS)*

The three Omani Air Force 485s all had freight doors fitted subsequent to completion. Here is 1003 (c/n 251) being converted with a large part of the forward fuselage removed which can be seen on the left of the photograph. *(BAE SYSTEMS)*

The penultimate One-Eleven built at the Hurn factory in early 1984. G-BLDH (c/n 262) was painted in a special BAC livery for photographic purposes. *(BAE SYSTEMS)*

The maiden flight of N650DH, the first BAC One-Eleven 2400 powered by Rolls-Royce Tays from San Antonio, Texas, on 2 July 1990. *(Dee Howard via Bill Hurley)*

The rarely photographed second Tay One-Eleven, N333GB (c/n 076), owned by Hanson Group, which was used for a trial installation of a 'glass cockpit' at Honeywell's in Phoenix. With the end of the programme it was broken up. *(Bill Hurley)*

One of the two One-Elevens used by Northrop Grumman for electronic warfare research, N162W (c/n 087), showing off a wide variety of excrescences used for electronic sensor development. *(Sunil Gupta)*

In 1984 the Ministry of Defence bought two 479s from Air Pacific, one of which, ZE432 (c/n 250), joined the Empire Test Pilots' School at Boscombe Down. *(QinetiQ)*

Right: This close-up of
the main gear of G-ASYD
during the Waterbeach trials
gives a real example of the
actual 'runways' that the 475
was certified to use. *(BAE
SYSTEMS)*

Below: In order to protect
the aircraft from damage
during rough field operation,
undercarriage gravel
deflectors were installed.
Antennae protected,
abrasion resistant paint was
sprayed onto the underside
of the fuselage and
glasscloth fitted to the inner
flaps. *(BAE SYSTEMS)*

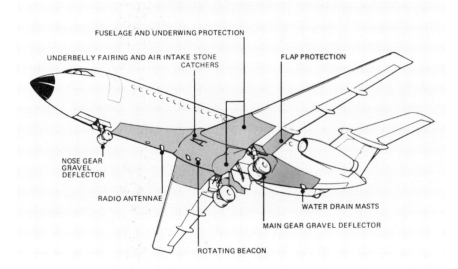

to make any stone strikes readily visible. For the first half of the trials, protective
cages were again fitted to the engine intakes. Additionally, high-speed cine cameras
were attached to a number of vantage points on the aeroplanes to record the path
of the debris kicked up by the nose and main wheels. The film evidence showed that
dust and stones were carried well clear of the APU and engine intakes.

The Waterbeach trials were carried out between 25 May and 4 June 1971. In all,
'SYD made twenty-five landings in conditions of pouring rain, hot sunshine and in

high cross winds and tail winds up to 20 knots, simulating 'hot and high airfields'. Roy Radford, who captained these trials, remarked to the author that on landing there was a tendency to bounce in random directions, which required careful control. Certification for this kind of operation was achieved in September 1971.

The 475 Demonstrations

Roy Radford described how challenging demonstration flying could be – much more demanding than test flying. The aircraft was away from base without support, often in an unfamiliar terrain for the pilots and crew. The demonstration pilot would have to 'sell' it to a local Chief Pilot who was often normally desk-bound with little recent relevant experience. Roy took the second production 475, G-AZUK on a two-week Sales Tour of South America in June 1972, visiting Peru, Chile, Ecuador and Argentina. 'ZUK was flown into strips that had never previously been visited by jets and made twenty-nine demonstration flights, ten of which were on unpaved runways. For instance, at Ayacuco in Peru the runway had a steep gradient, and Juliaca, also in Peru had just a 'runway' of grass and loose stones.

Roy also demonstrated the 475 in the Himalayas where on one occasion, when confronted by a large number of valleys, the local Chief Pilot could not point

The second production 475, G-AZUK (c/n 241) was flown by Roy Radford on a two-week Sales Tour of South America in June 1972, visiting Peru, Chile, Ecuador and Argentina flying into strips that had never previously been visited by jets. *(BAE SYSTEMS)*

out which he should land in and the navigational instruments were upset by the topography. Fortunately a seventy-year-old Pathan standing behind Roy's seat pointed out the destination!

BAC made strenuous efforts to sell the 475 to other customers in the region. This included hiring OB-R1080 from Faucett to demonstrate to Lloyd Aereo Boliviana of Bolivia. It was based at Cochabamba and flew into several rough airfields including the highest in the world at 12,090ft above sea level with a 6,000ft runway of sod and gravel. Though the demonstrations impressed the Bolivians, no orders were forthcoming mainly because of the difficulty of arranging finance.

The 475 in Service

The first and second production 475 series, 476s for Faucett of Peru, flew respectively as G-AYUW from Hurn on 26 March and G-16-16 on 7 July 1971, later becoming G-AZUK. They were both based at Wisley for the final aspects of the 475 certification. 'YUW was demonstrated at the 1971 Paris Air Show and delivered by Roy Radford, registered as OB-R-953 in July. G-AZUK had flown the South American demonstrations in a rather unappealing grey and white livery with no special titling, but for the Farnborough Show in September 1972 it was painted in BAC house colours and demonstrated on the ground and in the air. It was only finally delivered to Faucett as OB-R-1080 in July 1974.

Based at Lima, the first aircraft began revenue services on 5 September 1971 on key Peruvian domestic routes radiating from the capital to serve seven major cities. Peru boasted a number of unpaved runways, notable among these was Iquitos, deep in the Amazon jungle and Cuzco at 10,500ft above sea level in the Andes, both requiring the special abilities of the 475. Within one year of delivery OB-R-953 was achieving 60% load factors; utilisation was eight flights involving seven to eight hours' use daily and an average despatch reliability of 98%. Faucett's One-Elevens were laid out as seventy-four-seaters and were to spend ten years operating on domestic routes in Peru flying in and out of some of the least distinguished airfields in the world, but nevertheless providing a valuable service to the inhabitants scattered over that remote and difficult terrain.

Withdrawn from service in December 1982, both Faucett airliners were flown to Van Nuys, California, and put into open store and therefore exposed to the elements. There they remained mouldering and neglected possibly until their ultimate demise. However, some five years later, Mediterranean Express, a Luton-based charter line pinpointed them and asked British Airways Engineering to assess the cost of repair and return to the UK. An on-site examination was carried out and the BA engineers report stated matter-of-factly that the dents in the centre section were from 'llama strikes' when the aircraft had operated from the unprepared strips. A thousand hours were spent on refitting 'ZUK (back with its British registration) before it could be ferried to Heathrow and a full overhaul. The test flight with Civil Aviation Authority (CAA) Chief Pilot Peter Baker (one time One-Eleven project pilot with BAC) went well and it was awarded its British Certificate of Airworthiness. On 23 June 1987, it uploaded its first paying passengers for Mediterranean Express.

Its sister, the first production 475 G-AYUW was less fortunate, it returned to the UK in November 1987 but its overhaul was abandoned and it was purchased for spares by British Aerospace. The fuselage, sold to AIM Aviation, was delivered to Hurn for water demisting trials and placed outside the former BAC flight shed in June 1989. It was later scrapped. G-AZUK served with Baltic Airlines, Loganair, Ryanair and British Air Ferries, and though there was some discussion by BAe Filton of purchasing it to replace 'SYD, it joined the exodus to Nigeria.

The 475 series had all the hallmarks of a contemporary Regional Jet for which there is now a substantial market but which had not developed thirty years ago. Further orders were received for a single aircraft from Air Malawi, which had previously leased a 207 from Zambia Airways. Air Malawi took delivery of their 475, a

Two 475s at Hurn in February 1972, 7Q-YKF (c/n 243) for Air Malawi with incomplete tail livery and DQ-FBQ (c/n 245) for Air Pacific. The latter aircraft registered ZE433 flies with a Eurofighter Typhoon radar with an extended nose. *(BAE SYSTEMS)*

481 7Q-YKF, in February 1972, enabling them to provide a geographic expansion to their network radiating from Blantyre to neighbouring countries in Central and South Africa. The Air Malawi 475 served for twenty-one years and was joined in 1980 by a former Hapag-Lloyd 500, which was sold to Okada Air twelve years later. The 481 was sold to GAS Airlines of Nigeria in 1993.

The first Air Pacific One-Eleven 479, DQ-FBQ, made a 12,000 mile delivery flight to their Nausori Airport headquarters, Suva, on Vitti Levu, the principal island of Fiji, on 10 March 1972. After intensive crew training, inaugural flights begun on 2 April. The initial routes were from Fiji to New Hebrides, Papua New Guinea, Samoa, replacing the Hawker Siddeley 748s formerly used. The second aircraft ordered was delivered more than one year later at the end of July. Both aircraft returned to the UK in March 1984. DQ-FBQ became ZE433 for the RAE Bedford and DQ-FBV joined the ETPS at Boscombe Down as ZE432 (see Chapter 14).

Production of the One-Eleven actually stopped at the end of 1972, leaving a stockpile of six unsold aircraft. Orders came from the Omani Air Force for three in July 1974, helping reduce the stockpile, and the first of the trio made its first flight with 'Chuck' Thrower in command and was delivered before the end of the year.

Hush-Kitting the One-Eleven

In 1973, BAC and Rolls-Royce developed a hush kit to reduce the noise of the Spey to comply with stringent new regulations. G-ASYD carried out flight trials in two phases. The first phase involved twenty-four hours of aerodynamic trials in October 1973. In the following year the very noticeable hush kits with a 6ft addition to jet pipes were fitted and first flown on 14 June 1974. In the following two months twenty-five hours of noise calibration flying was carried out at RAE Bedford. The kits proved satisfactory, reducing the noise by up to four decibels and the land area affected by ninety decibel noise was halved. In September that year, 'SYD appeared at Farnborough sporting the hush kits, which were available to customers on new-build aircraft and as a modification to existing machines.

Freight-Door-Equipped 475s

BAC had proposed a fuselage-mounted freight door as a possible addition to the aircraft as early as 1967 for the USAF Aero-Medical version (see Chapter 10). This was 80in wide by 73in high. In the event, when the first examples were fitted seven years later the larger VC10 freight door, 120in x 73in, was used. It could be fitted retrospectively or during manufacture. So with a minimum of delay the One-Eleven's configuration could be altered from all-passenger to mixed passenger/freight or all-freight operation. The door, operated by its own hydraulic system, could be opened to near vertical for crane loading and its interior was trimmed to match the cabin furnishings, thus making it barely discernible to the passenger. (But Douglas was well ahead of BAC and offered large freight-door-equipped DC-9s from 1965 for which the Long Beach company received appreciable orders.)

The One-Eleven's freight handling system consisted of a removable overlay floor secured to the seat rails. In the doorway it was fitted with a ball mat for easy manoeuvring of loads inside the aircraft. The other floor sections were fitted with rollers to facilitate forward and aft movement of loads. Fitted with these facilities the 475 could carry almost eight tons more than 1,700 nautical miles. A 500 series would have been able to carry nearly ten tons over this distance but none was built.

Whereas the first two Omani aircraft were delivered without freight doors, for which they later returned to Hurn to have fitted, the third aircraft made its first flight at Hurn and then returned to the production line for its fitting. Delivered in November 1975, it was almost immediately severely damaged in an oxygen fire (see Chapter 13). All three machines still fly for the Omani Air Force and frequently visit Hurn for maintenance by Flight Refuelling.

Besides the freight-door-equipped Omani machines, one window-less dedicated freighter 475, a 487, was built on the Hurn production line for Tarom as YR-BCR. This proved very useful in transporting equipment from Hurn and other BAC sites during the setting up of the licence production line in Romania. It was leased to Anglo Cargo Airlines in 1986, later registered as G-TOMO, but returned to Romania in 1992 and went to Nigeria seven years later.

Only three other 475s were built. HZ-MAM was delivered in May 1978 to Mouaffak Al Midani of Saudi-Arabia and fitted out in California as an executive aircraft. In 1993 it went to Nigeria, then to Indonesian Air Transport and is now owned by an aircraft lessor, Aravco, as G-MAAH. The last two machines lingered complete but unflown at Hurn while there was talk of them going to the Queen's Flight.

The Last Hurn Deliveries

With the announcement in July 1983 of British Aerospace's decision to close the Hurn factory, it was decided to fly the two as yet unflown 475s. John Lewis, Deputy Chief Test Pilot at Filton, took the first on its maiden flight on 2 February 1984 as G-BLDH (LDH = Last Delivery Hurn) in a special colour scheme, with a blue cheat line and 'BAC One-Eleven 475' titling. Eight days later he captained its second flight and it was passed as ready for delivery. John Lewis also captained its companion, the final British-built One-Eleven, on its maiden flight on 9 May as G-BLHD (LHD = Last Hurn Delivery) in a grey and white colour scheme with no markings and a second flight final test flight two days later. (Incidentally the author saw this

The dedicated Tarom 475 freighter YR-BCR (c/n 267) being checked at Hurn in June 1981 before delivery. It was the only One-Eleven to be built with a reduced number of windows. Note the lengthy Stage 2 hush kits fitted to the exhausts of the Speys. *(BAE SYSTEMS)*

The last of 663 aircraft built by the Vickers-Armstrong, later BAC and finally BAe factory at Hurn. G-BLHD (c/n 260) and BAC Hurn senior management in May 1984. It was not unusual for aircraft to fly in this basic colour scheme while awaiting sale to a customer. *(BAE SYSTEMS)*

Following the closure of the British Aerospace (ex-BAC) factory at Hurn in May 1984, the last two One-Eleven 475s, G-ALDH and G-ALHD (c/n 262 and 260), were flown to the company factory at Woodford and placed in temporary storage with a partly complete Nimrod AEW3 between them. *(BAE SYSTEMS)*

flight not knowing at the time it was the last Hurn One-Eleven maiden flight and, having seen the prototype's first flight twenty-one years earlier, was very pleased to have witnessed it). Both aircraft were ferried by Al Smith and John Lewis to BAe Woodford, Cheshire, at the end of May. They were fitted out with executive interiors and long-range tanks by McAlpine Aviation and then sold to Indonesia and Saudi owners respectively.

The Development of the 475 into the 670

The idea that, with minor modifications, the 475 Series One-Eleven could be an answer to the very tough operating requirements of Japanese local routes, was first mooted late in 1975. From the start of discussions on building an aircraft to replace the Japanese-built YS11s it was apparent that the problem was a complex one. There was simply no aeroplane available that did what was wanted and, while plans to remodel the airfields did exist, practical politics, underlined by the experience of opposition to the new Tokyo airport at Narita, suggested they should not be taken too seriously.

Japan's air transport system is one of the world's densest, uplifting twenty-five million passengers per year, and with tremendous growth potential, since travel has such a high priority in Japanese discretionary spending. When there are Jumbo Jets, TriStars and DC-10's all flying on short-range routes, what prospect was there for small jets? The answer lay in the seventy YS11s, sixty/sixty-four-seater turboprops built in the sixties in Japan which still served no less than forty-nine of the cities receiving airline service. These aircraft were ageing and becoming less profitable. At the same time passengers were looking for jet standards of service. Originally the 737 and DC9 were selected to replace them, but the Ministry of Transport set very high standards for airports and a situation developed whereby improvements everywhere, from the YS11-length 4,000ft to a minimum 6,000ft jet runway, became impractical. The Japanese authorities set a ruling that neither of the short-haul jets should operate into runways shorter than 6,000ft, heavily influenced by a belief that, under Japanese conditions, the American certification procedures gave inadequate margins for safety in day-to-day operations. These factors combined to create a demand for a jet aircraft to serve the 4,000ft airfields without extension. The aircraft would have to show an actual level of performance, rather than just a legal one, which, under daunting conditions, satisfied the local interpretation.

To achieve a possible sale BAC decided to mount a demonstration operating 'SYD on the actual routes and, to prepare for it, 'SYD underwent a substantial refurbishment. Meanwhile the sales engineers had to negotiate with the individual airport operators and visit each one to assess their quality. Captained by Roy Radford, 'Yankee Delta' was demonstrated at the 1976 Japanese International Air Show in Iruma, which was used as a base. During the show it set out daily on simulated airline flying into these small airfields, some at high altitudes, often in appalling weather conditions, 'SYD impressed the airport managers and the competition alike, since their aircraft could not operate from 4,000ft runways at all.

During the demonstrations two BAC salesmen were tasked with transporting a very large picture of a Faucett 475 on public transport to promote these flights. At the end of the trip, they were only too happy to give it to Roy Radford, since they had grown rather tired of taking it on and off trains. Roy now has it on display in his conservatory at home.

At the end of 11,500 miles and thirty journeys, BAC was relieved to see that despite 'SYD's non-standard developmental nature it was an extremely reliable vehicle. From beginning to end, the flights were performed to British landing and take-off criteria, on schedule except for one diversion and because of one baggage delivery problem. But despite BAC's best efforts, no order was forthcoming. The Japanese authorities insisted on greater fuel reserves and performance margins if the One-Eleven was to be certified in their country.

The 670 Series

BAC was still anxious to achieve their aim of supplying the substantial YS-11 replacement market and decided to develop the 475 further. In a BAC brochure published in 1977 for the new 670 series it was proposed that there would be:

– a wing span increase of 40in, to 96ft 10in
– automatic wheel brakes with advanced hytrol anti-skid
– automatic ground spoilers and lift dumpers
– two overwing exits each side
– Spey ejector silencers – these silencers had a rearward-moving, acoustically lined shroud which would provide positive thrust augmentation and silencing in climb and on approach. During cruise the ejector would be stowed in the forward position covering the reverser cascades and eliminating the drag they caused.

During versioning as the 670 prototype G-ASYD was fitted with a modified wing leading edge, improved braking systems and a tail parachute for stalling tests with which it actually made her maiden flight as a 670. She is seen here on the Hurn Flight Test apron with the parachute prior to the maiden flight on 13 September 1977. *(BAE SYSTEMS)*

G-ASYD's Final First Flight – As the 670 Series Prototype!

Entering the Hurn hangars in March 1977, 'Yankee Delta' began its last metamorphosis, though not exactly to the aforementioned specification. BAC engineers found that wing extension would increase the bending moment of the wing and that the additional performance was obtainable by fitting a small triangular fillet or cuff between the wing leading edge and the wing fence. This cuff increased the lift coefficient by up to 20% and reduced the approach speed by 6 to 8 knots and take-off speed by up to 12 knots. Since 'SYD was a demonstrator, she was not fitted with the additional overwing exits nor most noticeably with the Spey ejector silencers.

On 13 September 1977, Roy Radford and John Cochrane made SYD's first flight as the 670 prototype from Hurn to Filton, where flight testing was based. Equipped with the rear parachute rig for stall protection, 'SYD immediately engaged on a full test programme, completing twenty-four stalls on the following day. Dynamic stalls were flown on 19 September and almost daily after that, with Dave Davies, Chief Test Pilot of the CAA taking the controls on 20 October when forty-three stalls were made. After the One-Eleven's earlier difficulties in this area the BAe was assiduous at fully testing this area. The following year, in April 1978, Roy and Dave Glaser carried out

A close-up of the wing cuff fitted to G-ASYD as a 670. This small cuff between the wing leading edge and the wing fence had a substantial effect on the aircraft's performance: it increased the lift coefficient by up to 20%, reduced the approach speed by 6–8 knots and take off speed by up to 12 knots. (Author)

runway performance measurement trials at Hurn, as these were paramount for the Japanese order. As Japan has so much rain, a series of tests were organised using RAF water tankers spraying a section of Hurn's main runway and then measuring 'SYD's stopping performance in the wet.

By late 1978, BAe felt confident to make an offer in a letter to Japan's TOA Airways of £5,350,000 each for twenty of the 670 series aircraft, but unfortunately TOA did not order. So after all this effort and expense there were no orders forthcoming.

These improvements fitted to the 670 provided a valuable increase in performance, allowing the One-Eleven to either use restricted runways or extend its range. BAe considered adding the first three improvements, i.e. the cuff, hytrol brakes and automatic lift dumpers to the 500 series, which would then be re-designated as the 600 series. BAC could then market the short-fuselage 670 and the longer 600 and could retrofit the improvements to existing 475s and 500s. Analyses took place as to costs and markets and though there seemed to be an appreciable market, nothing ever came of the project after this (see Chapter 10).

A close-up of the parachute fitting on G-ASYD just after a test firing. The anti-stall parachute fitting on the One-Eleven was large and fitted far back in order to provide a sufficient nose-down pitching moment and so that it would not become entangled in the tail. *(BAE SYSTEMS)*

G-ASYD made her last Farnborough appearance in 1978 but there were further demonstrations. In October 1979, Roy Radford and John Cochrane took a break from Concorde tests to fly 'SYD to Malaysia and Indonesia in the hope of sales. Now the 670 branding was dropped and the aircraft was once more titled as a 475. But there were no orders. Though this was the end of 'SYD's many sales tours she still had fifteen years of useful life ahead.

In 1980, BAe approached the Government for funding to pursue research into relaxed stability, manoeuvre and gust alleviation using 'SYD. The concept was to move the aircraft CG (Centre of Gravity) aft using water ballast to reduce stability to improve manoeuvrability. The aircraft remains flyable only because the stability is replaced artificially by a digital computer augmentation system which interprets pilot commands fast enough to drive the control surfaces in the right way. 'SYD was flown at 0.50 smc (Standard Mean Chord) which meant that the CG was behind the aft limit. This was unpleasant to fly and especially uncomfortable for the test crew in the back of the cabin. After nine flights the programme was wound down. It demonstrated that reductions of up to 25% in tail plane area were possible which would reduce structural weight and operating costs in a new design.

'SYD was then used for research into manoeuvre load alleviation followed by gust alleviation trials as part of the A320 research programme. This entailed detecting gusts and activating the spoilers to deploy very quickly and partly cancel out the wing bending caused. The load relief target was 33%, which would significantly improve aircraft ride.

Then in late 1981 'SYD was specially fitted with a Russian de-icing system. This employed electro-impulse induction in the leading edge, which was energised to de-ice the wing. On 30 April 1982, tests were flown behind the Boscombe Down Canberra, WV787, which sprayed water from a rear nozzle and iced the leading edge. The tests were to ensure that the system worked and that there was no injurious skin fatigue. Though the tests proved satisfactory no further development work took place.

Throughout the 1980s 'SYD continued flying, mainly on communications runs between BAe sites and collaborative projects offices, especially the Warton–Munich, Warton–Turin and Filton–Toulouse runs. The Military Division was keen to take it over so they could operate it on a full-time basis but Filton Flight Test resisted this as 'Yankee Delta' was still needed for the very occasional equipment test.

'SYD was also used on other roles by BAe, for instance to support jet stream test flying trials in Spain and, in April 1983, accompanying the two-seat Hawk Trainer demonstrator, G-HAWK/ZA101, on a successful sales tour of the Middle East. 'SYD travelled with the Hawk, which made the demonstrator's ground and flight crew tasks much easier. Flying from the Hawk's base at the well-known Hawker test airfield at Dunsfold, Surrey, they transited through Malta to Luxor then to Riyadh where the two aircraft were based for a week. They then flew on to Kuwait and finally Bahrain for more demonstrations and back to Dunsfold on 19 April 1983. Prior to the merger of BAC and Hawker Siddeley in 1977 to form British Aerospace, such co-operation was unheard of. In January 1991, with the start of Operation Desert Storm, the war to free Kuwait from the Iraqis, Yankee Delta spent time based in Riyadh, Saudi-Arabia, ready to pick up BAe people if necessary and fly them home.

The final tests in this long and distinguished career were with Lucas Industries light activated spoilers and ailerons and to herald this the fuselage was painted with the titling 'Fly by Light Control Technology' above the windows. 'Yankee Delta' was retired in October 1993 and parked outside at Filton but fortunately saved from the scrap heap and donated to the Brooklands Museum by BAe Airbus.

G-ASYD's Last Flight

John Faucett, Filton's Chief Test Pilot, invited his predecessor John Lewis to accompany him on 'SYD's last flight. The runway at Brooklands had never been long but six years after BAe's departure there was only approximately half of the original 3,600ft remaining. Aircraft can only approach the runway from the south because it is bordered to the north by the steep London–Bournemouth main line railway embankment. The Museum had to get permission to use the runway and remove lamp posts and arrange fire cover.

G-ASYD, the well-known One-Eleven development aircraft donated by BAe to the Brooklands Museum in 1994. After its last flight into the historic site it is preserved and frequently open to the public. *(Author)*

G-ASYD's final touchdown on the remaining part of the Brooklands runway at Weybridge on 14 July 1994. *(Cliff Knox)*

The flight crew practised their drills carefully and, with incidence vanes once more fitted through each fourth cabin window as so often on test flights, the crew took off from Filton for the last time on the morning of 14 July 1994. Coming from the Wisley direction, the several hundred spectators saw her make a long approach and a well-rehearsed landing with a maximum energy stop. In fact, John Lewis remarked that they stopped so sharply they had to power up to taxi to the end of the runway and park.

It is open to viewing regularly at the Brooklands Museum and visitors may be intrigued to find artefacts from the aircraft's history; the parachute canister, the parachute itself, a flight test observer's panel, the incidence vanes and a large raised patch in the floor where the escape chute was fitted. As 'SYD spent most of it's life test-flying, it was always felt that there might be a need for emergency escape facilities, so this feature was retained even when seats were fitted over it when the aircraft was used on the inter-factory shuttle services. (See Appendix 9)

G-ASYD has had a fascinating history and it is exceedingly fortunate that it is preserved and in good hands.

10

The Stillborn Civil and Military Proposals

Through the One-Eleven's history there were many schemes to develop it beyond the 500 series and special performance 475. BAC persevered with many projects through the late 1960s and up to Nationalisation in 1977 but none ever came to fruition. Though most of the developments were based on extending the fuselage to improve payload/range for commercial carriers, some were for military applications and there were civil and military collaborative proposals with Japan.

BAC Decision Making

A decision to develop the aircraft would have required the BAC Board to make a substantial investment in the project. But throughout its sixteen-year existence the Corporation had to fight for survival against many vicissitudes. The One-Eleven itself had a troublesome development which delayed it severely, the VC10 failed to penetrate the civil market and in 1965 a major blow struck the Corporation with the Labour Government's cancellation of TSR2, BAC's main military aircraft programme. The loss of TSR2 put the organisation in a parlous state, there were many redundancies, and the Luton factory, which made the One-Elevens' wings, was closed and the work transferred to Weybridge. Problems were exacerbated by the Government's lengthy negotiations on TSR2 cancellation compensation, which interfered with and delayed their financial support for the One-Eleven 500. Throughout this period the Labour Government continued to propose purchasing all of BAC as a step to merging it with Hawker Siddeley which had a deleterious affect on project development and investment.

Other problems confronting the Corporation were the result of a change in its make-up. In 1960, BAC was formed by the merger of three companies, Vickers-Armstrongs, English Electric and Bristol. But in 1966, Rolls-Royce purchased Bristol, enabling them to take over Bristol Siddeley Engines and become the sole British aero-engine manufacturer. This purchase gave them a 20% holding in BAC, which was unwelcome to them. Eventually this holding was bought from the receiver by Vickers and English Electric (now owned by GEC) after Rolls-Royce's bankruptcy in 1971, giving them equal shares in the Corporation. So now there was GEC's Sir Arnold Weinstock, a vigorous industrialist of the times with a say over half of the BAC Board but no background or interest in the aircraft industry. It is recorded that at a meeting of the Board in April 1971 Weinstock saw no reason for One-Eleven production to continue and that BAC was finished in the civil field. It is in the light of this tough, if not downright hostile atmosphere, that BAC had to make its investment decisions. As a result no major developments of the One-Eleven took place. This attitude also put paid to the production of aircraft 'on spec' which tied up capital but gave BAC the advantage of being able to offer early delivery decisions and clinch a deal.

In 1977, with the formation of the state-owned British Aerospace (BAe) from BAC, Hawker Siddeley Aviation and Scottish Aviation, the new Board examined their projects and in July 1978 decided to develop the mothballed Hawker Siddeley 146 as the BAe 146. The net result spelt the end for any substantial investment in the One-Eleven. But all was not over for this sturdy jet since BAe then followed another road and began licensed production with Romania.

The One-Eleven Civil Proposals

Between 1967 and 1983 BAC/BAe examined a number of proposals to develop the aircraft. Few of these took to the air but some of them had real potential and would have given the type the power and improved performance needed to compete with the Americans.

The 600 Series Mark 1

In 1967, BAC project teams began to look at a 600 series development of the 500 with extended fuselage, additional wing area and increased power. Deliveries were projected for the summer of 1971. The main thrust of this development was to scale up the design using the 500 series as a model. The 600 would have had a 146in fuselage extension, 120in in front of the wing and 26in behind, providing three more rows of seats. With the increase in size there was to be an additional toilet, extended galley facilities, additional emergency exits (a door either side behind the wing but one fewer over-wing exit) and a second freight loading door forward of the wing. The rear fuselage was to be extended and modified to give an improved aerodynamic shape and the wing area was to be increased by 202sq.ft to 1,233sq. ft. The engineers achieved this by moving the existing 500 series wing outboard and adding a new section, thus increasing the span by 120in and providing for additional flap sections each side.

The tailplane was extended by adding 62in to the end of each tail span and the fin was heightened. A very noticeable feature of this proposal was the drag-reducing deletion of the fin/tailplane bullet. As a result the tail was reminiscent of the DC-9.

Discussions with Rolls-Royce had produced the possibility of an 'aft-fan Spey'. This was a free-running fan installed behind the engine/thrust reverser unit of the Spey 512. This resulted in a bypass ratio of approximately 4:1, much improved specific fuel consumption and noise, and a take-off thrust of over 17,350lb. The aft-fan Spey was also intended to be fitted on the outboard engines of the Nimrod maritime reconnaissance aircraft but this was clearly a very difficult concept and did not proceed.

The 600 series Mark 2

With the advent of the 500 series in 1967 BAC realised that more could be obtained from the basic 500 airframe as long as there was more power and investigated a simpler, less developed version of the 500 under the 600 designation. So there was

The 600 series Mark 1.

The 600 series Mark 2.

The 700 series.

a later version of 600 Mark 2 in 1969 which required much less development than the 600 Mark 1. Instead of a widened 500 series wing and tailplane and additional exits, this proposal used exactly the same wing and empennage of the 500 except for a stub fin above the tailplane. The only appreciable alteration to the 500 series dimensions was an extended fuselage with an 80in plug ahead of the wing.

The 600 Mark 2 had similar aft-fan 19,730lb Spey power plants as the earlier version, Maximum Take-Off Weight (MTOW) was increased by 17,000lb over the 500 series of that date and with an additional fuselage fuel tank could have carried up to 129 passengers for 2,200 miles. Here was an aircraft capable of providing serious competition to the existing 737-200 series, which could have been in service in summer 1971.

Sadly, although the initial studies looked very promising, neither of these 600s went ahead. What were the reasons for this? Probably a combination of politics and a lack of finance. BAC did not have the money to develop the 600 and was fully engaged in the development of the Two-Eleven at Weybridge designed to compete with the Boeing 727-200 which BEA and other airlines were interested in. The Two-Eleven would have been assembled at Hurn and BAC did not have the capacity to run both projects and opted for the BAC Two-Eleven over the 600 series.

Two-Eleven and Three-Eleven

Sir George Edwards knew how difficult it would be to maintain the viability of the Weybridge plant since by the late 1960s VC10 production was slowing and the TSR2 had been cancelled. Plans to press ahead with the development of the Two-Eleven were driven by the need to provide work for the Weybridge workforce. The Two-Eleven was a very much scaled-up expansion of the One-Eleven design, seating 203 passengers and powered by the new 40,000lb thrust Rolls-Royce RB211. But the Labour Government would not support the project, even though BEA ordered it.

With hindsight it is easy to question the wisdom of BAC's decision to expend so much time, energy and money in pursuing the Two-Eleven project, especially when likely customers such as Air France and Lufthansa had already chosen the Boeing 727-200. The Two-Eleven had both a new airframe and new engine which is often regarded as a combination likely to prove troublesome, not least by people such as Brian Trubshaw who said as much in his in his autobiography. BAC should have developed the One-Eleven 600 Mark 2 and, if Rolls-Royce could not provide the power, chosen another company.

Deprived of the opportunity to develop the Two-Eleven, BAC then embarked on the Three-Eleven, an advanced technology wide-bodied airliner seating 245, eight-abreast, with a range of 1,450 miles and powered by RB211s. It was an aircraft very similar in capacity to the Airbus A310. It was intended that the Three-Eleven, like the

Two-Eleven, would be assembled at Hurn even though much of the fabrication would take place at Weybridge. There was intense lobbying of the Labour Government and especially Tony Benn the Minister of Technology, and many believe that if Labour had won the 1970 General Election the project would have received the launch aid needed. But Labour lost the Election and the new Tory Government under Edward Heath had to shore up Rolls-Royce – so there was no aid forthcoming for the Three-Eleven. BAC had spent £2 million on the stillborn project and the immediate result was redundancies at Weybridge.

700 Series

The next appreciable attempt to put more life into this excellent airframe came in 1974 when, with 211 aircraft already delivered and over 2,500,000 hours flown by One-Elevens around the globe, BAC proposed the development of a 700 series. This model was intended to take on the American manufacturers whose unstoppable DC-9 and Boeing 737 had taken order after order from BAC.

It is interesting to compare the 700 with the 600 series Mark 1 proposal of 1967. The 700 drew on both the earlier 600 series proposals with the greatly extended fuselage of the Mark 1, but with the Mark 2's use of the refined wing of the developed 500 series and the same fin and tailplane as all the other series. The fuselage was extended in a similar way to the earlier proposal with 100in added in front of the wing and 44in behind. Type 1 emergency exit doors were placed either side between the wing and the Spey engines. The MTOW was 117,000lb, just 3,000lb less than the 600. But like the 600 the engine of the 700 remained on the drawing board. It was another aft-fan Spey with 16,900lb thrust but was never built.

Three-Engined and Four-Engined One-Elevens

In 1974, in their search for more performance, BAC even sought inspiration from the Trident 3 and briefly considered a 700 with an RB 162 booster engine in the tail with the APU moved elsewhere, Kruger flaps and additional airbrakes. Considering the costs of operating an additional non-standard power plant it is not surprising that this idea did not develop far.

However, in 1972 much more serious consideration had been given to a four-engined lengthened aircraft. The engines were 8,000lb thrust Rolls-Royce Snecma M-45s (as fitted to the VFW-614) and the fuselage was to be extended by 144in to provide 129-seat capacity. This project would have provided the airframe with the power it needed and nor was it the only four-engined proposal; another very different version was projected for the Japanese Self-Defence Forces in 1975.

800 Series

Though not much was happening on the production line in 1974 the project engineers even proposed an 800 series, a maximal development of the 500 with some similarities to the 1967 600 series! This was powered by the Snecma/

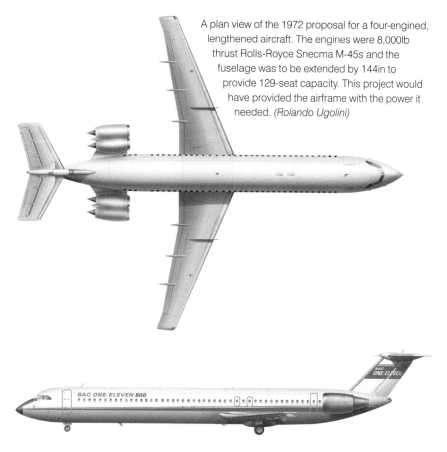

A plan view of the 1972 proposal for a four-engined, lengthened aircraft. The engines were 8,000lb thrust Rolls-Royce Snecma M-45s and the fuselage was to be extended by 144in to provide 129-seat capacity. This project would have provided the airframe with the power it needed. *(Rolando Ugolini)*

In 1974, BAC engineers proposed an 800 series, a maximal development of the 500 powered by the Snecma/GE CFM56 with a 290in plug ahead of the wing and 100in aft. There was an enlarged tail and a new wing centre section giving 120ins more span and 790 gallons more tankage. Four years later a new 700 series proposal emerged around two Rolls-Royce RB432s of 18,000lb thrust. The fuselage additions forward of the wing and behind provided room for 136 passengers. These proposals shared the bigger wheels and bulged undercarriage fairing of the 475. *(Rolando Ugolini)*

GE CFM56 and had a 290in plug ahead of the wing and 100in aft. There was an enlarged tail and a new wing centre section giving 120in more span and 790 gallons more tankage. Whereas the undercarriage and other features were the same as the 700, the ventral stairs were deleted.

Another 700 Series

Four years later in 1978, with BAC now part of the nationalised British Aerospace, a new 700 series proposal emerged around two Rolls-Royce RB432s of 18,000lb thrust. The fuselage additions were a little longer than the previous concepts, now being 106in forward of the wing and 58in behind. The door layout returned to the 500 series arrangement – essentially a front passenger door and ventral door with four overwing exits. This cabin could have seated as many as 136 passengers at 30in seating pitch. Both these proposals shared the bigger wheels in the bulged undercarriage fairing of the 475 series. Flight deck plans show considerable modification with a much more modern layout somewhat reminiscent of the Fokker 100. MTOW was lower than both the earlier proposals at 116,000lb.

British Airways and the One-Eleven 600/700

In 1978 when British Airways, the new UK national airline, indicated they were going to order nineteen Boeing 737-200s, British Aerospace did the best they could to compete with their rival and presented a new 600 series to the airline. This was a 500 with the 670 series wing cuff, brakes, lift dumpers and engine ejector cowl. BAe even proposed to supply the aircraft initially as 600s with Speys and then rebuild them as 700s with extended fuselages and 18,000lb thrust RB432s power plants when these became available in 1985.

Why did BAe not consider American engines, or BAC before them? The BAe 146 that was due to be launched had American engines, so why could the new organisation not make this leap?

Workers for the Hurn and Weybridge factories, together with their MPs, lobbied Parliament in an effort to persuade the Labour Government to force BA to order the British product. However BA, (sometimes interpreted as standing for Boeing Always!) needed delivery of the aircraft by 1980, and British Aerospace were unable to deliver the higher-powered larger 700 to that schedule. BAe was not in a competitive position so BA chose the Boeings, ordering them at a cost of £140 million on 19 April 1978 and took delivery of the first example in February 1980. Their total eventual purchase amounted to more than 100 of the American aircraft. As a sop to BAe, BA purchased three more 500 series built to the normal specification

The one-Eleven 600 of 1978 for BEA. This was fitted with the 670 series wing cuff, brakes, lift dumpers and engine ejector cowl. BAE proposed to supply the aircraft initially as 600s with Speys and rebuild them as 700s with extended fuselages and 18,000lb thrust RB432s powerplants when these became available in 1985. *(Rolando Ugolini)*

not the unique 510 arrangement. Small compensation for a long-term blow to the British aircraft industry.

In a last-ditch effort to convince the national airline to 'Buy British', BAe issued a press release, stressing the advantages of One-Eleven purchase in preserving British jobs, and how the BAe jets could be purchased for £129 million. But to no avail, in July 1978 the Department of Trade approved British Airways order.

So in the event none of these civil proposals went into production. Taking a long view some consolation can be drawn from knowing that all the hard work was not wasted, for the 1974 700/800 series CFM56-powered versions led onto the X-Eleven with a six-abreast fuselage, the outer wings of the One-Eleven mated to a new centre section. And in due course this proposal became a joint European project which metamorphosed into the very successful Airbus A320.

The More Unusual Proposals

Just as BAC examined possibilities for taking advantage of the sturdy One-Eleven as an airliner there was also considerable work put into military or research proposals.

In November 1967 a proposal was submitted to the USAF Military Airlift Command for a CASEVAC (casualty evacuate) One-Eleven. It was designated as a 417, and would have carried thirty patients on stretchers or forty seated patients. It had a small forward freight door for stretcher loading from an integral extendable covered ramp. *(Rolando Ugolini)*

USAF Aeromedical Version

In November 1967, BAC submitted a proposal to the United States Air Force Military Airlift Command for an aeromedical version of the One-Eleven to evacuate casualties from war zones. The order was expected to be for eight aircraft with an estimated value of £15 million in dollar exports. The aircraft proposed was a version of the 400, designated as the series 417, and would have carried thirty patients on stretchers or forty seated patients. It was to have been equipped with a small forward freight door for stretcher loading from an integral extendable covered ramp to protect casualties from the weather. Not surprisingly the USAF chose an American supplier for the specification, a version of the McDonnell Douglas DC-9.

RAF Airborne Early Warning

It is perhaps not well known that much work was done in 1970/71 on an Airborne Early Warning (AEW) version for the Royal Air Force. This used the basic 475 series aircraft but with the 500 series undercarriage, giving very good weight and performance capability to carry a fuselage-mounted 24ft diameter rotodome similar

These side and plan views illustrate the 1970 Airborne Early Warning (AEW) version capable of carrying a fuselage-mounted 24ft diameter rotodome proposed for the Royal Air Force. In December 1986, eleven years after the One-Eleven would have been in service and after the expenditure of more than £1 billion the 'cheaper' Nimrod AEW was cancelled and was replaced by imported Boeing E-3 AWACS. *(Rolando Ugolini)*

146 or 1-11? While investigating STOL in 1974 BAC looked at various high-lift devices, which would reduce approach speeds and field length. To test these, there were plans for a 475 with a high wing, four under-slung engines and the undercarriage accommodated in stub wings. *(Rolando Ugolini)*

to that of the United States Navy Grumman E2C aircraft. To provide the range, additional long-range tanks were fitted in the fuselage and a hatch as used in the test aircraft allowed for crew escape. Using the maximum 104,000lb take-off weight, which the 475 was structurally capable of, it could give two hours patrol time in the area of Gibraltar or six hours off Norway. The programme would have made the aircraft available by mid-1975, but it was rejected in favour of the Nimrod AEW on grounds of cost. One final comment: in December 1986, eleven years after the One-Eleven would have been in service and after the expenditure of more than £1 billion, the 'cheaper' Nimrod AEW was cancelled and was replaced by the imported Boeing E-3 AWACS.

Short Take Off and Landing (STOL)

For a study into Short Take Off and Landing (STOL) in 1974 BAC looked at various high-lift devices, involving blown flaps or slats and flaps which would bring the approach speed down to below 100 knots and field lengths of 2,300ft. Most surprisingly, to test these studies there were plans for a 475 with its One-Eleven wing mounted high on the fuselage, four underslung podded engines and the undercarriage accommodated in stub wings. It looked remarkably like the BAe 146!

Noise-Shielding Proposals

It is interesting to note that in 1974, twenty-seven years before the Stage 3 noise regulations came into effect, an examination for a Government contract was made of methods of shielding the forward and aft noise from the Spey engines. There were a number of stages in this process culminating in a repositioning of the Speys both upwards and forwards together with a dummy tailplane fitted to the lower rear fuselage. It was noted then that the results of these changes would achieve the Stage 3 requirements for the twenty-first century.

Japanese Collaborative Civil and Military Proposals

BAC perceived a substantial potential market for One-Eleven derivations in Japan in 1975 and put forward proposals for a collaborative programme with the Japanese aviation industry to fulfil some of the country's civil and military needs. The civil proposal was designed to fulfil the NAMC YS-11 replacement market, which also manifested itself in the 475D, and 670 One-Eleven. But the collaborative airliner project was much more radical than either of these, with a new wing to be built in Japan, a lengthened fuselage, taller fin, widened tailplane and the aft-fan Speys. The in-service date was projected for 1980.

Some of those same changes were planned for use in the military versions. The Anti-Submarine Maritime Surveillance version with a 400 series-length fuselage would have had the new wing plus two underwing Rolls-Royce Turbomeca Adours, a large chin radar, cabin fuel tanks, a sizeable weapons bay, underwing pylons, searchlight and a crew escape hatch. In another form most of these features were employed on an AEW version together with a fuselage-mounted rotodome previously proposed to the RAF.

In the mid-1970s there were several civil and military proposals involving co-production with Japan. The Anti-Submarine Maritime Surveillance version for the Japanese Self-Defence Force had a 400 series fuselage, new wing, two underwing Rolls-Royce Turbomeca Adours, a large chin radar, cabin fuel tanks, a sizeable weapons bay, underwing pylons, searchlight and a crew escape hatch. *(Brooklands Museum)*

Flight-Refuelling Tanker Versions

In 1985, as a spin-off from the VC10 tanker conversion programme, there was an examination of a One-Eleven flight-refuelling tanker. The concept was based on variants of Romanian-built 475s and 500s which would be fitted respectively with four or five VC10 tanker fuselage tanks, a flight-refuelling probe and two underwing pylons placed just inboard of the ailerons.

Rightly, the Project Office was examining ways to sell more aircraft but with many of these projects the overall problem remained the same – insufficient power to stretch the airframe and improve the aircraft's performance. The One-Eleven should have been developed beyond the 500 by 1970 and development should have continued in line with the competition.

11

Romania and the One-Eleven – Licence Production

Romania under Ceaucescu followed a somewhat independent policy from that of the other Soviet satellites. Over the years from the end of the Second World War, Romania had managed to gain some international legitimacy by promoting its independent national identity and refusing to slavishly support the USSR. For example it did not break relations with Israel over the 1967 Six-Day War and denounced the invasion of Czechoslovakia in the following year. The Czechoslovaks had entered negotiations with BAC to buy VC10s but after the Russian invasion were obliged to accept Soviet-made Ilyushin Il-62s. Romania decided it wanted to develop its aircraft industry and sought quality Western equipment. Whereas the purchase of American aircraft might have been too provocative, British airliners were acceptable. So in February 1968 an order was announced for six One-Eleven 400 series for Tarom, the Romanian national carrier. Part of the contract was an offset deal whereby Britten-Norman, the successful Isle of Wight manufacturer contracted for Romanian assembly of 212 'green', i.e. unfurnished ten-seater twin-engined Britten-Norman Islanders which were then flown to Bembridge on the Isle of Wight for fitting out.

In January 1968 the first Tarom One–Eleven 424 flew as G-16-4 prior to the announcement of the order but soon received the Romanian registration YR-BCA. All were laid out as eighty-four seaters. The order was delivered evenly from production lines at both Hurn and Weybridge with the final delivery, YR-BCF, on 13 December 1969. In 1972, two second-hand 400 series were purchased from BAC.

Even though BAC demonstrated a Philippines Airlines 527 series to Tarom in October 1970, it was only followed by an order several years later for five 525s due for delivery in 1977. The first of this order, YR-BCI, flew on 20 December 1976 and was the first aircraft to fly with hush kits. That deal also involved the manufacture of a further 100 Britten-Norman Islanders and parts for One–Elevens.

With the Labour Government's decision to nationalise the aircraft industry in 1977 and the new British Aerospace's decision to develop the BAe (Hawker Siddeley)

146, further substantial development for the One-Eleven was at an end. The BAe Board decided to enter into a licence production contract with Romania. After lengthy negotiations agreement was reached and a signing ceremony took place during President Ceausescu's state visit to Britain in June 1978. The One-Eleven agreement (valued in excess of £150 million) was covered entirely by hard currency payments from Romania via a long-term credit facility established by UK Banks. At the same time BAe also entered into a counter-trade arrangement with the Romanian Government to identify buyers for a wide range of Romanian products in markets throughout the world.

Most notable was the certification arrangement, whereby One-Elevens built locally by the Romanian company Romaero were certified by the DaVC (equivalent to the UK's Civil Aviation Authority). Because of BAe's on-site surveillance of One-Eleven manufacturing and assembly, each locally built aircraft received UK CAA certification. BAe retained overall design authority throughout the contract, and ROMBAC's Flight Operations Manager was Dave Glaser, former Chief Production test pilot on the One-Elevens. Quality was raised by training a considerable number of Romanians in the various skills of manufacture, assembly and testing. The partnership was indicated by the aircraft branding as ROMBAC One-Elevens, 'ROM' for Romania and 'BAC' for the original BAC.

The licensing agreement included the sale of three complete aircraft, to be built at Hum. But the main part of the deal was twenty-two aircraft sets of structural components, equipment, details and raw materials, to be supplied for the Romanian production line. After the twenty-second aircraft, indigenous One-Eleven production was to be established and the Romanian aircraft industry would be free to produce as many One-Elevens as it could sell.

The three Hum-built aircraft comprised a single 525 for delivery in January 1981, YR-BCN, followed by a 487 (475 Freighter), YR-BCR, in June and another 525, YR-BCO. This was ceremonially handed over on 12 March 1982 by Mick Wilde, Managing Director BAe Weybridge-Bristol Division, as the last One-Eleven to be completed at Hurn. Though there were still two unflown 475s in the factory, they had been completed prior to the Romanian 500 and were only flown just prior to Hurn's closure in 1984.

An Aeromaritime Guppy delivered the first complete fuselage from Hurn to Romania in January 1980 and the whole operation involved a considerable use of outsize freighter capacity. Tradewind's Canadair CL-44s carried wings and other major structural items to Romania and smaller components were flown containerised in Tarom An-26s. The One-Eleven 487 freighter was also employed in transporting equipment to the Romaero base at Baneasa, near the Romanian capital, Bucharest. Less critical parts were sent by Romanian-operated surface transport.

The Baneasa site was extensively developed as a centre of civil aircraft production (the Islanders were already in production there). As for workmanship,

The relationship with Romania was forged when the state airline ordered six 400s in February 1968. The first aircraft YR-BCA (c/n 130) is seen at Hurn in March of that year. It crashed two years later near Constanta in Romania. *(Author)*

Romania production teams had already acted as a subcontractor for the Hum One-Eleven line, supplying the entire tailplane so their workforce was experienced in the standards required. Paralleling the airframe agreement was a licence to Romania's Turbomecanica to assemble Rolls-Royce Spey 512s for its One-Elevens covering a total of 225 engines.

Whereas Romania was successful in the licence production of 165 Aerospatiale Puma helicopters, the bright plans for the One-Eleven were never fulfilled. The production of One-Elevens only made painfully slow progress in the 1980s. The main problems were caused by a lack of commitment at the top exacerbated by hard currency exchange problems. From 1981 the lack of currency meant that the Romanians had to wait months even to buy bolts. Senior staff would not make decisions without either BAe or Rolls-Royce authority. BAe engineers based at Baneasa remarked that in the winter months Romanian aircraft workers were obliged to walk long distances to report for work in unheated hangars. In the hangars temperatures were often recorded as low as -25°C, too cold for adhesives and paint to be applied. Conditions were so bad that the workers were often sent home.

The result was a terrible waste of potential for, between 1982 and 1989, just nine One-Eleven 561RCs were produced leaving a 475 freighter 85% complete (but not surveyed by BAe) and another 561RC series 70% complete. The workmanship

The first fuselage from the Hurn production line being loaded into an Aeromaritime Guppy for transfer to the Romanian assembly line on 26 January 1980. *(BAE SYSTEMS)*

sometimes left much to be desired and one aircraft had a tail fin with a camber, which resulted in the aircraft constantly trying to make a flat turn in flight. A specially re-rigged hinge had to be fitted and certified to rectify this. Apparently the unfinished 475 was removed from the jigs too early and BAe refused to sign off the work as having been completed to their quality standards. Since this 475 never flew there was no need for rectification on this occasion.

The first ROMBAC One-Eleven YR-BRA flew on 18 September 1982 from Baneasa and the second on 28 April 1983. The next three followed at approximately yearly intervals and the sixth, YR-BRF, flew in September 1986. There was then an eighteen-month hiatus before the flight of YR-BCG in March 1988 and then 'BRH followed in December with the final machine, 'BRI, flying in April 1989.

With this slow rate of production ROMBAC was never really a reliable supplier of aircraft and the nine built 561s were all initially delivered to Tarom. Had production really developed as planned sales could have taken place with other operators. Tarom used its British and home-built aircraft on international routes throughout Europe and North Africa. It withdrew the 400s from use in the late 1980s and none of the 525s or 561s is now in service.

Tarom also leased its One-Elevens far and wide to many operators; to UK operators such as Anglo-Cargo (with the freighter), British Island Airways, Dan-Air,

YR-BCO (c/n 272) a 525 for TAROM was ceremonially handed over on 12 March 1982 by Mick Wilde, Managing Director, BAe Weybridge-Bristol Division as the last One-Eleven to be completed at Hurn (though two 475s still remained unflown). *(Brooklands Museum)*

A very low fly over by the last Tarom aircraft to be completed in front of the production line hangars at Hurn. *(Mike Phipp)*

The Romanian ROMBAC One-Eleven production line at Baneasa. Unfortunately the programme was not sufficiently funded and only nine aircraft were completed. *(Author's collection)*

The beginning of Romanian production. The roll out of the first Romanian assembled aircraft, YR-BRA (c/n 401) at Baneasa on 27 August 1982. *(Rolls-Royce Heritage Trust)*

The end of Romanian production. An uncompleted freight-door-equipped 475 (c/n 410) originally destined for the Romanian Air Force on the Baneasa production line. *(Ken Goddard)*

London European Loganair, and elsewhere to Adria, Aero Asia, Air Memphis, Citylink, Jugoslovenski Aerotransport, Lauda Air, Ryanair, Romavia and the Romanian Government. Romanian aircraft also made their way south to serve in Nigeria.

The Romanian story does not end there but continues with the belated attempts to re-engine the One-Eleven in the United States and the Romanian desire to take advantage of this work. However, as related in the next chapter, these attempts came to nought and BAe ended the agreement with Romaero on 7 July 1993.

12

The Tay One-Eleven – A Tortuous Story

The One-Eleven had long been in need of more powerful engines and with the advent of the Rolls-Royce Tay engines in 1982, BAe Weybridge received enquiries from Corporate 400 series owners about the possibility of re-engining. The chief advantages were that with the greater power and lower specific fuel consumption, the Tay engine would give aircraft much greater range. In fact, with freight bay fuel tanks a Tay One-Eleven would have a transatlantic capability. Even though the Tay had a higher installed weight of 1,250lb over the Spey there were clear economic arguments in its favour taking into account all the re-engining aspects, initial purchase of engines, modification work and certification as the Spey was very noisy and costly to maintain. Using the Tay 650 with its powerful 15,100lb thrust, take-off performance would be increased by 32%, range by 500 miles and engine maintenance costs cut by up to 40%.

Whereas BAe was contemplating re-working existing aircraft, ROMBAC had indicated that from their thirteenth One-Eleven on their production line the Romaero wanted to use an alternative power plant. It had accurately identified that by 1990 the Spey One-Eleven's potential sales would be poor because of noise legislation and correctly identified that a Tay-powered One-Eleven would prove strong competition if marketed at competitive prices.

In July 1983, BAe Weybridge proposed a programme of re-engining both 400 and 500 series aircraft to existing operators with estimated development costs of $25 million on the basis of thirty-five conversions. The price for conversion of the each airliner to purchasers was to be $5.5 million.

There had been hope that one or other of the large operators, for example British Airways or British Caledonian, would express an interest in re-engining their fleet, but none was forthcoming from these quarters and at the end of year the proposal was withdrawn. British Caledonian did give the matter full consideration but concluded that the conversion was not viable and decided to expend £1 million on each of their fleet with the fitting of Stage 2 hush kits, wide-body interiors and repositioned toilets so that full facilities were available at both ends of the aircraft.

BAe's Internal Politics

Though BAe Weybridge was keen on the proposal, other sections of the organisation would have been much less pleased to see an additional rival to the BAe 146, which was being produced at BAe Hatfield. The Tay One-Eleven promised to out-perform the BAe 146 so it is reasonable to speculate that re-engining of the One-Eleven would not fit well within BAe corporate strategy.

The withdrawal of this BAe proposal really spelt the beginning of the end for the Tay One-Eleven project, for without the whole-hearted involvement of the manufacturer there was unlikely to be a viable programme. But attempts were to continue for many years with a significant number of parties who were perspicacious enough to see that the combination of the proven, rugged airframe and a new, superior engine was a cheaper and better prospect than much of the competition. These included Dee Howard (DHC), then an innovative aircraft engineering concern based in San Antonio, Texas.

Dee Howard Corporation

Mr Dee Howard, Chief Executive of Dee Howard, discussed the programme with various executive One-Eleven operators including Salem Bin Laden, (half-brother of Osama Bin Laden) who operated two One-Elevens, and wanted to improve their range. The Tay engine's much lower specific fuel consumption would provide the

A close-up of the new engine installation with reversers deployed on the first Tay-powered aircraft while still registered N700JA. For the maiden flight it became N650DH (c/n 059). *(Dee Howard via Bill Hurley)*

range improvement. DHC talked to British Aerospace about the programme but BAe was not very interested in the project because of their other products. But, since the project appeared to fit very well with Dee Howard's capabilities and provided another first-class engine to fit the patented DHC aluminium thrust reverser, Dee decided to go ahead with it. BAe, as design authority, and Rolls-Royce entered into an agreement with Dee Howard to provide expertise and technical data. BAe's involvement was driven by contractual responsibility to ROMBAC, not by any real desire on its own part, and Rolls-Royce appear to have always been half-hearted about the programme, viewing the re-engined One-Eleven as competition for the Tay-powered Fokker 100.

Technical Alterations

Technically the alterations to One-Eleven to take the Tay were surprisingly few, for besides the new engines there were only changes to the electrical power and starter motor. The power plant used the existing frames, which were reinforced as the installation increased the weight of the aircraft by 3,000lb and new pylons fitted owing to the greater girth of the Tay. Dee Howard designed the cowling and reverser and taking all factors into account there appeared a good case for the re-engining, especially for the 500 series which could outperform the BAe 146-300 and was probably equal to the Fokker 100.

The programme was formally launched on 28 January 1986, with first flight of the Tay prototype (c/n 059, originally N5019, a series 401AK built for American Airlines) planned for July 1987 with FAA certification in December of that year. Publicly, no mention was made of the fact that the 475 and 500 series were also included in the agreement, possibly at BAe's behest.

Market Survey Report on the Tay Programme

A market survey report on the Tay programme of 1986 highlighted the following:

1. The re-engining programme of the type was straightforward and BAe structural audits confirmed there were no difficulties in the aircraft staying in service beyond 2010.
2. The first re-engining needed to be available in 1987-1988.
3. The conversion would not be in competition with the BAe 146.
4. The Tay 400 was not particularly attractive because of its limited MTOW but the 475/500 series would be more attractive to re-engine because of their higher MTOW.

5. The 500 series would be the best conversion for airliner use and the 475 for executive purposes but neither had FAA certification.
6. A Tay 500 would compete very strongly with the Fokker 100 having more range but be much cheaper to purchase.
7. Purchase price was the main deciding factor for corporate users, not lower operating costs. An executive Tay 475 or 500 with additional tankage would have the range of the Gulfstream IV or the Falcon 900 and a larger cabin, but cost half the price.
8. Breakeven for a conversion programme would be fifteen aircraft but there was demand for thirty-five to fifty-five of the re-engined 475 and 500 series.
9. The Romanians should be part of the programme from the start producing new Tay-powered aircraft – albeit at a very slow rate.

Alenia takes over Dee Howard

In spring 1988, Alenia of Italy took a 40% holding in DHC and then as the year progressed and the costs of the One-Eleven programme rose, Alenia increased its holding to 60% giving it overall control. But the schedule had slipped substantially and as a result in early 1990 Guinness Peat Aviation (GPA), a major airliner lessor who had proposed purchasing fifty Romanian-built Tay 500s, withdrew. Gradually parties were perceiving that the project was under-resourced, under-financed, poorly marketed and managed and way behind schedule.

The First Flight

In fact it was only on Monday 2 July 1990, three years behind schedule, that the Tay One-Eleven N650DH, marketed as the BAC 1-11 2400 made a one hour forty-seven minute first flight. The captain was John Lewis, Chief Test Pilot, British Aerospace, Filton, who led the flight test programme, co-pilot, Ron Franzen, Dee Howard Project Pilot, with two Flight Test Observers.

The first Tay One-Eleven N650DH and its flight test crew drawn from British Aerospace and Dee Howard. *(Bill Hurley)*

Demonstration at Farnborough 1990

Eager to promote the aircraft, John Lewis and Johnnie Walker (originally a One-Eleven test pilot with BAC) flew comparative noise trials at Birmingham Airport late in August where its startling reduction in noise was amply exhibited with average flyovers of 70db, about 20db less than the Spey-powered aircraft. The team then visited BAe Filton on 30 August before departing to Farnborough for the airshow. At Farnborough commentators were generally impressed but also noticed the shaking of the tailplane when full reverse was operated during the landing run.

Despite the positive first impressions following their UK visit, Dee Howard had only two orders for Tay One-Elevens – one from Hanson Trust and one from Turbo-Union. There were expressions of interest from others, for instance Anglo-Cargo, which was keen on conversion of its 487 freighter, but no other firm orders.

N650DH piloted by John Lewis and Johnnie Walker on finals at the Farnborough Airshow in September 1990. *(Rolls-Royce Heritage Trust)*

N650DH landing at Farnborough showing the operation of the Tay clamshell reversers, very different to the Spey installation. Airbrakes also deployed to assist in braking the aircraft. *(Rolls-Royce Heritage Trust)*

Progress Report, March 1991

In March 1991, the President of DHC spoke of sixty to eighty conversions as a realistic target with perhaps a third being corporate 400s (2400s) and the remainder airliner 500s (2500s). The 500 would need an order for ten or more from an airline or leasing company because it would need a separate certification programme owing to centre of gravity issues and differing aerodynamics. A price for the 2400 conversion was quoted at just under $9 million with an optional Honeywell electronic flight instrumentation system costing $2.3 million more.

Substantial progress had been made in the flight testing: stall testing to both FAA and CAA requirements, take-off and landing tests and noise certification tests which showed excellent margins over requirements.

But some problems had been revealed: the shaking of the tail by the reverse thrust, in the meantime it was decided that the aircraft was to be initially certified with idle reverse thrust only, subject to modification of the reversers. The failure of the wet runway water ingestion trials (i.e. ingestion of water into the engines) could probably have been cured with a re-designed chine to the nose wheel tyre.

As BAe had design authority any certification flying had to be captained by a BAe pilot, either John Lewis, John Fawcett or Johnnie Walker with BAe's Chief Engineer, Roger Back, signing it off.

The Second Tay One-Eleven

The second Tay One-Eleven, N333GB, owned by Hanson, was first flown by Mark Mannweiler and Ron Franzen in June 1991. The pair then flew it to the Honeywell facility in Phoenix, Arizona on 11 August, to start the new avionics test programme which involved the fitting of a new 'glass' cockpit somewhat reminiscent of the Fokker 100's. The aircraft had a very successful programme testing the new Honeywell avionics suite, but now ugly rumours were spreading that the project would be cancelled and confidence dwindled. On 17 November the first aircraft, N650DH, made its 178th flight, which proved to be its last, and a few days later had the engines removed having flown a total of 338 hours. N333GB was initially parked at the Honeywell facility at Phoenix but was then returned to Dee Howard's facility at San Antonio on 26 November, piloted by Johnnie Walker, having flown a mere ninety-seven hours. There they remained, N650DH was broken up but N333GB's fuselage and wings were still intact in February 2002.

Dee Howard had cancelled the project and the parties issued lawsuits and though there was an attempt to revitalise the project nothing came of it.

The Views of some of those Involved

John Lewis (at that time BAe Chief Test Pilot, Filton) who captained the aircraft on her first flight and had led the test programme said that it was a superior machine to the 146 and the tail shake was not much of a problem. After the Farnborough demonstration in 1990, Roger Back, the One-Eleven designer, told John not to use full reverser again, but re-angling of the plumes would have sorted out the problem and even idle reverse provided sufficient stopping power. There was some flow separation around the rear end, which would have been solved by vortex generators. The stall on Tay was not as good as the Spey version due to fitting of Tays on stub wings bigger than Speys, so the aircraft had a tendency to roll and oscillate laterally. In Back's view, BAe and the CAA were always very helpful, but DHC was mainly interested in the Boeing 727 Tay re-engining contract.

Johnnie Walker, who was a test pilot on the programme from July 1990 to November 1991 said nearly all the essential testing had been completed, including in-flight reverse operation, handling, performance, noise measurements, comparative performance and stability when the decision was made to cancel.

In Johnny's opinion the Tay One-Eleven was of course a much better aircraft than the Spey; if he had any criticism of the re-engined aircraft it was the higher idling thrust, resulting in greater use of brakes during taxiing. He believed it was a pity that Alenia did not allow them to complete the certification. There was so little more to be done.

Bill Hurley, formerly Dee Howard Director of Flight Test and Certification, expresses some views below that echo the views of those on this side of the Atlantic:

> The Tay engine and the BAC One-Eleven were a good fit. The airplane is very reliable and has a good service history, but needed a change to meet the noise requirements. The engine met the noise requirements plus added improved efficiency and performance. The Tay One-Eleven combination provided a cost effective, life extension of an excellent airframe with added performance and range and with reduced noise.
>
> Many airlines and bizjet operators were visited and the response was positive. Also, there was excellent support from BAe and Rolls-Royce. In addition, there were discussions with ROMBAC, the Romanian aircraft manufacturer, for the manufacture of new airplanes with the DHC design. All in all, the program success looked very good. This potential of this program was a large factor influencing Alenia to help finance the program.
>
> There were some delays in getting the airplane prepared for flight testing, but the testing program went very well. Overall, there was an excellent team on the test program. BAe and Rolls-Royce provided great support, which included on-site personnel. And, DHC employed seconded BAe personnel to assist. The

FAA certification flight test program was very close to completion. But, there was a FAA airspeed limit on the test airplane because of needed basic airframe structural substantiation. DHC flew the airplane to the required flight envelope because BAe assured the airframe was satisfactory. But, the FAA would not let their pilots fly beyond the imposed limit until they had reviewed the structural data. BAe was never able to produce the original airframe structural analysis from their records, so the FAA certification program was terminated.

So why was it cancelled?

1. Timescale and management: The programme had taken too long and interested purchasers had withdrawn.
2. Sales: There were only two orders for the 400. The 500 version, a better prospect, would require FAA certification and more testing.
3. Certification: There were still technical difficulties with the structure that needed a substantial BAe input.
4. Company profits: Alenia realised money could be made more easily and more quickly from the Boeing 727 Tay programme.
5. Partners: Arguably neither BAe nor Rolls-Royce was wholly committed to the programme. The ROMBAC operation was working so poorly that no one would have confidence in their supplying new Tay One-Elevens. (See below)

Romania and the Tay

As early as 1983 the Romanians expressed an interest in fitting Tay engines to their machines. With the agreement between Dee Howard and BAe, Romaero saw a chance of buying the Tays and nacelles from Dee Howard and fitting them on the production line. So, in 1988, a proposal was put together between Swift Aviation of the UK and the Romanians for the purchase of fifty ROMBAC Tay One-Eleven 560s but it foundered three years later through lack of financing.

Romaero met BAe, Rolls-Royce and Alenia (owners of Dee Howard) in September 1991 and proposals were made to use c/n 409, YR-BRI, which had already flown, and refit it with Tays. There were many difficulties to overcome that blurred the vision and dampened the morale of those involved. The three main factors were the lack of finance to the tune of $100 million, BAe's justifiable and crucial lack of confidence in the Romanians being able to carry it through and Rolls-Royce's desire to be supplier not an investor.

In February 1993, BAe and Rolls-Royce were surprised to learn that Romaero had signed a deal with Kiwi International Airlines of Newark, New Jersey, to build eleven

A Kiwi International AIRSTAR 2500. The last chance for the Tay programme and the Romanian licence production was an order by Kiwi International Airlines of New Jersey for eleven Tay-powered 560s. To be called AIRSTAR 2500s, they would be have been assembled in Romania and flown 'green' to Hurn for fitting out with avionics and interiors at Hurn. *(Rolando Ugolini)*

Tay 560s. Branded as AIRSTAR 2500s they would have been assembled in Romania and flown 'green' to Hurn for fitting out with Honeywell 'glass' cockpit avionics and cabin interiors by FLS at Hurn. But this idea soon foundered.

Then, on 7 July 1993, BAe withdrew from the Romaero operation entirely, apparently because of money owed by the Romanians. Licence production then ceased. Too late, TAROM, the Romanian airline, announced they wanted to re-engine their One-Eleven fleet and Dee Howard offered the second Tay 400 series, N333GB, to Romaero who were unable to afford it.

This was the final attempt to make something of the Tay and Romanian production. The ninth ROMBAC One-Eleven was the last to fly in 1989, leaving a 560 and a freight-door-equipped 475 incomplete on the production line and presumably now scrapped.

13

Notable Accidents in Service

During the initial test flying the One-Eleven had the misfortune to suffer three accidents, one fatal, and there have been twenty-nine accidents in airline service to date resulting in the write off of the aircraft. Of those in airline service, twelve have resulted in fatalities.

Many of the accidents were caused by poor navigation so that the ground or sea was hit, or were the result of badly executed landings. Between 1989 and 1997 there appear to have been eight landing accidents resulting in write off in Nigeria – two caused by running out of fuel in the vicinity of the airports. A typical example befell Oriental Airline's 5N-IMO which crashed at Tamanrasset, Algeria, on 18 September 1994. After circling for almost one and a half hours and four aborted landings in adverse weather conditions, it ran out of fuel and crashed. Five of the thirty-nine on board were killed.

A further write-off of a Nigerian aircraft took place in a 412, 5N-BDC, of Eagle Aviation landing at Libreville in August 2001. This was followed less typically in March 2002 by an Albarka Air 401 5N-MBM being written off on the ground after a storm.

One of the worst One-Eleven commercial accidents happened in Kano, Nigeria, on 4 May 2002. Lagos-bound Executive Air Services 5N-ESF, a 525 built at Hurn as YR-BCN and delivered to Tarom in 1981, crashed into a densely populated part of Kano immediately after take-off. The crew of seven and sixty-six passengers out of seventy-nine on board were killed along with at least fifty on the ground (see Chapter 15).

N1553 was the first passenger-carrying One-Eleven to crash on 6 August 1966, killing forty-two passengers and crew. A series 203 delivered to Braniff on 8 December 1965, it was flying from Kansas City to Omaha when it became the victim of an extremely strong gust of wind which hit the aircraft from behind at 140ft per second. The elevators were smashed upwards, the rudder forced from side to side beyond the normal limit of travel and then the tailplane broke off. Under these loads the right wing then failed. BAC was very concerned about this accident but after a thorough investigation by the FAA it was accepted that the aircraft had been struck by an extreme storm.

The second accident in the One-Eleven's airline service career occurred on 23 June 1967 and happened to a Mohawk series 204, N1116J, *Discover America*, and killed all thirty-four on board. The airliner was flying from Elmira to Washington when parts of the tail were seen to separate from the fin. The cause was the failure of a non-return valve allowing hydraulic fuel to flow back into the APU which then ignited, burnt through the spars and led to failure of the tail. The inevitable consequence of such a serious failure was that all eighty aircraft then in service had to be inspected and similar symptoms were found in many of the non-return valves. These were redesigned and replaced to ensure no recurrence of the accident.

The forced landing of BUA's G-ASJJ, eighteen months later on 14 January 1969 at Milan Airport, fortunately did not result in any casualties. It was caused by the pilots not following procedures correctly after an apparent engine failure, switching one engine off and not noticing that the throttle of the remaining Spey had been partly pulled back so that there was insufficient power for the aircraft to fly.

Almost two years later, on 6 September 1971, twenty-two of the 121 on board the Paninternational 515 series D-ALAR, were killed when it crash-landed shortly after take-off on the Hamburg-Kiel autobahn because of a maintenance error. Both engines failed because the water injection system had been wrongly filled with kerosene. The water injection system was designed to cool the engines and allow them to operate at full power for longer periods. The aircraft hit a bridge, both of the wings broke off and the fuselage was burnt out but mercifully many of those on board survived.

Over their twenty-six years of One-Eleven operation, Philippine Airlines suffered a disproportionate number of incidents to its aircraft. PAL's first accident was to one of its 402s in 1969 when PI-C-1131 flew into a hill while on approach, killing most on board and on another occasion, fifteen years later, a 527 registered RP-C-1182 overshot the end of a runway into the sea but everyone was saved.

N1553 (c/n 070) of Braniff International at Hurn. The first passenger carrying One-Eleven to crash, on 6 August 1966 killing forty-two passengers and crew. It was the victim of an extremely strong gust of wind, which hit it from behind at 140ft per second. *(BAE SYSTEMS)*

It has to be said that three of these incidents were caused by terrorist action. The first involved RP-C1184, a series 524, on 3 June 1975 when a terrorist exploded a grenade at 20,000ft in an aft toilet, tearing a hole in the side through which a terrorist himself was sucked out to his death and injuring several passengers. Patched up in Manila and flown back to Hurn in August 1975 for repair it returned to service in February 1976. Amazingly, just over three years later on 18 August 1978, a similar incident befell the same aircraft on approach to Manila at 24,000ft, with an explosion in the same toilet and the same fate for the would-be saboteur. The explosion blew away part of the roof, distorted the floor and gutted the toilets. The airliner, with fifty-nine passengers on board, lost all pressure and made an emergency descent from 24,000ft to 10,000ft followed by an emergency landing. After the event the pilot, Captain Antonio del Costello, coolly remarked, 'We were amazed at the chaos when we looked round'. BAC presented Captain Costello with an inscribed silver model of a One-Eleven as an acknowledgement of his bravery and presence of mind. Hurn workers flew out to Manila to patch up the aircraft and so for the second time RP-C1184 flew into Hurn for repair and redelivery after a slow, unpressurised, low altitude, eleven-stop flight. Incontrovertible proof of airframe strength. This veteran of terrorism was finally retired from service in January 1992 having flown 42,000 hours.

In between these bomb attacks on the Philippines aircraft there was a hijack of another on 23 May 1976 when RP-C1161, a series 527, was taken over by six Moslem rebels. Security forces stormed the aeroplane and three rebels and ten passengers were killed in the fracas. This time the airliner was damaged beyond repair.

To attest for the strength of the One-Eleven, on 27 July 1989 another 527, RP-C1193, ran off the end of a wet Manila runway, crossed a road colliding with several vehicles and ended up on a railway track. None of the passengers or crew

RP-C1184 (c/n 190) a PAL 524, was twice the victim of terrorism. On each occasion a bomb in a toilet severely damaged it and killed the perpetrator. But each time the aircraft survived. This shows the damage after the first attempt in 1975. *(BAE SYSTEMS)*

The second return of Philippines Airlines' RP-C1184 to the Hurn plant after terrorist bomb damage. This photo shows the large reinforced patch fixed over the rear fuselage so that the aircraft could make an unpressurised flight back to Hurn and repair in October 1978. G-ASYD is in the background. *(BAE SYSTEMS)*

was seriously injured but eight of those in the vehicles lost their lives. An aviation magazine commented (in rather poor taste in view of the fatalities) that the One-Eleven's structural integrity was renowned since they were made by the British Aircraft Corporation, one of whose forbears was Vickers-Armstrongs, best known for building battleships.

In almost thirty years of safe operation with British Airways and BEA there was only one serious incident involving the Hurn-built jets. On 10 June 1990, G-BJRT, while climbing through 17,300ft (not 23,000ft as the press reported), on an early morning flight from Birmingham to Malaga suffered a highly unusual incident. There was a loud bang on the flight deck as the left windscreen in front of the captain blew out and the fuselage filled with condensation mist. It was at once apparent to the cabin crew that an explosive decompression had occurred. Since the captain had released his shoulder harness and loosened his lap-strap he was partly sucked through the window, but two stewards entering the flight deck were able to grab hold of him while the co-pilot took control of the aircraft. The two men tried to pull the commander back within the aircraft and, although they could see his head and torso through the left windows, the slipstream frustrated their efforts. However, they kept a grip on the captain's legs while he lost consciousness and an emergency landing was made at Southampton Airport. The captain was taken to Southampton General Hospital suffering from bone fractures in his right arm and wrist, a broken left thumb, bruising, frostbite and shock. The other crew members and passengers were fine apart from one of the stewards who had cuts and bruising to his arm.

This highly unusual incident occurred because when the windscreen was replaced during maintenance prior to the flight, eighty-four of the screws fitted were fractionally too narrow and six too short which resulted in the failure of the windscreen outwards because of the aircraft's pressurisation.

Nightmare at 23,000ft as crew cling to captain

PILOT SUCKED FROM JETLINER

On 10 June 10 1990, while climbing through 17,300ft (not 23,000ft as the newspaper reported), the left windscreen of British Airways' G-BJRT (c/n 234) blew out and the Captain was partly sucked through the window, but did survive the event. *(Author)*

D-ANDY (c/n 127) formerly of Bavaria Fluggesellschaft being unloaded from a Canadair CL-44 at Hurn in November 1970 after crashing at Gerona. It rejoined the production line and in December 1971 was delivered as G-AZED to Dan-Air. *(BAE SYSTEMS)*

Besides the twice-damaged PAL machine mentioned above, other One-Elevens returned to Hurn after various accidents, wars and hijacks to be refitted and returned to their owners or other customers. Some of these were sold on after repair. The first of these rebuilds was G-ASJD in 1964/65, but it was not until 1970 that another took place. This time the wreckage of a Bavarian series 414, D-ANDY which crashed at Gerona, was air-freighted back to Hurn by Canadair CL-44. It rejoined the production line and on completion in December 1971 was sold to Dan-Air as G-AZED.

A LANICA (Nicaragua) owned One-Eleven AN-BB1 came back for similar treatment in early 1972 and spent five months at the Hurn factory being repaired

In January 1972, LANICA's AN-BBI (c/n 111) returned to the Hurn factory for repair after a hijack attempt in San José, Costa Rica. The fuselage was pierced by bullets and the interior was so badly damaged that it had to be totally refitted. Five months later it was redelivered.

A view of the cabin and flight deck of Omani Air Force 485, 1003 (c/n 251) gutted by an oxygen fire just after delivery in November 1975. Initially assessed as beyond repair she was dismantled, shipped to Poole and then transported by road to Hurn and rebuilt. *(BAE SYSTEMS)*

after an attempted hijacking, only flying back to Nicaragua in June. Two months later British Caledonian 501 G-AWYS limped into Hurn having flown back from Corfu with its undercarriage down. It had slipped off the runway into a lake and had been pulled out, dried off and fitted with another undercarriage to make the journey home. In December 1972 it, too, returned to service.

During the Turkish invasion of Cyprus in 1974 a number of aircraft including a One-Eleven were damaged during the fighting. A team from Hurn went to Nicosia to plug the bullet holes in the fuselage with what Roy Radford referred to as 'pot menders'. So after eighteen months of being stranded there, 5B-DAF, a 518 series was returned to Hurn for full repair in December 1975. When repairs were complete and the aircraft registered as G-AXMG, it was leased first to Bavaria Fluggesellschaft and then Monarch Airlines, which sent it back to Hurn again in March 1978 after a wheels-up landing at Stansted during crew training. Fortunately not much damage was done (except to the pilots' reputations!) and this repair only took six weeks. The aircraft went on to fly with Ryanair and then with Nationwide of South Africa.

It took BAC much longer to manage the major repair of an Omani Air Force 485 registered 1003. This machine had been thoroughly gutted by an oxygen fire just after delivery in November 1975. The initial BAC assessment was that repair was not viable. However, the Omani Government decided to proceed with a rebuild so it was dismantled and shipped to Poole Quay in Dorset only ten miles from Hurn. From there, 1003 was transported by road the short distance to Hurn Airport arriving in April 1976. The lengthy rebuild was completed in February 1977 and 1003 was re-delivered shortly after.

A view of the fire-damaged Omani aircraft's fuselage and wings in the ship's hold on arrival at Poole Quay. *(BAE SYSTEMS)*

14

Bizjets and Test Beds

The Viscount, the One-Eleven's predecessor, made its mark not only as a commercial transport but also as an executive aircraft and as a military test bed. No surprise that the One-Eleven followed suit. Though there were a number of orders by executive users, a large part of the demand for the One-Eleven in this market segment was to be satisfied by former airline aircraft.

Executive Layouts

Typically the layout of the executive would include a large lounge and galley area forward of the wing, with more private areas aft. Others were kitted out to carry large numbers of staff in part of the cabin with more private areas partitioned off. BAC did not carry out this furnishing themselves but customers would choose a contractor. For example, Marshall's of Cambridge carried out a number of these contracts and there were other suppliers in the USA, such as Dee Howard. The work might include fitting additional fuel tankage in the forward freight bay to extend the range as well as bespoke luxurious furnishing.

First Executive

Just prior to the first flight in August 1964 two orders for executive versions were announced for delivery in two years' time. One order was placed by Helmut Horten, a German retail chain, named after its founder. The Helmut Horten aircraft was appropriately registered D-ABHH, and made its maiden flight on 15 January 1966. The first machine to be assembled at Weybridge, D-ABHH, flew from the short Brooklands runway to nearby Wisley, though it did visit Hurn prior to delivery two weeks later.

Tenneco ordered two aircraft; both assembled at Weybridge, here N503T (c/n 183) the second example is seen landing at Wisley in June 1969. *(BAE SYSTEMS)*

Many American Airlines aircraft were sold for executive use and several carried the registration N111NA (c/n 065). This is the former American Airlines N5025 on display at Farnborough 1974. *(BAE SYSTEMS)*

American Executives

Based on their Viscount experience, BAC regarded the USA as a major market for executive One-Elevens. BAC employed an agency, Page Airways, to market the executive One-Eleven in the USA and it contributed to the sales of all the American executive models.

The second executive machine, and first for North America, was for an executive Viscount user, Tenneco of Houston. Like Helmut Horten's aircraft, Tenneco's also flew from Weybridge and after fitting out with an executive interior was delivered as N502T in March 1966. A second One-eleven, N503T, also assembled at Weybridge was delivered in July 1969. Then in 1975, Tenneco bought the Horten aircraft, registering it as N504T. After more than twenty-one years' operation all three were sold in 1987 to other executive users.

In September 1966, BAC delivered the former second 400 series prototype, G-ASYE, to an American company, Victor Comptometers. BAC had first flown the aircraft a year earlier and it had flown three long demonstration tours for the manufacturer. The aircraft probably had a much quieter life as an executive aircraft machine than as a demonstrator since executive aircraft usually fly relatively few hours. Another 400 series executive, N270E, crossed the Atlantic on delivery to Engelhard Industries in September 1967 and like its counterparts went on to serve in the corporate role with other customers.

American Airlines' One-Elevens Turn Executive

In 1972 the biggest operator of One-Elevens, at that time, American Airlines, decided to sell its thirty-strong fleet. A number were sold to other airlines but 16 were purchased by National Aircraft Leasing of the United States for conversion to executive/corporate transports. American Airlines overhauled the machines and then Dee Howard fitted them out with executive interiors to customer specification. Additional fuel tanks were fitted in the rear section of the forward freight hold to extend their range. Once ready for their new role the aircraft were then generally sold to American corporations.

In order to promote the conversions, National Aircraft Leasing exhibited N111NA, formerly American Airlines N5025, at Farnborough '74, and the former N5040 also registered as N111NA at Farnborough '76. In addition to the National Aircraft Leasing contract other American 401s were also sold separately to private companies.

It was not only American Airlines' One-Elevens that joined the ranks of executive fleets, but also British examples, notably the first production aircraft, British Caledonian's G-ASJA. After conversion by Marshall's of Cambridge in 1970 it became N734EB for Barwick Industries, and flew with many other organisations in a similar role until it was scrapped in 1989.

Saudi Executives

More than twenty One-Elevens have been registered in Saudi-Arabia for executive purposes, including Mouffak Al Midani who bought an executive 475, a 488 in 1978. Most notable among Saudi owners was Sheikh Salem Bin Laden, the half-brother of Osama Bin Laden, who owned three at various times. The Saudis were very interested in the Tay re-engining project as they realised how the more powerful and fuel efficient Tay would greatly improve the range of a strong, well-engineered airframe.

Many aircraft were used in Saudi-Arabia as executive aircraft; HZ-GRP (c/n 060) owned by Saudi Research & Development, was originally built for American Airlines as N5020 and later bore the oft-used registration N111NA. *(BAE SYSTEMS)*

An Executive User Profile

On 12 November 1971, the *Bournemouth Echo* reported that Mr Robin Loh, Chairman of the Robin Group of companies of Singapore and Hong Kong had taken delivery of a One-Eleven 400 Executive twin-jet registered 9V-BEF for wide-ranging business, executive and charter operations in south-east Asia. This One-Eleven had initially operated with Autair, the Luton-based airline and was then readied for sale to Berni Cornfeld, the Swiss financier, but Cornfield's order was not confirmed so Mr Loh snapped it up.

The *Echo* went on to report that Mr Loh, 'whose business was in shipping, banking, real estate, ship-building and oil exploration, and who operated a mixed cargo and tanker shipping fleet – was an experienced business aircraft user of both piston and jet powered types.

Plush executive interior of the Saudi Research & Development aircraft, HZ-GRP. *(BAE SYSTEMS)*

His One-Eleven incorporated a 12 seat executive compartment forward and airliner type seating for 35 passengers in the rear. The interior was such that the aircraft could be quickly converted to all executive or all-airliner accommodation. Mr Loh also specified that the aircraft be fitted with an extra 350 gallon long-range tank and additional navigational equipment.'

After two years' use by Mr Loh, the aircraft went on to fly in the same role with Pelita, an Indonesian oil company, before reverting to normal airline use with British Island Airways as G-CBIA, and finally joining the Okada Air fleet in Nigeria.

Air Force Executives

BAC tried very hard to sell the Hurn jets to the two major Australian Airlines, Trans-Australian Airlines and Ansett but lost out to their Long Beach competitor, the DC-9. It was some compensation when, at the end of 1965, the Royal Australian Air Force ordered two 217s fitted with the higher-powered Spey 25s which were delivered in early 1968. Registered A12-124 and A12-125 the RAAF operated them as executive transports for the Government until 1990 when European Aviation purchased them. They returned to Britain registered as G-EXPM and G-KROO before being re-exported to Nigeria and used by Okada Air until 2002. Other Air Forces that flew the One-Eleven include the Omani and the Philippines, which briefly flew a 400 series. Another Air Force purchaser was the Forca Aerea Brasileira (Brazilian Air Force) which bought two 423s delivered in 1968 and 1969.

Ford and Rolls-Royce

In 1976 the two Forca Aerea Brasileira 423s were purchased by the Ford Motor Company which registered them G-BEJM and G-BEJW and operated them from its

The first of the Royal Australian Air Force's One-Elevens A12-124 (c/n 124) at London Heathrow, possibly on its delivery flight in January 1968. The two RAAF One-Elevens flew in an executive role from 1968 until 1990. *(BAE SYSTEMS)*

base at London Stansted Airport. The following year Ford bought a further aircraft, formerly D-ANNO of Bavaria Fluggesellschaft and re-registered her as G-BFMC the last three registration letters standing for Ford Motor Company. They were to transport Ford engineers on flights between Ford's European plants in the UK, Belgium, Germany and Spain. Two of the Ford One-Elevens joined the general southward trip to Nigeria in 1993 and were followed by the third and final machine in 1997.

One 400 series, formerly TI-1056C for LACSA of Costa Rica and later TACA, returned to British Aerospace Hurn in 1979 for fitting of a freight door for Turbo-Union. This enabled her, as G-BGTU, to carry freight in the front portion of the cabin and up to thirty-nine passengers in the rear. Operated by the Rolls-Royce Flying Unit it transported personnel and parts between the UK, Germany and Italy. Though due to become the third Tay One-Eleven this never happened and it was sold in 1994 to Nationwide Air Charter in South Africa as ZS-NNM.

The Queen's Flight One-Elevens – Never Realised

The first proposals for use by the Queen's Flight came in 1971 when BAC produced a detailed brochure on how the aircraft might be versioned to suit Royal and

Ford Motor Company operated three aircraft in their executive fleet from Stansted. G-BEJW (c/n 154) seen at Hurn was originally delivered to the Brazilian Air Force in 1969, bought by Ford in 1976 and sold to Nigeria in 1993. *(BAE SYSTEMS)*

There was definite interest in some circles that the Queen's Flight should operate One-Elevens and two proposals were made by the manufacturers; the final one concerned the sale of the last two 475s on the Hurn production line which later became G-BLDH and G-BLHD. This is an artist's impression of how the One-Eleven might have appeared in Queen's Flight livery. *(BAE SYSTEMS)*

Governmental needs. They would have been two special 475s, designated as 480GB, with a specialist navigator's station, commodore's position, larger galleys, extra fuel tanks and easily convertible to suit different layouts. The initial proposal was deemed too expensive and executive Hawker Siddeley 748s were delivered instead. In April 1973 the Ministry of Defence (MoD) looked again at the 475s on the Hurn line but no decision to purchase was made. However, there must have been definite and continuing pressure for the sale because in 1980 the RAF carried out an appraisal of 'SYD and Roy Radford was asked to train the Duke of Edinburgh to fly the One-Eleven. Roy found the Duke to be an astute and skilful pilot but found it a little strange that Royal protocol demanded the instructor call his pupil, 'Sir'. When the Hurn production line closed in 1984 again there were belated efforts to sell the last two 475s to the Queen's Flight again but they were delivered to McAlpine Aviation (see Chapter 9).

British Military Test Beds

Four One-Elevens, three based at Boscombe Down, are used by the military in the UK, though until recently there were five in operation. These can continue flying after noise restrictions came into force on 1 April 2002 because military aircraft are exempt from such restrictions.

XX105

The first One-Eleven to serve with the MoD was the former G-ASJD, a 201, which had first flown on 6 July 1964. It has had a chequered history, beginning with an ignominious forced landed on Salisbury Plain on 20 August 1964 while carrying out stalling tests and was dismantled and returned to Hurn (see Chapter 4). It first flew again on 13 June 1965 and was delivered to British United Airways on 5 August 1965, survived BUA's merger with Caledonian Airways and continued in service until 21 September 1971.

The British MoD then bought the aircraft, which was sent to Hurn for conversion and repainting, then delivered to the Experimental Unit of RAE Bedford. As XX105 the aircraft was firstly used as a part of the Blind Landing Test Programme and later participated in another task, the testing of Direct Lift Control Systems.

The UK Defence Evaluation Research Agency (DERA now QinetiQ) used XX105 during trials of the European Geostationary Navigation Overlay Service System as its on-board equipment makes it one of the most technologically advanced aircraft in the sky. The Boscombe Down-based QinetiQ Air Fleet Department now operates XX105 on avionics navigational and flight management research. XX105 is the oldest flying One-Eleven and one of the only examples not to be hush-kitted.

XX919 (c/n 091) formerly used by Philippines Airlines was sold to the Ministry of Defence in 1974 and broken up in June 2000, though the forward fuselage is preserved at Boscombe Down. In the background at Hurn is N5021 previously delivered to American Airlines and sold to Tristar Western for executive use in 1973. *(BAE SYSTEMS)*

Formerly a Philippines Airlines One-Eleven, XX919 (c/n 091) was a military research aircraft for twenty-three years when it was withdrawn from use and scrapped in 2000; the nose was saved for the Boscombe Down Aviation Collection. Here next to it is the nose of Andover XS790. The collection was relocated to Old Sarum in 2012. *(Author)*

XX919

BAC One-Eleven series 402, XX919, undertook many trials within the UK in addition to making the occasional airshow appearance in between a busy flight test programme. Built at Hum, it first flew on 7 April 1966 and was delivered to Philippines Airlines as PI-C1121 the same month, where it remained in passenger service for the next five years.

Repurchased by BAC in part-exchange for a 500 series aircraft it was flown to Hum for refurbishment for the MoD. From there, it was delivered on 16 May 1974 to the Royal Aircraft Establishment, Farnborough, for research duties.

Whilst at Farnborough XX919 was used as a flying laboratory, engaged in high-frequency communications research and was also modified with a Sonobuoy rack and dispenser in the rear fuselage, launching its load through the modified rear stairwell. XX919 continued flying in these roles from Farnborough until relocation to Boscombe Down on 24 March 1994 where it continued as a research aircraft, still undertaking the aforementioned duties, with the DERA. It remained in operational service until 4 March 1997, but was then placed in open storage after over thirty years, and 19,421 hours, of civil and military service. XX919 was put up for sale and during June 2000 underwent spares recovery, most of the aircraft being scrapped with the front fuselage saved for the new Boscombe Down Museum, and now resides undercover though bereft of many parts.

ZE432

The Empire Test Pilots School's (ETPS) BAC One-Eleven 479 was manufactured in July 1973 and delivered to Air Pacific registered as DQ-FBV. It operated with them for eleven years and was purchased by the MoD, reregistered as ZE432 in May 1984, and transferred to the ETPS at Boscombe Down.

Fitted with a specially lengthened nose for Eurofighter Typhoon radar trials this former Air Pacific One-Eleven 479 was purchased by the Ministry of Defence in 1984 and registered ZE433 (c/n 245). It is seen here at the engine silencers at Hurn now used by European Aviation but originally installed by BAC. *(Mike Phipp)*

ZH763 (c/n 263) was delivered as G-BGKE to British Airways in 1980. She entered service with the Defence Research Agency in 1994 and is now used on radar research based at Boscombe Down. *(QinetiQ)*

The One-Eleven is fitted with incidence meters (as originally fitted to all One-Elevens on test), cockpit-mounted flight control position indicators, air data acquisition module, cockpit voice recorder, accident data recorder, and a right-hand seat EFIS display.

The aircraft provides students with experience of captaining a large multi-engined civil aircraft and is used for performance and handling exercises. Specific exercises are level flight performance, climb performance, take-off performance and civil certification exercises.

ZE 433

The sister of the ETPS One-Eleven, ZE433, was delivered to Air Pacific in 1972 as DQ-FBQ and operated for them for twelve years. At the end of its airline service it was purchased by the MoD and was based at RAE Bedford from 1984. Its nose was substantially extended to accommodate radar for the Eurofighter Typhoon and first flew with the 'A' version of the Eurofighter Typhoon ECR 90 radar in the nose at Bedford, on 8 January 1993. The 'C' version which is the first ECR 90 packaged to fit Eurofighter was flown in the One-Eleven from July 1996.

ZH763

A former BA 539 delivered in 1980, ZH763, was purchased from BA by GEC Ferranti in 1991 with the intention of becoming the Eurofighter radar test bed. However since this would have required nose alterations it was exchanged for the MoD's ZE433 which had already undergone such changes. ZH763 was extensively modified with housings under and on the upper side of the front fuselage for Enhanced Surveillance Radar and operates for QinetiQ at Boscombe Down.

A dynamic shot of Northrop Grumman's N164W (c/n 090) taking off, note the non-standard radome and aerial array. Seeing this shot one can appreciate how the One-Elevens were sometimes referred to as the 'pocket rocket' in the USA. *(Sunil Gupta)*

American Military Test Beds – Northrop Grumman's One-Elevens

Northrop Grumman owns two former American Airlines' One-Eleven 401s, N162W and N164W, which though they carry civil registrations are engaged in military research. These aircraft have served as test beds for many developmental programmes such as the B-1B, F-16 and F-22 radar, and the YF-23 avionics.

Lockheed Martin modified one of the One-Elevens to prepare it for the Joint Strike Flight (JSF) flight test program in which it will serve as a flying test bed for prototype multisensor JSF avionics. Integrating the avionics systems on a flying test bed will reduce the need for sensor flights during the engineering and manufacturing development phase of the programme.

Flight testing the Lockheed Martin prototype JSF sensors and systems began on the One-Eleven in late 1999. The tests demonstrate its all-weather, air-to-air, and air-to-ground capabilities in urban and simulated-threat environments. Lockheed Martin was granted the JSF contract on 26 October 2001 and more test work was given to their One-Elevens.

15

Serving the World into the Twenty-First Century

During the 1990s, the number of One-Eleven operators dwindled substantially. When Dan-Air ceased operations its One-Elevens went into store and BA began disposing of its examples. Increasingly the One-Eleven was used on the periphery by small up-and-coming users or for standby charters. No longer the star of airline fleets, from now on the One-Eleven would just have the bit parts, for there were younger and quieter performers to take the starring roles.

However, it was still in service, or entering service, and making money for airlines that had never operated it, such as Ryanair, Nationwide in South Africa, and in Nigeria. More importantly with the UK's European Aviation the One-Eleven found a dynamic champion which demonstrated the strength of a great airframe and how much potential still remained in a far from new design. European even sought to extend the life of that aircraft beyond the imposition of the stringent Stage 3 noise regulations which came into force in April 2002.

According to *Flight International* in May 2002 there were still 104 One-Elevens in existence throughout the world of which seventy were active and thirty-four stored. However, after the tragic crash of a in Nigerian One-Eleven in May 2002 the number active fell drastically.

The One-Eleven and Ryanair's Growth

Ryanair, now one of Europe's most forceful airline brands and market-maker grew from small beginnings. Along with other budget airlines it has marketed its 'no frills' product so vigorously that well-established national carriers have had to rethink their product and follow the Ryanair, Easy Jet and Go approach for short-haul routes.

In the 1980s, air routes were still heavily regulated, but in 1986 the UK and Irish Governments agreed to expand services between the two countries and gave a licence to Ryanair to run services between Dublin and Luton. In November of that

Ryanair first started their 'no frills' services with One-Elevens. This machine, EI-BVI (c/n 256) 'The Spirit of Connaught' was built for Tarom as a 525 and leased to the Irish carrier from 1988 to 1993 and then returned to the Romanian operator. *(Author)*

year the Irish company introduced its first One-Eleven, a Romanian-built Tarom-leased 561, formerly YR-BRB, which became EI-BSS. This was the beginning of eight years of Ryanair One-Eleven operation during which a total of sixteen were bought or leased.

Ever on the lookout to expand their business, Ryanair bought into London European Airways and leased another Romanian One-Eleven 561, YR-BRF, for use on scheduled flights to Amsterdam from Luton starting in May 1987. Within a few months the scheduled services were dropped and the aircraft given a British registration, G-BNIH, for the short-lived Ryanair Europe but then joined the Ryanair fleet proper in 1990 as EI-CAS.

In March 1987 the Irish Government granted licences for more Dublin flights to newly popular destinations in Europe such as Stuttgart and Malaga as well as other routes such as Knock–Luton and Knock–Birmingham. Granting these licences still gave Aer Lingus, the Irish flag carrier, the best pickings, that is, Heathrow–Dublin, etc. With these additional services Ryanair took on more One-Elevens and also other aircraft.

Throughout the rest of the 1980s, Ryanair grew its services and also its losses. It added three more One-Elevens to its fleet and briefly a series 476, G-AZUK. Fortunately, in September 1989 the Irish Government, anxious to foster Ryanair and to continue to protect Aer Lingus, carved up the market between them allowing Ryanair to have sole rights on Stansted–Dublin services. But with losses reaching almost IR£20 million in 1990, Ryanair had to rethink its business strategy if it were to survive. To offset its liabilities the leased One-Eleven fleet was further reduced to just two. EI-BVH, 'BVI and four others formerly used by British Island Airways and London European were passed onto Ryanair and received Irish registrations as

EI-CCU, 'CCW, 'CCX and 'CDO, bringing the fleet up to a total of six. Luton was replaced by the newly developed Stansted as the hub of Ryanair's operations with seven daily flights to Dublin and flights to other destinations in the Republic.

As an indication of the turbulence and the vagaries of the airline business, after making a slender profit in 1991, Ryanair felt confident enough to briefly lease back in two more One-Elevens from Tarom giving them a fleet of eight in all while the non-jet equipment was disposed of. The One-Elevens started to appear in a new livery, a white overall fuselage with blue titling and a yellow harp on an all-blue tail. In 1993, the last full year of Ryanair One-Eleven operation, the fleet was still eight, consisting of the four former London European aircraft and four leased former BA 501s, EI-CIB, 'CIC' 'CID, 'CIE. Traffic had grown to 1.15 million passengers and turnover to IR£56 million.

In 1994, the company began to purchase second-hand 737-200s and the rest of the story is the all-too familiar one. By the end of that year the company had withdrawn all the sturdy One-Elevens that had served Ryanair so well as it struggled to establish itself and helped it become the force that it is today.

The four longer-serving One-Elevens, formerly EI-CCU, 'CCW, 'CCX, 'CDO, were eventually sold on to Nationwide of South Africa, while three of the leased 501s went to Shabair of Zaire and the other worked first for Maersk, a BA franchise, and later flew southwards to Executive Aviation Services of Nigeria.

Nigeria – A One-Eleven Graveyard?

A significant destination for the British type is Nigeria where as many as seventy-nine examples of all series have found their way. Very few aircraft have returned from Nigeria, a large number are referred to as stored which almost certainly means that they will never fly again. This massive demand for the One-Eleven and other older aircraft was caused by the Nigerian airline deregulation in the mid-1980s.

In total, there have been twelve airlines which have come and gone in the volatile Nigerian economic and political climate. These are: ADC, Albarka, Changchangi, Chrome, Executive Air Services, Fassey Aviation, Gas Air, Hold Trade Air, Kabo, Okada, Oriental and Savannah. Okada must take pride of place having used a total of twenty-five One-Elevens of all series except the 475 since 1983.

Okada started by purchasing 300s and 400s in the late 1980s and the two former Royal Australian Air Force 217s, the only 200s, joined their numbers in 1991. In the following year it almost purchased seven ex-BA 510s stored at Hurn which were repainted in their colours but the sale fell through. However, Okada soon bought three other 500s bringing their total purchases to twenty-five aircraft. Okada's livery is familiar to British eyes since it is a version of the old British Caledonian scheme. Okada adopted this livery when it purchased some One-Elevens from British Caledonian that were still in those colours.

Seen at Southend in 1991 is 5N-SKS (c/n 100) a former Mohawk and US Air series 204 which on arrival in Nigeria was sold to Kabo Air. Behind her is EI-BWI (c/n 007), third production aircraft first flown as G-ASJC for BUA and then flown with Pacific Express and Braniff. *(Rolando Ugolini)*

Just outside the hangars where it was built, G-AVMM (c/n 141) constructed as a 510 for BEA and British Airways, sold to European Aviation which sold it in turn to the Nigerian operator, Changchangi in whose livery it is seen. It later became 5N-BCG. *(Mike Phipp)*

Okada seems to be very much an airline steeped in the contemporary 'disposable culture' and as aircraft needed maintenance, they were cannibalised or replacements purchased and at least two were written off in accidents.

Kabo Airlines did not quite achieve Okada's record and never used any of the longer fuselage 500 series, preferring to purchase eighteen 200s and 400s many of which had originally been delivered to US airlines such as Braniff, Mohawk and American Airlines where they will have seen intensive service.

The other Nigerian One-Eleven operators all have much smaller fleet sizes. Owing to the difficulty in obtaining information from the country it is hard to know how many may exactly still be in use. European Aviation of Hurn sold two 510s to Changchangi and two 500s to Savannah, the two newest Nigerian One-Eleven operators.

The Nigerian aircraft have had more than their fair share of the more recent accident write-offs, with eleven of the thirteen One-Eleven incidents between 1991 and 2002 occurring to their machines. (The other two were with TAROM operated aircraft.) Additionally four One-Elevens were apparently damaged by a storm while on the ground on 27 May 2002.

A Permanent End to Nigerian One-Eleven Operations?

The accident on 4 May 2002 to Executive Aviation Service's 5N-ESF and the death of 145 people was Nigeria's worst air accident in five years. In the previous month, concern over the use of ageing aircraft by the country's de-regulated airline industry had resulted in the Government banning the use of aircraft older than twenty-two years. However, this triggered strong protests from the private carriers and so a five-year phasing-in period was allowed, but on 8 May 2002 the Nigerian Government grounded all One-Elevens pending investigation of the accident.

South Africa's First One-Elevens

Even though the BAC jet entered service in 1965 it was not until thirty-one years later, towards the end of its commercial life that the first One-Eleven joined the South African register to fly for Nationwide Air Charter. Services began in January 1996 using three One-Elevens on the country's prime domestic route between Johannesburg and Cape Town and on international routes in the region.

The One-Elevens, five 400s and six 500s, were fitted out in a two-class seventy-two and ninety-four all-leather seat layout respectively. The 500s had previously been with Ryanair and Cyprus Airways, the passenger 400s had had more chequered

Another former European aircraft about to leave Hurn for Nigeria. Still carrying the registration G-AXLL (c/n 193) due to start services with Savannah Airlines in November 2001. (Mike Phipp)

ZS-NUG (c/n 237), originally built for LACSA, flew with Nationwide of South Africa until withdrawn from use in 2000. It is shown here at Lanseria, near Johannesburg, in 2009. *(Rainer Bexten)*

careers, and include the former G-AVGP and G-AWEJ built as 408s for Channel Airways, the former N5026 an American Airlines 401 and Autair's 416 G-AWBL. An exception is the 409 freighter, which is the only one of its type and originally was delivered to LACSA and later especially converted at Hurn for Rolls-Royce and became G-BGTU. Now registered as ZS-NNM it can carry a 10-ton load and has typically been used for transporting domestic mail.

Nationwide owns its One-Elevens and maintains them at its maintenance base at Lanseria Airport, north of Johannesburg, where its simulator and crew training is also centred.

The One-Elevens have gradually been phased out because though Nationwide regards them as rugged and easy to operate, the high temperatures and altitude of Johannesburg limit their performance. It is the familiar story; Boeing 737s are superseding them.

British World Airways

British World Airways grew out of British Air Ferries (BAF) which itself was spawned by British United Air Ferries which once operated Carvairs and Bristol Freighters in car ferry services across the Channel.

Their association with the One-Eleven began in 1990 with some early 201s, which had once been used by its sister British United. These were the former G-ASJC, fourth-production aircraft which flew the low-speed handling trials with BAC's Trubshaw and Oliver in the latter part of 1964, G-ASJG which had been the final Certificate of Airworthiness trials aircraft and G-ASJH. The first of these was flown back across the Atlantic after service with Florida Express and put into store at Southend as EI-BWI, never to fly again and gradually stripped for spares. The other

G-OBWA (c/n 232) still bearing British World livery being prepared at Southend for a ferry flight to Sierra Leone in July 2002. First flown in 1971 it had also flown with Court Line, British Caledonian and Dan-Air. *(Author)*

two registered as G-DBAF and G-OCNW served for two years before being put into store. The latter was broken up but G-BDAF moved on to Liberia, then Afghanistan and finally Rwanda (Central Africa). Another well-travelled One-Eleven, G-AZUK, also briefly served with BAF.

With Dan-Air's demise in 1992, BAF bought their complete fleet of eleven One-Eleven 500s, replaced their short-body versions and reserved the registrations G-OBWA to G-OBWK inclusively. As the 500s were being put into service BAF re-branded itself as British World Airways with a totally new livery on the sensible grounds that the old name was a hangover from its car-ferrying days and not representative of the contemporary airline. Five of the eleven 500s taken on were pressed into service on charters from Manchester, Gatwick and Stansted and an isolated scheduled service to Bucharest was trialled but soon withdrawn. The other aircraft remained stored, used for spares recovery and then scrapped. Besides the charters, at least one One-Eleven could typically be seen at Stansted acting as standby aircraft to help out airlines in busy periods or when aircraft were unserviceable.

In 2000, British World announced that Boeing 737s were to replace the British jets and the One-Elevens were advertised for sale in *Flight International* magazine. Two were sold to Albarka Air Services of Nigeria but British World went out of business in December 2000 and the three remaining, G-OBWA, 'BWD, 'BWE were left stored in the open at Southend. These aircraft were sold to Air Leone in Sierra Leone and three were delivered.

Guatemalan 400s

Over its many years of operation the One-Eleven served a number of airlines in Central America and still continues to fly with Tikal Airlines of Guatemala. The airline uses two 401s, registered TG-TJF and TG-TJK, which were originally delivered to American Airlines as N5043 and N5023 respectively in 1966. Tikal bought their first jets in 1995; uses them mainly on an internal route from Guatemala City to Flores and into Mexico at weekends.

European Aviation

European Aviation's involvement with the One-Eleven started with the purchase of the two RAAF 217s in 1990 sold to Okada Air the following year. In May 1993, Paul Stoddard, European's owner, bought sixteen One-Eleven 510s and spares from British Airways. The original intention was to scrap them but European realised that it was more profitable to fly them. This purchase made European the most important European-based One-Eleven operator in the late 1990s. In September 1993, European Aviation Air Charter was formed, targeted at tour operators, charter and schedule airlines needing additional capacity on short and medium-term leases. European toyed with operating its own flights but concluded that leasing aircraft to other operators was its niche.

 Though originally based at Filton, when European Aviation decided to move to Hurn in 1994, it was homecoming for the One-Elevens to the hangars in which they were first assembled and among the staff there are some who had worked on One-Eleven production with BAC.

European's One-Elevens

The former BA 510s had certain unique features specified by BEA, the original purchaser, to make them similar to the Trident. They had a Smiths flight control system and substantial differences to the standard One-Eleven layout. As an added inconvenience they were not fitted with forward airstairs, being ballasted instead with a piece of concrete. European gradually removed the ballast and fitted airstairs and installed the usual Collins flight control system to a number of 510s. Some such as 'VMR, 'VMS, 'VMV, 'VMX were never flown and were used for spares, like 'VMJ, which with its tail and wings removed became a cabin trainer.

 From 1998, the 510 series aircraft were gradually withdrawn from service, stored, broken up or sold. 'VMN was donated to the Bournemouth Aviation Museum in May 2000 in AB Airlines colours – a pity it is not in European colours! 'VML and

'VMM went to the Nigerian operator Changchangi in December 2000. The last 510 in operation was 'VMT, which operated in 'Minardi Formula One' black livery in a fifty-seat executive layout. Executive charter is a niche at which European has excelled with clients from leading companies, heads of state, film stars and members of several royal families. The Minardi Formula One team belongs to Paul Stoddard, owner of European, so the One-Eleven was useful for transporting them and other F1 people.

In 1994, European bought four former BA/BCAL 500s, G-AWYV, G-AXLL, G-AYOP, G-AZMF. These were equipped with Collins flight systems, forward airstairs and could operate at higher weights than the 510s. Two years later European also purchased two Austral 500s which flew back to Hurn where they became G-HKIT (for Hush Kit) and G-IIIH (for Stage 3 Hush). They were to fly with hushed power plants but the programme did not prove viable and like two Philippines 500s purchased at

Photographed in European Air Charter colours is G-AVMI (c/n 137) originally built for BEA and sold to European Aviation in 1993. European leased it to Sabena and Jersey European. *(European Aviation)*

Delivered to Austral in November 1969, this One-Eleven (c/n 196) served with the Argentine airline until 1996, when it was bought by European Airlines and flown back to Hurn for possible Stage 3 hush-kitting and registered as G-HKIT. However, it never flew again as the Stage 3 hush-kitting programme for 500s was abandoned by European Airlines and the aircraft was broken up in 2001. *(Author)*

the same time they never flew again. The operating fleet peaked at fourteen and at one time European even owned twenty-four One-Elevens. Gradually these numbers were reduced by sales and scrapping.

By the summer of 2001, European were operating only five; G-AWYV, G-AXLL, G-AYOP and G-AZMF in the airliner role, with the specially branded G-AVMT for executive charter. But in November 2001, 'XLL and 'YOP were sold and painted in the colours of Savannah Airlines of Nigeria leaving just three One-Elevens running during that winter; 'WYV in a standard 104-seat layout and red livery, 'ZMF in black livery and 'VMT for the Minardi Formula One team.

The European One-Eleven Simulator

Initially the airline used the BA simulator at Cranebank, near Heathrow, but then wisely decided to purchase it rather than pay for its use. This was the nucleus for the development of European's training arm, which has other simulators for other types at Hurn.

The simulator was built by Rediffusion in 1969 and has three-axis movement and a night facility showing runway lights, but no day vision. The author had the opportunity to 'fly' the simulator in November 2001 in a take-off, left-hand circuit and landing at Shannon. He found it very challenging and was grateful to Steve Costello, European's Simulator Engineer who ensured the 'aircraft' landed safely! The life of the simulator seems likely to exceed that of the European fleet and was certified for use until 31 October 2002.

One-Eleven Operations with European Aviation

European's Hurn-built jets had a far wider field of operations than they ever had with their former owners, especially the 510s that were built for BEA and then joined the BA fleet. European's One-Eleven operated in many colours and for other airlines on short-term leases in their own colours. They flew for almost every British airline and over fifty airlines internationally. AB, Euroscot, Maersk (in BA colours), Sabena, Jersey European, Air France, Air Liberté, and Air Littorial used One-Elevens in their colours and other frequent users were BA, Ryanair, Air UK and even Cathay Pacific in European's red colour scheme.

With all these operations the BAC One-Elevens trekked far and wide, to Keflavik in Iceland, Evenes in northern Norway, Riyadh in Saudi-Arabia, and to many places in the former Soviet Union, such as Dzkhankhan and Samarkand. One of the longest sectors covered non-stop was Moscow–Paris with a full load, helped by a long runway and low temperatures at Moscow and favourable winds.

Stage 3 Hush Kitting

Though the Spey One-Elevens were satisfactorily Stage 2 hush-kitted in the 1980s there was a deadline of April 2002 for the end of operations in Europe and North America for aircraft not Stage 3 noise compliant.

Rolls-Royce took the view from the start that the prospects of achieving effective hush-kitting to Stage 3 standards on the Spey was very difficult. Though it might be possible on the 400 series, it was deemed impossible for the heavier 500 series. In 1994, there were about twenty operators who were bothered about Stage 3 compliance and so a conference was called at Fort Lauderdale to discuss the problem. Since Rolls-Royce did not see much likelihood of success it fell to an American company, Quiet Technology Corporation (QTC), to carry out the work.

With such a large One-Eleven fleet, European seriously investigated the possibility of extending the life of their 500 series fleet beyond the 2002 deadline. In 1997, it was

European Aviation promoted the One-Eleven Stage 3 hush kit at Farnborough 1998. G-AVMM (c/n 141) flew into Farnborough and was fitted with a mock-up for the spectators to view. *(Author)*

G-AVML (c/n 140) flew to Quiet Technology's base at Opa Locka in Florida, for Stage 3 hush-kit trials in autumn 1998. A Stage 3 nacelle was fitted and fully tested. This made the aircraft noise compliant but the weight, cost and lack of support prohibited conversion. Had this scheme worked, One-Eleven airliner services would not have come to an end in Europe and North America in 2002. *(European Aviation)*

The One-Eleven's last stand. VP-CCG (c/n 081) one of the three 400s fitted with the attractive Stage 3 hush kits at the rear of the engine seen at Hurn in February 2002. These quieten the Speys sufficiently to allow the aircraft to continue flying in Europe and North America. This is a very different fitting to the Stage 2 hush kits fitted to most One-Elevens. Though there were trials with the 500 series as well, costs proved prohibitive to fit the Stage 3 hush kits to them. *(Colin K. Work)*

reported that European had been working with Quiet Technology on a $40 million project to develop a hush kit that would bring the BAC One-Eleven to Stage 3 levels. G-AVMM was displayed at Farnborough 1998 with a mocked-up Stage 3 Spey on its right engine but it was G-AVML that flew to Quiet Technology's base at Opa Locka in Florida, for Stage 3 hush kit trials in autumn 1998. A Stage 3 nacelle was fitted to the right Spey and was fully tested. Though this made the aircraft noise compliant the weight penalty, development costs and lack of support made conversion of the 500s prohibitive. Had this scheme worked, One-Eleven airliner services would not have been forced to come to an end in the UK in April 2002.

Quiet Technology did achieve hush-kitting of the 400 series and the FAA awarded a Supplementary Type Certificate. The test aircraft used was VP-CCG, which carried out tests at Williams Gateway Airport in Arizona. Rolls-Royce were not made aware of this at the time and nor initially were the CAA. To date, three 400 series have been converted, the others being VP-CLM and N999BW. QTC's system consists of a translating ejector (optimised for Mach 0.8 cruise) installed on sliding rails that require no changes to the aircraft's thrust reverser. Total installed weight is approximately 110lb per side. (Cost of installation of a similar system to a Spey Gulfstream was $1.35 million.)

The Last British Commercial One-Eleven Flights

With European and North American services ending at the end of March 2002 it was fortunate that there was still a substantial and experienced operator most appropriately based at Hurn in the shape of European Aviation to provide hardware for a number of enthusiasts' flights.

The first of these was on Saturday 16 March 2002. There were three flights from Hurn, all fully laden, flown by a spick and span G-AZMF which two weeks later operated similar flights from Manchester and Luton. On the last day of operations, Sunday 31 March, two more public flights and a final, private, last-ever flight was suitably flown from Hurn. The first of these, at 14:00, was organised by a Bournemouth Travel Agent, Bath Travel, which first used British United One-Elevens on Majorca charters from Hurn in April 1965. Two hours later, Ian Allan operated the final public flight and at 18:30 European Aviation flew a final brief flight for themselves and the enjoyment of their staff.

Those making the pilgrimage to Hurn in March mostly comprised aircraft enthusiasts, from many countries but more significantly many who had been intimately connected with the project at BAC and BAe. Amongst these were test pilots, flight test observers, aerodynamicists, engineers, designers and salesman for whom the occasion was an opportunity to meet former colleagues and at the same time to bid a fond farewell to a great aircraft which had proved its worth over almost four decades of flying.

One of the last One-Elevens in UK commercial service was European's G-AZMF (c/n 240) seen on the Hurn apron, and which flew a series of enthusiasts' last commercial One-Eleven flights at the end of March 2002. *(Author)*

16

Conclusion – What Held the One-Eleven Back?

The BAC One-Eleven achieved some success, but not nearly as much as it might have done. Some 241 delivered over almost thirty years does not compare with the thousands of Boeing 737s produced over forty-five years and still in production. So what lessons can be learnt from the failure to achieve the same sales, not forgetting the employment opportunities, for a British product?

To some extent the principal lesson to be learned from the One-Eleven's history is that if the advantages of good design, technical innovation and pioneering are not consistently exploited and developed, and if company and Government support is lacking at crucial phases then rivals will take the lead.

The aircraft's strengths can be summarised as follows.

Specification

The decision to aim for a worldwide specification, rather than that of British Airways' predecessor BEA, and simultaneously to achieve British and American certification for the first time ever was clearly right.

The Basic Design Concept

The basic design concept was sound. The structural philosophy and construction have proved first class, amongst the most robust of any modern aircraft. Fourteen One-Elevens formerly with US Air, (ex-Mohawk, Aloha or Braniff) achieved over 70,000 flights, an average of ten flights per day from 1965 until their withdrawal from service in 1989. Currently approved operating life is 85,000 hours/landings and a number of aircraft, especially those initially delivered to Braniff and Mohawk, made over 80,000 landings. Total One-Eleven fleet performance exceeds 8.5 million flying hours and 9 million landings.

Export Success

Until development was inhibited in the late 1960s the aircraft met direct US competition to a greater degree than any European product had done and still achieved reasonable sales. It was Britain's biggest ever dollar earner before the Rolls-Royce RB 211 engine was introduced and given the kind of determined development that has been shown by Boeing with the 737, it could have achieved several times its actual level of sales.

The aircraft's weaknesses can be summarised as follows.

Design

The original choice of the servo-tab operated elevator proved to be flawed. The three accidents during the development period did grave harm to its credibility – the first of these, the deep stall accident, certainly produced a new degree of practical knowledge of this phenomenon which was freely shared with the rest of the industry. The second and the third should not have happened but also did untold harm to sales.

Some aspects of the design were not as well optimised as they should have been. Almost certainly the selection of the circular fuselage cross-section was a weak spot and Douglas's slightly wider 'double-bubble' provided operators with a cabin that felt appreciably wider.

Powerplant

The use of the Rolls-Royce Spey engine with its limited growth potential stymied growth of the One-Eleven and allowed Douglas with their higher-powered engines to virtually deny the European market to BAC at a stroke by the early development of the extended DC-9 30. The same growth potential of the Pratt & Whitney power plant led the Boeing 737's early success and from the 737-300 series Boeing fitted an even better, different power plant, the SNECMA-General Electric CFM 56-3. The revamped 737 even held its own against the much newer Airbus A320.

With hindsight, BAC should have pushed American into selecting the JT8D so as to offer an alternative power plant. This would have revolutionised the programme allowing the development of a much better 500 series and ultimately a 700/800 series equivalent of the DC-9 80 and Boeing 737-300. Alternatively, a much earlier Rolls-Royce Tay could have saved the day but, in any event, BAC should have introduced a different, more powerful engine as an alternative at a time when the project still had many years to run.

Production

The programme was a swift one by European standards but nonetheless the build-up to production was slow and was further hampered by months of delay following the prototype's fatal crash just two months after the first flight. Douglas, with their US-style production programme, was able to offer very large numbers of aircraft to a market where traffic growth had blossomed just at the right time for them. Consider that within two months of the 737's start-date, Boeing had a stretched 737! BAC did not offer an enlarged One-Eleven until six years after the initiation of the project.

Lack of Focussed Direction

In the late 1960s, relatively early in the One-Eleven's development, BAC started to talk about a Series 600 and a Two-Eleven, the latter with more than double the capacity of the One-Eleven. BAC shelved the 600 series to develop Two-Eleven, which was never built and was eventually superseded by plans for a Three-Eleven, which also never flew. Rather than pursuing these new schemes, efforts should have been put into realising the already proven potential of the Hurn-built machine by stretching it and re-engining it to produce a 600 series and further larger developments. The 475 was a sprightly performer but there was no real market for it as evidenced by the poor sales.

Management and Political Difficulties

The lack of corporate interest in the programme in the early 1970s when the bankruptcy of Rolls-Royce changed the balance of power in BAC towards GEC (who had little interest in the risks of civil aviation) curtailed development. Subsequently, the uncertainties of merger and nationalisation followed by denationalisation caused effective development to cease with the 500/475 series and further sales prospects became meagre.

Later Developments

Romanian licence production was much too slow and stymied by a lack of decision-making at all levels. It was never a viable alternative to British production and without an alternative powerplant there was no market for the Romanian-built aircraft.

The Tay One-Eleven 400 programme was technically near to being a success but seemingly predicated on the wrong series of the aircraft, for the performance advantages were far greater for the 500 than the 400. To add to this there were difficulties at Dee Howard and possibly some lack of co-operation from the British end, so the programme took too long and customers lost interest. Had the Romanian production been working much better it might have saved the programme.

The Boeing View

In a presentation in 1985, Joe Sutter, former Executive Vice-President of the Boeing Company, talked of the difficult decisions the manufacturer has to make in allocating limited resources between derivative and new design programmes. Sutter noted the

XX105 (c/n 008), one of the longest serving One-Elevens. Her maiden flight as G-ASJD was in July 1964, she crash-landed on Salisbury Plain six weeks later during stall testing, was delivered to BUA in 1965 and sold to the Ministry of Defence in 1971. She only made her last flight in 2003. *(BAE SYSTEMS)*

The last British-built 500 series, YR-BCO (c/n 272), taking off from Hurn in March 1982. (BAE SYSTEMS)

upsurge in interest in the 100-seat market and a number of new entrants jostling for place. He said, 'In retrospect, wouldn't it have been more cost effective for both the airlines and the manufacturing industry if British Aerospace had kept their BAC One-Eleven in production by updating the airframe and re-powering with the Rolls-Royce Tay engine?'

Conclusion

A great UK opportunity was wasted by failure to develop the BAC One-Eleven and thus allowing the only European team with continuity or experience in airliner design, production, marketing and support to scatter and atrophy. There is perhaps some consolation to be drawn from the significant share the UK has in Airbus, which has not repeated the mistake of the BAC One-Eleven programme by losing confidence in its product, and has proved to be able to compete with Boeing by offering a full portfolio of airframes to equal those of its American rival.

The BAC One-Eleven was the only civil project conceived and produced solely by the British Aircraft Corporation and which stayed in production throughout BAC's existence. The earnings from it were a major factor in keeping the Corporation afloat during its troubled history. It is self-evident that the One-Eleven should have been further developed – it obviously possessed the potential. Maybe Douglas outsold the One-Eleven with the DC-9, but it was bankrupted as a result, as indeed was Fokker with its Tay-powered Fokker 100 in 1996. Let it not be forgotten that BAC did not over extend itself but went on to produce Concorde.

The One-Eleven achieved substantial sales, bested in Britain by only the Viscount and BAE 146/RJ. It gave work to Rolls-Royce and many British ancillary equipment

BAC One-Eleven 500.
(Rolando Ugolini)

suppliers and helped the national balance of payments. Over forty years it provided much employment in the UK, transported many thousands of passengers throughout the world and won the deserved affection of many.

The tenacity and determination of BAC's staff must not go unmentioned here. The manner in which the team worked to address the challenges of One-Eleven design, testing, production and sales is a tribute to their combined skills, devotion and hard work. At times in the early years the employees at Hurn, Weybridge and Filton must have felt discouraged and downhearted but perseverance and a certain determination shone through.

Addendum

The first edition of the book was completed and published in 2002 when the BAC One-Eleven's activities had just been seriously circumscribed following the introduction of Stage 3 noise regulations in Europe on 1 April that year. The last UK airliner operator, European Airlines, grounded its small fleet of One-Elevens and began the gradual process of disposal.

Up to 2002, all series of One-Elevens had been successfully hush-kitted by the manufacturer to be compliant with the Series 2 regulations but these later regulations proved a greater obstacle to overcome. Neither the manufacturer nor Rolls-Royce were interested in pursuing the matter of achieving a Stage 3 compliant aircraft. Even though the 400 and 475 series aircraft could have been satisfactorily hush-kitted to achieve the Stage 3 regulations, trials with a European Airlines 500 series had indicated that the weight penalty was too great and meant that conversion was not a viable option. It should be noted that the European noise legislation did not apply in other parts of the world where operators remained interested in working with these well-built, efficient and inexpensive aircraft, either as airliners or as executive aircraft.

One-Elevens were displayed at the Farnborough Show for many years and in even 2008 appeared in an anonymous role. The nose of G-AVMZ (c/n 153), the last of British Airways' fleet of 510s exhibited by Air Salvage International, a firm specialising in the breaking up and disposal of aircraft. *(Author)*

Three One-Elevens at Medevia, Malta, in 2003. Two for Air Leone of Sierra Leone, 9L-LDL (c/n 232) still in British World livery and 9L-LDJ (c/n 242). The third One-Eleven is Albarka Air's 5N-BBP. All three were scrapped in 2006. (Roberto Benetti)

The End of Nigerian Operations

Nigeria had been a strong market for One-Elevens and almost eighty had been sold to operators there. However, following the terrible crash of the Executive Air Service's One-Eleven 5N-ESF in May 2002, with the loss of seventy-one passengers and crew and seventy-eight on the ground, the aircraft were grounded. They began to deteriorate and, despite appeals, in 2004 the Nigerian Aviation Authorities told operators finally to dispose of their aircraft as the restrictions would remain in force.

The crash of 5N-ESF had been caused after take-off from Kano when the aircraft suffered an engine failure and crashed into a heavily populated area. The One-Eleven was quite capable of flying on one engine in this eventuality, even though engine failure in that phase of the flight would not have been easy for the pilots to handle. A full investigation by the authorities should have determined what happened. Whether this took place or not is unclear, but the knee-jerk grounding of One-Elevens by the authorities and the eventual permanent grounding leaves questions unanswered as to the veracity of any investigation into the accident's causes.

The Last Flight of XX105/G-ASJD

After almost thirty-nine years of airline and Government research service XX105 made its final flight on 5 June 2003 from Boscombe Down. Following its eventful

XX105's (c/n 008) much modified flight deck with a 'glass' cockpit on the left side and a standard One-Eleven arrangement on the right. *(QinetiQ)*

period as a One-Eleven test aircraft (see Chapter 4), it was delivered and flew with British United/British Caledonian as G-ASJD until 1971, when it was purchased by the MoD and heavily modified by the manufacturers at Hurn for research purposes.

The author had the good fortune to fly in this aircraft at Boscombe Down only four months prior to its final flight. In terms of passenger comfort, the cabin interior left much to be desired, with the forward and middle sections of the cabin crammed with observer panels, leaving room for just eight seats to the rear. The flightdeck had been extensively modified, with a standard One-Eleven cockpit layout on the right side while on the left there were two Smiths Electronic Information System 'glass' cockpit displays. In the centre a huge autopilot control panel was positioned on the coaming, as is common with contemporary airliners (but was not the case with a standard One-Eleven). The central panel between the pilots was extended rearwards and fitted with GPS and Flight Management Control Unit.

During its long test career, XX105 carried out numerous research programmes concerning flight control, navigation and flight deck displays. These included fully automatic curved microwave approaches and flying on converging courses with an American Sabreliner to trial TCAS (Traffic Collision Avoidance System). In 2002, the aircraft acted as a pseudo-UAV (Unmanned Aerial Vehicle) to test data transfer between a ground station and an airborne unit.

Boscombe Down, 28 May 2003: a never-to-be-repeated trio of One-Elevens. There is one each of a series 200, 475 and 500. The formation comprised crews of the Aircraft Test and Evaluation Centre and the Empire Test Pilots' School flying: XX105 (c/n 008), a series 201AC in the lead; ZE432 (c/n 250); the ETPS series 479FU nearest the camera; and, furthest away, ZH763, a 539GL (c/n 263). A QinetiQ Alpha Jet was the photo ship. *(QinetiQ)*

One-Eleven
XX105 following
its retirement at
Boscombe Down
next to Lockheed
Hercules *Snoopy*
XV208, which was at
that time withdrawn
from use, but later
resurrected to
become an engine
test bed for the
A400M. *(QinetiQ)*

On 28 May 2003, Boscombe Down organised a three-aircraft One-Eleven farewell photo sortie to XX105, consisting of XX105 itself, their 500 series ZH763 and the ETPS's 475 series ZE432, with an Alpha Jet as photo ship. XX105 then continued on to its final trials sortie. On 5 June it made its last flight, with an overshoot at Hurn – the very same place where it had made its maiden flight in 1964 – before landing at Boscombe Down at 16:00. Although initially stored as part of the Boscombe Down Aviation Collection, in 2008 the aircraft's owners QinetiQ decided to scrap it.

An earlier military One-Eleven XX919 had been scrapped in 2000 but its nose was saved for the Boscombe Down Aviation Collection. This collection has now moved to Old Sarum Airfield near Salisbury, Wiltshire, and is open to the public.

The two other One-Elevens of the trio, plus ZE433 which was used by Marconi for Eurofighter Typhoon radar trials, continued in use at Boscombe Down for a number of years. However, both ZE433 and the ETPS's ZE432 were grounded in 2009 owing to corrosion. With the demise of these two there was only ZH763, a former British Airways series 539GL, remaining. It flew a handful of times in 2011 and enthusiasts were hopeful that it would remain flying until 20 August 2013, so that the fiftieth anniversary of the One-Eleven's maiden flight could be celebrated in style, but most disappointingly it made its final research flight on 13 December 2012. Thankfully, QinetiQ donated it to the Classic Air Force Collection at Newquay and ZH763 made its final flight there on 26 April 2013.

Preserved One-Elevens

Preservation of One-Elevens in the UK has been patchy; three are currently preserved though regrettably all of them are externally stored and so suffer from the elements.

When British Airways ended its One-Eleven operations it donated two standard series 510s to museums: G-AVMU to the Imperial War Museum Collection at Duxford and G-AVMO to the British Airways Collection at the RAF Museum, Cosford. Duxford's One-Eleven is fortunate in having had a full repaint in the winter of 2012–13 and is in a reasonable condition. However, when BA decided it could no longer fund its collection at Cosford in 2006 it appeared likely that G-AVMO would be scrapped. In the event it was sectioned, transported to and reassembled at the National Museum of Scotland at East Fortune, which is in the vicinity of North Berwick. The third preserved UK One-Eleven is clearly the most significant of the three: G-ASYD, the prototype 400, 500 and 475 series test aircraft. This is on show at the Brooklands Museum, the site of the former BAC factory. There was a further preserved One-Eleven, G-AZMF, at the Bournemouth Aviation Museum which had replaced G-AVMN, initially preserved there in 2001 but exchanged in 2004 as unlike the latter it was painted in European Airlines livery. Most unfortunately, in 2007, Bournemouth Airport ended the lease of a hangar and land to the museum at very short notice; the collection was partly dispersed though some remains on a site away from the airport. The One-Eleven was returned to European Aviation on the other side of Hurn Airport, where its wings and tail were removed and the hull transported to the Newcastle College Aviation Academy in November 2008.

There are other One-Elevens stored or decaying around the world, but in Argentina, Austral, a long-time user of the One-Eleven, has 500 series LV-MZM

G-AVMO (c/n 143) pictured at the RAF Museum, Cosford, as part of the British Airways Collection. It was delivered in 1993 but with the airline's decision to end support for its collection in 2006, it was sectioned and transported to the National Museum of Scotland at East Fortune where it was reassembled and is now displayed. *(Author)*

The first of three Omani Air Force One-Elevens registered 551. Quite unusually for the One-Eleven these three aircraft only ever flew with their initial customer. This freight-door-equipped aircraft was withdrawn from use at Muscat in August 2008. *(Author's collection)*

preserved at Morón. As the longest continuous operator of the One-Eleven with thirty-five years of operation, the Royal Air Force of Oman has preserved 553, one of its three freight-door-equipped 485GDs. All three were regular visitors to Hurn over the years for maintenance and 553 excited many when it appeared at the 2009 RIAT Display at Fairford, Gloucestershire.

One-Elevens in Romania

Although the scheme to build One-Elevens in Romania (see Chapters 11 & 12) stalled after the ninth aircraft was completed at the Romaero factory at Baneasa, work continued to maintain these and other One-Elevens. Over the passage of time the One-Elevens were gradually withdrawn from service or used as spares sources. Among these other One-Elevens in Romania was a former American Airlines 401AK which first flew in August 1966 and was sold by the airline into executive jet service. After storage at Bucharest Airport it returned to service in 2006 in Kazakhstan with East Wing as UN-B1110 and continued in use for several years.

Tarom, the Romanian state airline, ceased to exist in 2000, but operations continued with Romavia airline while limited operations continued with two 561s, YR-BRE and 'BRI, which were engaged in Government flights; they were later withdrawn from use in 2009 and 2008 respectively. In addition, Mia Airlines, a privately owned Romanian company, had four Stage 3 hush-kitted One-Eleven 400s (YR-CJL, YR-HRS, YR-MIA) which flew executive and VIP air transport services to a wide range of destinations. As these aircraft had Stage 3 hush kits they were still able to operate legally in Europe after 2002. These three aircraft were leased to Tombouctou Aviation in Mali in 2005 but none is now in service.

Airbus withdraws support

In late 2006, Airbus, which had taken over support of the One-Eleven from BAE Systems, closed its One-Eleven Spares and Support Department at Filton, further compounding matters in February 2010 when Airbus withdrew the One-Eleven's type certificate. The ramifications of this regulatory change were that any One-Eleven registered in a European Union country was no longer eligible with a normal Certificate of Airworthiness. This did not affect Boscombe Down's One-Elevens as they were military test beds, nor did it affect those aircraft with the Royal Air Force of Oman.

American One-Elevens

Although One-Elevens are to be found in various stages of decay in places such as the Mojave Desert in Utah, USA, there are still several that are airworthy and occasionally fly. Northrop Grumman has two of its electronics systems test beds N162W and N164W still in the air, and to keep them in this state two others, N161NG and N111JX, are slowly being cannibalised for spares in the suitably bone-dry environment of the Mojave. N162W and N164W sport various odd nose shapes, bumps and excrescences under which lie trials devices. It is expected that during 2013 only N164W will still be in the air.

On 27 August 2011, Classic Jet Tours executive One-Eleven N999BW flew an enthusiasts' flight from Dallas Love Field. The aircraft in question was originally built as an executive aircraft for Engelhard Industries as a 419EP and, registered as N270E, it first flew from Hurn. Throughout its life it always served as an executive

Mia Airlines of Romania's Stage 3 hush-kitted executive VP-CJL (c/n 086) at Innsbruck in December 2004. She was originally built as a 401AK and registered as N5040 for American Airlines. This aircraft was last heard of operating with Tombouctou Aviation in Mali. *(Wolfgang Hut)*

YR-BRE (c/n 405) was completed at the ROMBAC production line at Baneasa in March 1986 and flew with the Romanian state airline, Tarom, and then on lease to Aero Asia. Fitted with an executive interior, it was observed in 2001 engaged on Government flights in Western Europe. It was reported as withdrawn from use in 2009. *(Author's collection)*

aircraft. During an extensive refit in 2006–07 it was fitted with a 'glass' cockpit, Stage 3 hush kits and its luxury interior was refurbished. On the day of the flight twenty-one enthusiasts from many countries had the opportunity (at quite a price!) to fly for almost two hours in this pristine aircraft.

The Fiftieth Anniversary of the One-Eleven's First Flight

So the number of One-Elevens flying at the end of 2012 was a grand total of three. There were Northrop Grumman's two aircraft and Classic Jet Tours N999BW, all in the USA. Those enthusiasts celebrating the fiftieth anniversary of the One-Eleven's maiden flight at Hurn on 20 August 2013 will most regrettably have to do so without the star of the show. However, they can remember the large number of One-Elevens built, its success and the endeavours of those at BAC who achieved this.

Appendix 1

Flying the One-Eleven 500

By Capt. R.E. Gilman (Senior training captain, Trident flight, BEA)

Inevitably there is a temptation to compare the One-Eleven with the ubiquitous Viscount. There we had a small short-haul airliner which proved spectacularly successful in the international market. Here we again have a small short-hauler from the same stable, very handy to fly and offering economic attractions that have already produced an impressive order list.

That everything about the One-Eleven 500 is businesslike is confirmed as soon as one arrives on the flight deck, for it is immediately obvious that a great deal of thought has gone into the layout of the controls, indicators and switches, bearing in mind that it is already a two-pilot aeroplane. Something of the order of 9,000rpm are required to get the machine rolling, and it then becomes apparent that the undercarriage is somewhat firm. The nosewheel steering is positive in its control, which is supplemented by a limited amount of direct steering control from the rudder. On long taxi tracks with slight bends, and during the take-off roll, one tends to use the rudder steering alone. Here it is an advantage, as directional control can be achieved precisely with the feet, leaving the hands free for the control column.

Two take-off flap settings are used by BEA, according to the runway concerned. Where the take-off distance is the more limiting factor, then 18° of flap is used; but when the net flight path is critical, and the take-off distance permits, then 8° of flap with its longer ground roll and better gradient of climb is set up.

For simplicity's sake, a standard tailplane setting of 3° nose-up is employed regardless of aircraft loading, and this requires the pilot to bear in mind that a lightly loaded aeroplane, being more tail-heavy, will rotate that much more easily. The fact that the control column loads at unstick are never high, and at 74,000lb gross weight an unstick distance of 3,000ft is ample.

Depending on c.g. position, as one comes out of ground-effect after lift-off a slight trim-change may occur, and this must be countered to achieve V2; thereafter one continues rotation to hit V2 plus 30kt for the noise-abatement climb. However, if a pitch attitude of 20° is arrived at first, as may happen in a lightly loaded aircraft, then this is held – for under those conditions the noise limitations will not be exceeded.

At the noise-abatement cut-back point the flaps are raised to 8° (if they are not already there) and the power reduced to the pre-determined thrust index; very little out-of-trim condition results. At 3,000ft climb power is restored and, as the speed increases, flap is fully retracted and an acceleration to the 300kt climbing speed is undertaken.

During a climb out of Wisley at 12,000rpm and a t.g.t. (turbine gas temperature) of 505°C, the v.s.i. (vertical speed indicator) registered 2,000 ft/min initially. By 20,000ft this was down to 1,200ft/min and at 30,000ft it had dropped to 600ft/min at a fuel flow of 3,200kg/hr. Levelling-off at this height and reducing the power to 11,000rpm, the speed settled at 265kt IAS (indicated airspeed) and the fuel flow was 2,000kg/hr.

Rudder loads at this speed are very high, and in pitch it is expedient to use the elevator first and trim out residual loads with the powerful adjustable tailplane. In this axis the aircraft is extremely stable. The ailerons are manually operated, and after about a quarter of their travel are assisted by differential spoiler action, resulting in an impressive rate of roll. However, having flown both the 300 series and the 400 series, I got the impression that directional stability had not been improved by the stretch to the 500 series.

By increasing the power to 11,700rpm the speed rose to 295kt indicated, with an appropriate 0.77 Mach, which is the MMO (Maximum Mach Number) indicated (Mach 0.78 true). At this power the fuel flow was 2,600kg/hr.

At the higher Mach numbers a nose-down trim asserts itself; an automatic Mach trimmer takes care of this, a caution light flashing during its operation. At Mach 0.79 or 345kt, a high-speed warning is given in the form of an intermittently ringing bell. Extension of the air brakes at this speed gives a slight nose-up couple and some buffet. When the throttles are closed for the descent there is an adequate supply of pressurising air provided that the anti-icers are not in use, and at Mach 0.73 the rate of descent is around 2,000ft/min.

Levelling off at 17,000ft, the aircraft was slowed down for the stalling tests. There is no pitching moment on initial extension of the Fowler flaps, but as they turn down past the 3° point a progressive nose-up couple develops. By 18°, and with the falling speed, this changes into a slight nose-down couple which persists with further flap lowering; but the total effect right up to the 45° landing flap setting is not severe. Extension of the undercarriage does not influence the trim at all; once the doors are closed the loss in speed is only 5kt. In the flaps and gear-down condition the elevator is light and crisp, giving the sort of pitch control which makes it easy to reduce the speed by the classic 1kt/sec.

The weight was now down to 32,000kg (75,000lb), and at 113kt static interference from the igniters could be heard in the earphones. Actuated by the deformation of the airflow around the intakes at high angles of attack, sensory vanes initiate the switching on of the relight igniters purely as a precautionary measure, and the static interference which they produce gives the first warning of the approach to the stall.

Five knots later the stick shakers produced a high-frequency vibration of the control columns. Just before the stall some buffet became apparent and the port wing started to drop, but it was held by the ailerons without difficulty. At 100kt the warning horns sounded and the stick push occurred.

The initial force was around 100lb until the column passed the neutral position, whereupon it fell away quickly to some 20lb before tailing off. The pusher action had caused the nose to pitch down sharply to just below the horizon, and it was necessary to follow through manually in order to achieve the 20° nose-down attitude desirable for rapid recovery. The subsequent pull-out had to be made with care to avoid beating the phase-advance system and suffering a further push. BAC claim that it is impossible for the One-Eleven 500 to get into a super stall when it is trimmed within the normal c.g. range.

Back in the circuit at 1,000ft, light turbulence was ridden very well provided one was careful in the use of the ailerons, to avoid breaking out the spoilers. Rash use of aileron led to over-controlling; it was found easier not to use the rudder, but to accept the slight amount of sideslip associated with turns made on aileron alone. Pursuing this further, I found that when carrying out a very high rate of roll at 135kt

The Flight deck of N111NA (c/n 065). Note the well-appointed layout designed from the start for two-crew operation. The BEA series 510s had a different flight deck layout, which led to problems with crewing in later years when BA had other aircraft with the standard layout. *(BAE SYSTEMS)*

the induced slip resulted in a strange and sudden resistance as the ailerons passed through their neutral position; when this was passed the aileron loads fell off again, and the final timing through a roll of 60° was in the order of 5 sec. By using rudder assistance this can be reduced still further; and by the eradication of the slip, the aileron impediment disappears.

On the landing approach at 122kt (Vat+10kt) at the now reduced weight of 30,000kg (66,000lb) the excellent pitching stability made accurate speed-holding easy, and the centre line was maintained with the judicious use of aileron.

Landings are best made with power – prolonged hold-offs do not give the best results. As the throttles are closed with the stick eased back to maintain about 2° nose-up pitch, she settles nicely. However, if the rotation is overdone, the situation can often be corrected by allowing the control column to come forward gently, thus lifting the mainwheels and cushioning the contact. Using normal reverse thrust, lift dumpers and the Hytrol brakes, the landing run is impressively short.

Not unnaturally, where a twin-engined aeroplane is concerned, pilots are interested in the engine-out performance and the loss of ancillary services. With an engine failure at V1 the rudder displacement required to keep straight is surprisingly

The first aircraft for BEA, G-AVMH (c/n 136), during an early test flight. This machine flew for many years with BEA, British Airways and finally with European Aviation. *(BAE SYSTEMS)*

large on an aircraft with turbofan engines tucked into the side of the fuselage; but the foot loads themselves are moderate and easily held without trimming. It is important not to allow large angles of sideslip to develop if the best gradients of climb are to be achieved; and, on this aeroplane in particular, the turn-and-slip instrument needs to be watched carefully at this stage. If one snatches at the control column in turbulent conditions it is possible to bring on the stick shakers at V2 – particularly if they are set a little high.

So far as the ancillary services are concerned, the powered controls are, of course, of major concern. Should a total hydraulic failure occur, manual reversion is possible. In this mode the elevator has no self-centring capability and there is some backlash either side of the neutral point; thus it is easy to over-control in pitch. However, an electrically operated trim tab eases the task considerably.

For the landing it is better to revert to the emergency elevator control, which has no 'q' feel but a fixed feel set for 180kt. As one slows for the approach, a marked nose-down pitching develops and has to be held manually as there is no tailplane trimming to assist. The out-of-trim force can become very high under certain load conditions, but the more positive control in this mode is to be preferred to full manual reversion. The emergency elevator is powered by a completely separate hydraulic system with its own reservoir.

I enjoyed flying this aeroplane; it is compact, handy and without vices. I would think that its operating economics will endear it to managements too.

(Reprinted with kind permission from Flight International *7 November 1968)*

N.B. The article refers to the early One-Eleven 510s built to the BEA specification which had less power and operated to lower weights than later 500 series.

Appendix 2

On Flight Deck of European Aviation BAC One-Eleven G-AZMF Hurn-Turin-Hurn

This is an extract from an article that first appeared in April 2002 Airliner World Magazine

Hurn – Turin (EAF3202 BOH-TRN)

I arrived early at Hurn, on 30 December to see G-AZMF, a series 530, waiting on the frosty tarmac. Originally delivered to British Caledonian in 1972, later leased to Austrian Airlines and Air Malawi, she then became part of the British Airways fleet after the takeover of British Caledonian. In 1992 she was bought by European Aviation and used as a fifty-seater executive airliner for a time, which is why she was painted in the black European livery. With 43,927 hours and 39,155 landings she was one of the more experienced airliners operating!

I checked in, receiving my flight deck pass, watched a thorough de-icing take place and then boarded in the dark the aircraft via the front airstairs. I went straight onto the flight deck to meet Captain John Belson and First Officer John Gillies and extended the jump seat, sitting directly behind the centre console.

The crew were going through the pre-start checks. Then I witnessed the Spey start process with HP cocks, air, etc. Captain Belson instructed me that in the event of emergency, my exit was through the First Officer's window using the rope available. As push back was completed the First Officer called for the full-length of runway 26 since 'ZMF was almost fully loaded with 8 metric tons of fuel and 100 passengers. Flaps were set at 8°, take-off speeds were set for VR at 140 knots, V2 at 150 knots based on the runway length available and bugs (pointers) on the speedometers marked these by the crew.

At the threshold of 26 we turned sharply to make the most of the runway length available. All around there were the coloured lights of the taxiways and runway with additional illumination provided by a full moon. Then throttles were advanced, we accelerated quickly, passing the cross-runway intersection and as the runway was running out climbed away. Then turning east as the APU was switched off we climbed higher, affording us a breath-taking pre-dawn view of the Isle of Wight with the South Downs highlighted by the deep frost and turned South over the Channel.

It was fascinating to watch the instruments, not only the standard ones but the GPS (Global Positioning System) indicating the distance to the next waypoint, ground speed, heading, etc. An even more fascinating instrument is the TCAS (Traffic Collision Avoidance System) where the aircraft's transponder 'talks' to other aircrafts' transponders to alert them to the possibility of collision, indicating position, altitude and if necessary giving an audible warning to instruct the pilots to climb or ascend. The crew remarked that they had only used the TCAS for a year but now relied on it and it was important for a One-Eleven where the Collins Autopilot system was no longer state-of-the-art and altitude oscillated by $\pm$ 60ft. The autopilot needed an upgrade, which was not viable for an old type.

On achieving cruising altitude the GPS indicated we were cruising at a very high speed because of a jetstream from the West pushing our speed up to 545kts (9 miles per minute). The Captain discussed the descent into Turin with the First Officer who had never flown in there before. It is an unusual approach with the aircraft having to lose altitude in a short time after crossing the Alps. If we lost an engine before the Alps we could not climb over and would have to divert into Geneva.

There was full cloud over Southern France only pierced by the peaks of Alps pushing through the cloud tops. Then we crossed the Alps emerging in clear sky with Turin immediately below us. We descended to 19,000 feet as number 5 on approach and with the runway clearly in sight far below. The APU was re-started as the One-Eleven flew the descent pattern, which demanded rather graceful, steep, sharp turns one of them over a beautiful hilltop mausoleum, which contains the tombs of the Kings and Queens of Savoy.

There was a high workload as the crew went through the checks – bumpy because of wind off the top of the Alps, and then gear down, more and more flap out, the trimmer automatically balancing the aircraft so that we could fly slower and slower. Speed down to 180 knots with 6 miles to run and then at 5 miles, 45° flap, and 160 knots at the outer marker. We could clearly see the apron and an Italian Falcon waiting to take off after our landing. Then down with that typical, flat, rock-steady One-Eleven approach, sweeping in to touch down on all three wheels, the stick forward, reverse thrust, lift dumpers out. A rapid turn off, then looking for the 'FOLLOW ME' van which led us to a stand away from the Terminal. Then the experience, novel to the author, of turning sharply on the nosewheel, with mainwheels braked onto the stand, the batwoman waving us in. Parking brake on, windows open, engines off, APU remaining on. On the ground 9:30 GMT.

Turn round at Turin

Turin had a busy tarmac with 15 machines on the ground, various Boeings, Airbuses, but only one One-Eleven, 'ZMF which for all its age looked smart in the black European colour scheme – a hangover from its Minardi executive use.

For the turn round I decamped to the very pleasant, wide-body look, 104-seater cabin, arranged with one toilet on the front left side and one at the right rear. In fact none of the passengers would have had any reason to know the machine was 29 years old. Having flown on 737s I was impressed by the generous seating pitch provided.

The ventral steps were down too, so there was a breeze ventilating the cabin. Outside it was 10°C, and the crew continued with their jobs, the first officer pumping some oil into engine number 2 with a large hand pump and the APU roaring away, air-conditioning the cabin.

A tanker refilled the fuel tanks, the galley restocked and the luggage was loaded into the two under floor bays. With increased airport security the processing of passengers was taking a long time and the crew became anxious about losing their departure slot at 10:35. However we were then given a slot for 10:47.

G-AZMF on the tarmac at Turin. *(Author)*

I regained the jump seat as the flight crew went through the pre-start checks; a ritual-like questioning and responding to the checklists. We continued to wait for the passengers and it seemed we would miss our second slot but they arrived and we were cleared to start, even though it was now 10:45. Then there was confusion on the apron delaying us more but finally we were cleared, taxied fast to the runway and stopped, awaiting final clearance at 10:57, but fortunately were cleared to go.

Turin – Hurn (EAF3203 TRN-BOH)

Then the take-off on the generous Turin runway, flown by the First Officer with the Captain monitoring. With 8 tons fuel and 100 passengers the take-off speeds were, VR, 144kts and V2, 152kts. At VR John Gillies made a positive pull back on the control column followed by slight forward motion to maintain positive climb attitude. Then in brilliant sun, turning north towards the majesty of the Alps encircling us and into some turbulence over the peaks as the air spilled over them. We had to reach 18,000 feet to clear them and as before if we lost an engine, we would return to Turin for we would be unable to climb over the mountains. Over the Alps in excellent visibility to see Lake Geneva and routing via Dijon and Paris. Having benefited from the jetstream outbound we now had to pay the cost inbound to

The pilots of G-AZMF, Captain Belson and First Officer Gillies photographed at Turin. *(Author)*

Hurn. At cruise power on 90% rpm our ground speed was 310 knots against the 110 knot headwind.

At 12:33 we were cleared to descend from 31,000 to 22,000 feet, so the throttles were retarded and the rpm fell to 80%. London Control cleared us for a Threadneedle approach into Hurn. At 12:45 at 12,500 feet with 36 miles to run the Needles were in sight. Then good views of Dorset and the Isle of Wight but as we came over the Needles we heard the TCAS warning 'Traffic', 'Traffic', the crew did a swift visual check – there was a light aircraft passing well below us – so no problem. Turning west over Hurst Castle with Lymington and the old Beaulieu airfield to the right.

Descending over the New Forest to 2,000 feet and 6 miles to run to Hurn, runway 26, at 160 knots. Down to 128 knots with 3 miles to run and then the threshold and a gentle touchdown and the full procedure to stop her. Turning off at the end of the runway and along the bumpy perimeter track by the road, where I had so often stood and watched One-Elevens taxi by. Onto the apron, parking a little behind schedule at 13:00 at stand 4, the same one we set out from earlier in the day.

Before I vacated the flight deck I still had one treat in store. Captain Belson demonstrated the stick shaker (stall warning) and stick pusher (stall recovery) systems – the din of the first was incredible and in the event of a stall that exceedingly definite push of the stick would certainly force the aircraft's nose down.

The author would like to thank European Aviation for giving him the opportunity to fly on their One-Elevens.

Appendix 3

Aircraft Data

General dimensions

One-Eleven series	200/300/400	475	500
Length overall	93ft 6in	93ft 6in	107ft 0in
Wing span	88ft 6in	93ft 6in	93ft 6in
Height	24ft 6in	24ft 6in	24ft 6in

Operating weights

One-Eleven series	200	300/400	475	500
Maximum take-off weight	79,000lb	88,500lb	98,500lb	104,500lb
Maximum payload	17,600lb	20,000lb	21,300lb	26,420lb
Maximum passenger capacity	89	89	89	119
Maximum cargo volume	534cu.ft	534cu.ft	510cu.ft	687cu.ft
Fuel capacity	24,600lb	24,600lb	24,680lb	24,680lb

Engines

Series	200	207/217/300/400	475/500	510
Rolls-Royce	Spey 2 Mk 506-14/14W	Spey 25 Mk 511-14/14W	Spey 25 Mk 512-14DW	Spey 25 Mk 512-14E
Thrust (lb)	10,410	11,400	12,550	12,000

Appendix 4

Table of Type Numbers

Each One-Eleven type was identified by a number derived from the series to which it belonged, and a two-letter individual customer code. For instance the two BAC 400 series development aircraft, G-ASYD and G-ASYE were allotted the 400 code and American Airlines, as the first customer for the 400 series were allocated the number 401. On the production line large boards above the aircraft identified the aircraft as Type AK (i.e. for American Airlines) number one, two, etc. So in fact it was the two-letter code that stipulated the changes due to an individual type.

BAC negotiated with many airlines and sometimes allocated type numbers for sales that were not finalised. These are included in the list below even though no aircraft may have been built to that specification, and are marked with a *.

Initially aircraft were built for definite orders and allocated the type numbers. This was the case for all 200s, 300s and 400s. However a number of the 500 and 475 series were built on expectation of an order to a basic standard and would nowadays be referred to as 'White tails'. For example, these were given the type numbers 500EN or 475EZ and were only modified to suit customer requirements on receipt of an order. This enabled BAC to offer competitive delivery dates and to regularise its production cycle even if it proved challenging for the Sales staff.

BAC built 200 series

200AB	BAC owned prototype – G-ASHG
200AT	BAC owned prototype – G-ASVT*
201AC	British United Airways
202AD	Undisclosed customer (Western Airways)*
203AE	Braniff Airways
204AF	Mohawk Airlines
205AG	Kuwait Airways
206AH	Bonanza Airlines*
207AJ	Central African Airways
208AL	Aer Lingus
209	Hawaiian Airlines*

211AH   Helmut Horten Gmbh
212AR   Tenneco
214   Page Airways*
215AU   Aloha Airlines
217EA   Royal Australian Air Force

BAC built 300 series

301AG   Kuwait Airways
303   British Midland Airways*
304AX   British Eagle
320L AZ Laker Airways

BAC built 400 series

400AM   BAC-owned prototype – G-ASYE (later 410AM)
400AQ   BAC-owned prototype – G-ASYD
401AK   American Airlines
402AP   Philippines Airlines
403   Page Airways*
405   Aviaco*
406   British Eagle*
407AW   TACA
408EF   Channel Airways
409AY   LACSA
410AM   Victor Comptometers (formerly 400AM)
412EB   LANICA
413FA   Bavaria Fluggesellschaft
414EG   Bavaria Fluggesellschaft
416EK   Autair International
417EJ   United States Air Force*
419EP   Engelhard Industries
420EL   Austral/ALA
422EQ   VASP
423ET   Forca Aerea Brasileira
424EU   TAROM
432FD   Gulf Air

BAC built 475 series

475AM   BAC-owned prototype – G-ASYD
475EZ   Basic 475 series (built prior to order)
476FM   Faucett
479FU   Air Pacific

480GB   RAF Queen's Flight*
481FW   Air Malawi
485GD   Sultanate of Oman Air Force
487GK   TAROM (freighter)
488GH   Mouffak Al Midani
492GM   McAlpine Aviation

ROMBAC Built 475 series
496RD   Romanian Air Force (not completed)

BAC built 500 series
500AQ   BAC-owned prototype – G-ASYD
500EN   Basic 500 series (built prior to order)
501EX   British United Airways
509EW   Caledonian Airways
510ED   BEA
511EY   BKS*
515FB   Paninternational
516FP   Aviateca

Type numbers. Three British Caledonian One-Elevens at Gatwick. The sixth production aircraft, G-ASJF (c/n 010) a type 201AC, G-AWYU (c/n 177) a 501EX and G-AXYD (c/n 210) a 509EW. *(BAE SYSTEMS)*

517FE   Bahamas Airways

518FG   Autair/Court Line

520FN   Sadia/TransBrasil

521FH   Austral/ALA

523FJ   British Midland Airways

524FF   Germanair

525FT   TAROM

527FK   Philippines Airlines

528FL   Bavaria Fluggesellschaft

529FR   Phoenix Airways

530FX   British Caledonian Airways

531FS   LACSA

534FY   LANICA*

537GF   Cyprus Airways

538GG   Faucett*

539GL   British Airways

ROMBAC built 500 series

561RC   TAROM

562RC   Basic Romanian 560 series*

DEE HOWARD Tay One-Eleven

2400   Dee Howard Tay-engined 400

2500   Dee Howard Tay-engined 500 series*

Appendix 5

BAC One-Eleven Production List

This is the complete production list of the One-Eleven. This listing provides construction number, type number, registration on first delivery, initial customer, the first flight dates and delivery. Note that twenty-three aircraft first flew with 'B' Class registrations, e.g. G-16-1. Others flew with temporary British 'A' registrations for demonstrations or testing. British-built aircraft were assembled at Hurn, except for thirteen completed at Weybridge. (These are indicated by 'W'.) Nine were completed in Romania and two left incomplete. (These are indicated by 'R'.)

Construction number	Type	Registration	Customer	First Flight	Delivery	Built
004	200AB	G-ASHG	BAC	20/08/63		1
005	201AC	G-ASJA	British United	19/12/63	11/10/65	
006	201AC	G-ASJB	British United	14/02/64		2
007	201AC	G-ASJC	British United	01/04/64	06/11/65	
008	201AC	G-ASJD	British United	06/07/64	05/08/65	3
009	201AC	G-ASJE	British United	05/05/64	23/07/65	
010	201AC	G-ASJF	British United	28/07/64	22/05/65	
011	201AC	G-ASJG	British United	31/10/64	06/07/65	
012	201AC	G-ASJH	British United	17/09/64	17/04/65	
013	201AC	G-ASJI	British United	22/12/64	15/04/65	
014	201AC	G-ASJJ	British United	24/02/65	06/04/65	
015	203AE	N1541	Braniff International	09/06/64	10/08/65	4
016	203AE	N1542	Braniff International	30/10/64	20/04/65	
017	203AE	N1543	Braniff International	10/02/65	11/03/65	
018	203AE	N1544	Braniff International	26/03/65	06/04/65	
019	203AE	N1545	Braniff International	10/05/65	12/05/65	
020	203AE	N1546	Braniff International	30/05/65	02/06/65	
021–028	202AD		Western Airways			5
029	204AF	N2111J	Mohawk Airlines	04/05/65	15/05/65	
030	204AF	N1112J	Mohawk Airlines	19/06/65	25/06/65	

031	204AF	N1113J	Mohawk Airlines	03/08/65	10/08/65	
032	204AF	N1114J	Mohawk Airlines	26/09/65	29/09/65	
033	301AG	G-ATPJ	British Eagle	20/05/66	08/06/66	W
034	301AG	G-ATPK	British Eagle	14/06/66	24/06/66	W
035	301AG	G-ATPL	British Eagle	13/07/66	22/07/66	
036–8	206AH		Bonanza Airlines			6
039	207AJ	G-ATTP	British Eagle	19/02/66	22/04/66	
040	207AJ	G-ATVH	British Eagle	16/04/66	27/05/66	
041	203AE	N1547	Braniff International	18/07/65	20/07/66	
042	203AE	N1548	Braniff International	15/08/65	18/08/65	
043	203AE	N1549	Braniff International	20/09/65	24/09/65	
044	203AE	N1550	Braniff International	01/10/65	04/10/65	
045	203AE	N1551	Braniff International	03/11/65	08/11/65	
046	203AE	N1552	Braniff International	22/11/65	24/11/65	
047–8	202AD		Western Airways			7
049	208AL	EI-ANE	Aer Lingus	28/04/65	14/05/65	
050	208AL	EI-ANF	Aer Lingus	09/06/65	12/06/65	
051	208AL	EI-ANG	Aer Lingus	24/07/65	31/07/65	
052	208AL	EI-ANH	Aer Lingus	27/08/65	09/09/65	
053	400AM	G-ASYD	BAC	13/07/65		8
	500AM		BAC			
	475AM		BAC			
	670AM		BAC/BAe			
054	400AQ	G-ASYE	BAC	16/09/65		9
	410AQ	N3939V	Victor Comptometers		08/09/66	
055	401AK	N5015	American Airlines	04/11/65	23/12/65	
056	401AK	N5016	American Airlines	08/12/65	22/01/66	
057	401AK	N5017	American Airlines	03/01/66	29/01/66	
058	401AK	N5018	American Airlines	15/01/66	15/02/66	
059	401AK	N5019	American Airlines	29/01/66	24/03/66	10
060	401AK	N5020	American Airlines	06/02/66	13/03/66	
061	401AK	N5021	American Airlines	16/02/66	04/03/66	
062	401AK	N5022	American Airlines	03/03/66	17/03/66	
063	401AK	N5023	American Airlines	05/03/66	21/03/66	
064	401AK	N5024	American Airlines	24/03/66	15/04/66	
065	401AK	N5025	American Airlines	25/03/66	07/04/66	
066	401AK	N5026	American Airlines	08/04/66	23/04/66	
067	401AK	N5027	American Airlines	16/04/66	29/04/66	
068	401AK	N5028	American Airlines	26/04/66	10/05/66	
069	401AK	N5029	American Airlines	03/05/66	21/05/66	

070	203AE	N1553	Braniff International	05/12/65	08/12/65	
071	203AE	N1554	Braniff International	19/12/65	22/12/65	
072	401AK	N5030	American Airlines	12/05/66	27/05/66	
073	401AK	N5031	American Airlines	21/05/66	09/06/66	
074	401AK	N5032	American Airlines	06/06/66	21/06/66	11
075	401AK	N5033	American Airlines	10/06/66	27/06/66	
076	401AK	N5034	American Airlines	25/06/66	09/07/66	12
077	401AK	N5035	American Airlines	01/07/66	22/07/66	
078	401AK	N5036	American Airlines	23/07/66	04/08/66	
079	401AK	N5037	American Airlines	06/08/66	19/08/66	
080	401AK	N5038	American Airlines	23/08/66	08/09/66	
081	401AK	N5039	American Airlines	01/10/66	12/10/66	
082	204AF	N1115J	Mohawk Airlines	19/11/65	21/11/65	
083	211AR	N502T	Tenneco	02/03/66	05/04/66	W
084	211AH	D-ABHH	Helmut Horten	15/01/66	29/01/66	W
085	201AC	G-ASTJ	British United	25/10/65	09/11/65	
086	401AK	N5040	American Airlines	14/10/66	28/10/66	
087	401AK	N5041	American Airlines	29/10/66	10/11/66	
088	401AK	N5042	American Airlines	09/11/66	19/11/66	
089	401AK	N5043	American Airlines	21/11/66	10/12/66	
090	401AK	N5044	American Airlines	06/12/66	16/12/66	
091	402AP	PI-C1121	Philippines Airlines	07/04/66	19/04/66	W 13
092	402AP	PI-C1131	Philippines Airlines	17/09/66	24/09/66	
093	407AW	YS-17C	TACA	05/12/66	14/12/66	
094	402AP	G-AVEJ	Bavaria Flug.	03/01/67	23/03/67	
095	200AT	G-ASVT	BAC			14
096	215AU	N11181	Aloha Airlines	06/04/66	15/04/66	W
097	215AU	N11182	Aloha Airlines	30/05/66	07/06/66	
098	204AF	N1116J	Mohawk Airlines	01/08/66	05/08/66	
099	204AF	N1117J	Mohawk Airlines	26/08/66	30/08/66	
100	204AF	N1118J	Mohawk Airlines	20/09/66	26/09/66	
101	204AF	N1119J	Mohawk Airlines	11/10/66	15/10/66	
102	204AF	N1120J	Mohawk Airlines	06/01/67	24/01/67	
103	204AF	N1121J	Mohawk Airlines	10/08/67	17/08/67	
104	204AF	N1122J	Mohawk Airlines	19/12/67	30/12/67	
105	215AU	N11183	Aloha Airlines	26/05/67	31/05/67	
106	407AW	YS-18C	TACA	03/02/67	21/02/67	
107	320AZ	G-AVBW	Laker Airways	17/02/67	25/02/67	
108	409AY	TI-1056C	LACSA	06/03/67	14/04/67	
109	320AZ	G-AVBX	Laker Airways	28/03/67	08/04/67	
110	304AX	G-ATPH	British Eagle	19/04/67	28/04/67	

111	412EB	AN-BBI	LANICA	08/04/67	20/04/67	
112	304AX	G-ATPI	British Eagle	12/05/67	22/05/67	
113	320AZ	G-AVBY	Laker Airways	01/05/67	09/05/67	
114	408EF	G-AVGP	Channel Airways	09/06/67	14/06/67	
115	408EF	G-AWEJ	Channel Airways	01/05/68	10/05/68	
116	413FA	G-AWGG	Bavaria Flug.	20/06/68	25/06/68	
117	420EL	LV-JGX	ALA	10/08/68	25/09/68	
118	423ET	VC-92-2111	Forca Aerea Brasileira	12/10/67	15/10/68	
119	422EQ	PP-SRT	VASP	18/10/67	19/12/67	
120	419EP	N270E	Engelhard Industries	08/08/67	21/09/67	
121	432FD	VP-BCY	Bahamas Airways	28/08/68	11/11/68	
122	420EL	LV-IZR	Austral	21/06/67	12/10/67	
123	420EL	LV-IZS	Austral	05/09/67	08/11/67	
124	217EA	A12-124	RAAF	03/11/67	12/01/67	
125	217EA	A12-125	RAAF	10/01/68	08/03/68	
126	422EQ	PP-SRU	VASP	08/11/67	19/12/67	
127	414EG	D-ANDY	Bavaria Flug.	06/12/67	29/12/67	
128	408EF	G-AWKJ	Channel Airways	29/01/69	31/03/69	
129	416EK	G-AVOE	Autair International	08/03/68	19/03/68	
130	424EU	YR-BCA	TAROM	23/01/68	14/06/68	
131	416EK	G-AVOF	Autair International	18/01/68	08/02/68	
132	416EK	G-AWBL	Autair International	22/04/68	01/05/68	
133	320AZ	G-AVYZ	Laker Airways	08/04/68	11/04/68	
134	204AF	N1124J	Mohawk Airlines	04/03/68	25/03/68	15
135	204AF	N1125J	Mohawk Airlines	11/06/68	17/06/68	
136	510ED	G-AVMH	BEA	07/02/68	12/06/69	
137	510ED	G-AVMI	BEA	13/05/68	02/04/69	
138	510ED	G-AVMJ	BEA	15/07/68	29/08/68	
139	510ED	G-AVMK	BEA	08/08/68	16/09/68	
140	510ED	G-AVML	BEA	30/08/68	04/10/68	
141	510ED	G-AVMM	BEA	28/09/68	25/10/68	
142	510ED	G-AVMN	BEA	14/10/68	20/11/68	16
143	510ED	G-AVMO	BEA	29/10/68	27/11/68	17
144	510ED	G-AVMP	BEA	05/11/68	11/12/68	
145	510ED	G-AVMR	BEA	28/11/68	05/05/70	
146	510ED	G-AVMS	BEA	14/12/68	13/01/69	
147	510ED	G-AVMT	BEA	10/01/69	28/03/69	
148	510ED	G-AVMU	BEA	29/01/69	19/03/69	18
149	510ED	G-AVMV	BEA	21/03/69	21/04/69	
150	510ED	G-AVMW	BEA	27/04/69	02/05/69	
151	510ED	G-AVMX	BEA	02/06/69	20/06/69	

152	510ED	G-AVMY	BEA	09/07/69	21/07/69		
153	510ED	G-AVMZ	BEA	05/08/69	15/08/69		
154	423ET	VC-92-2110	Forca Aerea Brasileira	09/10/68	13/05/69		
155	420EL	LV-JGY	ALA	09/11/68	17/12/68		
156	424EU	YR-BCB	TAROM	11/12/68	17/12/68		
157	432FD	VP-BCZ	Bahamas Airways	27/11/68	04/12/68		
158	414EG	D-AISY	Bavaria Flug.	17/04/70	22/04/70	W	
159	424EU	YR-BCD	TAROM	22/07/69	30/07/69	W	
160	414EG	D-ANNO	Bavaria Flug.	19/12/70	22/12/70	W	19
161	402AP	EC-BQF	TAE	20/09/68	15/03/69		
162	409AY	G-AXBB	BAC	14/02/69	13/03/69		20
163	414EG	D-AILY	Bavaria Flug.	26/01/70	26/02/70	W	
164							21
165	424EU	YR-BCE	TAROM	29/09/69	23/11/69	W	
166	416EK	G-AWKJ	Autair International	27/02/69	20/03/69		
167	424EU	YR-BCC	TAROM	26/06/69	03/07/69		
168	424EU	YR-BCF	TAROM	18/11/69	13/12/69	W	
169–173							22
174	501EX	G-AWYR	British United	25/03/69	11/04/69		
175	501EX	G-AWYS	British United	16/04/69	24/04/69		
176	501EX	G-AWYT	British United	06/05/69	13/05/69		
177	501EX	G-AWYU	British United	10/06/69	17/06/69		
178	501EX	G-AWYV	British United	20/06/69	26/06/69		
179	204AF	N1126J	Mohawk Airlines	15/07/68	02/08/68		
180	204AF	N1127J	Mohawk Airlines	10/12/68	31/12/68		
181	204AF	N1128J	Mohawk Airlines	10/01/69	21/01/69		
182	204AF	N1129J	Mohawk Airlines	12/05/69	17/05/69		
183	212AR	N503T	Tenneco	07/06/69	08/07/69	W	
184	509EW	G-AWWX	Caledonian Airways	11/02/69	29/03/69		
185	509EW	G-AWWY	Caledonian Airways	11/03/69	31/03/69		
186	509EW	G-AWWZ	Caledonian Airways	18/04/69	28/04/69		
187	515FB	D-ALAT	Panair International	22/05/68	13/06/69		
188	517FE	VP-BCN	Bahamas Airways	17/07/69	23/07/69		
189	517FE	VP-BCO	Bahamas Airways	21/07/69	29/07/69		
190	524FF	D-AMIE	Germanair	02/09/69	17/10/69		
191	501EX	G-AXJK	British United	14/08/69	05/03/69		
192	521FH	LV-JNR	Austral	15/10/69	21/11/69		
193	523FJ	G-AXLL	British Midland	25/09/69	17/02/70		
194	521FH	LV-JNS	Austral	08/10/69	18/11/69		23
195	524FF	D-AMUR	Germanair	20/10/69	16/12/69		24
196	521FH	LV-JNT	ALA	06/11/69	25/11/69		

197	524FF	D-AMOR	Germanair	09/12/69	20/03/70	25
198	517FE	VP-LAN	Court Line/LIAT	12/01/70	20/06/72	
199	523FJ	G-AXLM	British Midland	26/12/69	05/03/70	
200	518FG	G-AXMF	Court Line	25/11/69	05/12/69	
201	518FG	G-AXMG	Court Line	08/12/69	18/12/69	
202	518FG	G-AXMH	Court Line	12/01/70	11/02/70	
203	518FG	G-AXMI	Court Line	27/01/70	24/03/70	
204	518FG	G-AXMJ	Court Line	17/02/70	12/03/70	
205	518FG	G-AXMK	Court Line	07/03/70	21/04/70	
206	518FG	G-AXML	Court Line	22/04/70	30/04/70	
207	515FB	D-ALAR	Panair International	01/05/70	13/05/70	
208	515FB	D-ALAS	Panair International	13/05/70	20/03/70	
209	501EX	G-AXJL	British United	20/02/70	03/03/70	
210	509EW	G-AXYD	Caledonian Airways	06/03/70	18/03/70	
211	523FJ	G-AXLN	British Midland	04/02/70	12/03/70	
212	529AR	HB-ITL	Phoenix Airways	14/05/70	01/04/71	
213	527FK	PI-C1161	Philippines Airlines	15/09/70	26/10/71	
214	501EX	G-AXJM	British United	17/03/70	25/03/70	
215	527FK	PI-C1171	Philippines Airlines	09/10/70	29/10/71	
216–225						26
226	527FK	PI-C1181	Philippines Airlines	03/11/70	05/11/71	
227	528FL	D-AMUC	Bavaria Flug.	28/10/70	03/12/70	
228	520FN	PP-SDQ	Sadia	21/09/70	15/10/70	
229	515FB	D-ALAQ	Panair International	04/12/70	04/03/70	
230	520FN	PP-SDR	Sadia	11/11/70	31/12/70	
231	516FP	TG-AZA	Aviateca	16/12/70	25/03/71	
232	518FG	G-AYOR	Court Line	29/01/71	18/03/71	
233	518FG	G-AYOP	Court Line	03/03/71	31/03/71	
234	528FL	D-ALFA	Bavaria Flug.	08/02/71	26/02/71	
235	524FF	D-AMAT	Germanair	17/04/71	08/05/71	
236	520FN	PP-SDS	Transbrasil	30/04/71	23/09/72	
237	531FS	TI-1084C	LACSA	13/05/71	26/05/71	
238	528FL	D-ANUE	Bavaria Flug.	28/02/72	15/03/72	
239	476FM	OB-R-953	Faucett	05/04/71	23/07/71	
240	530FX	G-AZMF	British Caledonian	04/03/72	14/03/72	
241	476FM	OB-R-1080	Faucett	07/07/71	19/07/74	
242	531FS	TI-1095C	LACSA	17/10/72	06/11/72	
243	481FW	7Q-YKF	Air Malawi	20/01/72	23/02/72	
244	531FS	TI-1096C	LACSA	11/05/73	14/05/73	
245	479FU	DQ-FBQ	Air Pacific	08/02/72	04/03/72	
246	527FK	RP-C1182	Philippines Airlines	01/06/74	14/06/74	

247	485GD	1001	Sultanate Oman AF	21/11/74	18/12/74	
248	527FK	RP-C1183	Philippines Airlines	29/06/74	05/07/74	
249	485GD	1002	Sultanate Oman AF	20/12/74	29/01/75	
250	479FU	DQ-FBV	Air Pacific	16/07/73	14/08/73	
251	485GD	1003	Sultanate Oman AF	19/03/75	01/11/75	
252	525FT	YR-BCI	TAROM	20/12/76	21/03/77	
253	525FT	YR-BCJ	TAROM	17/03/77	04/04/77	
254	525FT	YR-BCK	TAROM	28/04/77	14/05/77	
255	525FT	YR-BCL	TAROM	17/06/77	09/07/77	
256	525FT	YR-BCM	TAROM	08/08/77	25/08/77	
257	537GF	5B-DAG	Cyprus Airways	16/11/77	08/12/77	
258	537GF	5B-DAH	Cyprus Airways	18/01/78	28/01/78	
259	488GH	HZ-MAM	Mouffak Al Midani	28/04/78	15/05/78	
260	492GM	G-BLHD	McAlpine Aviation	01/05/84	09/07/84	27
261	537GF	5B-DAJ	Cyprus Airways	28/09/78	06/10/78	
262	492GM	G-BLDH	McAlpine Aviation	02/02/84	09/07/84	
263	539GL	G-BGKE	British Airways	26/01/80	03/03/80	
264	539GL	G-BGKF	British Airways	09/05/80	13/06/80	
265	539GL	G-BGKG	British Airways	06/08/80	18/08/80	
266	525FT	YR-BCN	TAROM	13/11/80	16/01/81	
267	487GK	YR-BCR	TAROM	26/06/81	28/07/81	
268–271						28
272	525FT	YR-BCO	TAROM	15/02/82	12/03/82	
273–277						29
401	561RC	YR-BRA	TAROM	18/09/82	24/12/82	R
402	561RC	YR-BRB	TAROM	28/04/83	07/83	R
403	561RC	YR-BRC	TAROM	26/04/84	08/84	R
404	561RC	YR-BRD	TAROM	02/04/85	02/86	R
405	561RC	YR-BRE	TAROM	27/03/86	03/86	R
406	561RC	YR-BRF	TAROM	30/09/86	10/86	R
407	561RC	YR-BRG	TAROM	21/03/88	03/88	R
408	561RC	YR-BRH	TAROM	01/12/88	12/88	R
409	561RC	YR-BRI	TAROM	04/89	04/91	R
410	496RD		Incomplete			R 30
411	561RC		Incomplete			R 31

Production List notes

1   Prototype crashed near Chicklade, Wilts, 22/10/63
2   Second production aircraft, crashed Wisley, 18/03/64. Planned to be rebuilt as
    095 but scrapped
3   Fourth production aircraft, crash landed near Tilshead, Wilts. 20/08/63.
    Dismantled and returned to Hurn for rebuild. Made 'second' first flight after
    rebuild on 13/06/65
4   First for Braniff, temporarily registered as G-ASUF
5   Order cancelled
6   Order cancelled
7   Order cancelled
8   G-ASYD, first 400 series development aircraft. Subsequently prototype 500,
    475 and 670 series. Preserved at Brooklands Museum in BAe colours. Last
    flight Filton to Brooklands, 14/07/94
9   G-ASYE, second 400 series development aircraft. Flew worldwide
    demonstrations then reconfigured as N3939V, series 410AQ for Victor
    Comptometers
10 First Tay One-Eleven. First flew as N650DH, 21/06/90
11 First flight as G-ATVU for demonstration to SAS in Sweden
12 Second Tay One-Eleven. First flew as N333GB, 06/91
13 As XX919 front fuselage preserved at Boscombe Down Museum, 07/00
14 G-ASVT, planned rebuild of G-ASJB as BAC 200 series demonstrator, not built
15 First flight as G-AWDF for braking trials at Torrejon, Spain, 03/68
16 Preserved Bournemouth Aviation Museum in AB Airlines colours, 05/01
17 Preserved RAF Cosford Aviation Museum in BA colours, 22/3/93
18 Preserved IWM Duxford RAF in BA colours, 04/03/93
19 Final Weybridge assembled One-Eleven
20 Leased Quebecair
21 Not built
22 Not built
23 First flown as G-16-9. Later G-AXPH for demonstration in Amsterdam
24 First flown as G-AXSY for demonstrations in Canada, USA & Caribbean
25 First flown as G-16-11. Later G-AXVO for demonstrations in Africa
26 Not built
27 Final British-built aircraft to fly
28 Built as 401-404 by Rombac
29 Built as 405-409 by Rombac
30 475 series freighter, incomplete in Romania, fate not known
31 560 series, incomplete in Romania, fate not known

Appendix 6

Chronology the of BAC One-Eleven

1956–1960	Initial studies by Hunting into twin-jet P107
January 1960	British Aircraft Corporation formed
May 1960	BAC takes over Hunting Aircraft and 107 studies
March 1961	Decision to use the Rolls-Royce Spey
March 1961	Vickers VC11 abandoned in favour of the BAC One-Eleven
9 May 1961	BAC One-Eleven launched with an order for ten aircraft from British United
October 1961	Braniff initial order for six aircraft
December 1961	BAC 107, a smaller version of the One-Eleven dropped
April 1963	Douglas DC-9 launched
May 1963	300/400 series announced
July 1963	American Airlines announce an order for fifteen aircraft
28 July 1963	Roll out of the prototype – G-ASHG
20 August 1963	First flight of the prototype
22 October 1963	Crash of prototype and death of crew on Salisbury Plain
19 December 1963	First flight of the first production aircraft, G-ASJA
18 March 1964	Crash of the second production aircraft, G-ASJB at Wisley
20 August 1964	Forced landing of the fourth production aircraft, G-ASJD on Salisbury Plain
19 February 1965	Boeing 737 launched
25 February 1965	Douglas DC-9 first flight
5 April 1965	British Certificate of Airworthiness awarded to the 200 series
9 April 1965	First service, British United flight Gatwick to Genoa
16 April 1965	Federal Aviation Administration Certification
13 May 1965	First flight of the prototype 400 series – G-ASYD
22 November 1965	Federal Aviation Administration Certification of the 400 series
29 November 1965	Douglas DC-9 first service
6 March 1966	First 400 series service by American Airlines
27 January 1967	BAC One-Eleven 500 series launched
9 April 1967	First flight of the Boeing 737

30 June 1967	First flight of the prototype 500 series – G-ASYD
2 February 1968	First flight of the first production 500 series – G-AVMH
15 August 1968	British Certificate of Airworthiness awarded to the 500 series
1 September 1968	First 500 series service by BEA
January 1970	BAC One-Eleven 475 series launched
27 August 1970	First flight of the prototype 475 series – G-ASYD
September 1971	Certification for rough field operation for 475 series
15 September 1971	First 475 series service by Faucett
29 April 1977	Formation of the nationalised British Aerospace from BAC and Hawker Siddeley Aviation
13 September 1977	First flight of the prototype 670 series – G-ASYD
June 1978	Licence production of the BAC One-Eleven agreed between British Aerospace and the Romanian Government
18 September 1982	First flight of a Romanian-built One-Eleven from Baneasa – YR-BRA
9 May 1984	Final first flight of a British-built One-Eleven from Hurn – G-BLHD
28 January 1986	Launch of Tay re-engining programme by Dee Howard
April 1989	Final first flight of a Romanian-built One-Eleven from Baneasa – YR-BRI
2 July 1990	First flight of the first Tay One-Eleven from San Antonio – N650DH
July 1991	First flight of the second Tay One-Eleven from San Antonio – N333GB
17 November 1991	Last flight of the first Tay One-Eleven – N650DH
26 November 1991	Last flight of the second Tay One-Eleven – N333GB
7 July 1993	British Aerospace withdraws from Licence agreement with Romania
14 July 1994	Last flight of G-ASYD – Filton to Brooklands
31 March 2002	End of One-Eleven commercial operations in Europe and North America because lack of compliance with Stage 3 noise regulations

Appendix 7

Preserved One-Elevens

G-ASYD – Series 670AM. Former series 400, 500, 475 and 670 prototype donated by BAe Airbus to Brooklands Museum. Last flight 14 July 1994, Filton to Brooklands captained by John Fawcett with John Lewis and Flight Observer Robin Morton. Preserved in BAe colours with 'Fly by light technology' titling.

Weybridge assembled thirteen One-Elevens between 1966 and 1970. The last of these was D-ANNO, (c/n 160) a series 414, originally intended for TAE of Spain and seen here in that livery in one of the large assembly halls built for VC10s. It was sold before delivery to Bavaria Fluggesellschaft and on 19 December 1970 made its first flight. This was the final first flight of the many aircraft completed at this famous site. *(BAE SYSTEMS)*

G-AVMO – Series 510ED. Formerly with BEA and BA. Preserved in BA colours. Delivered to RAF Museum, Cosford on 22 March 1993 and transferred to the Museum of Flight East Fortune in September 2006.

G-AVMU – Series 510ED. Formerly with BEA and BA. Preserved in BA colours. Delivered to Imperial War Museum, Duxford on 4 March 1993.

XX919 – Series 402AP. Front fuselage only. Formerly with Philippines Airlines. Then 1974 to the RAE Farnborough and later DERA Boscombe Down. During June 2000 most of the aircraft was scrapped but the front fuselage was saved for the new Boscombe Down Museum, and now resides undercover though bereft of many parts.

ZH763 – Series 539GL. Formerly with BA. Sold to GEC Ferranti in 1991 but transferred to QinetiQ and used for radar research. Last flight from Boscombe Down to Newquay on 26 April 2013 to join Classic Air Force Collection.

Appendix 8

One-Eleven Test Pilots

A large number of BAC/BAe pilots were involved in testing of the One-Eleven. This list though not exhaustive, provides details of eight test pilots frequently mentioned in the text.

Jock Bryce, Chief Test Pilot, BAC from 1961–65 captained G-ASHG on her maiden flight on 20 August 1963. He also made the first flight of the first production One-Eleven in December 1964, but had to retire from flying in 1965 after having flown approximately seventy-five hours on the type.

As Chief Test Pilot of Vickers-Armstrongs from 1951–61 he made the first flights of the Viscount 700, Valiant B.2, Viscount 800, Vanguard and the VC10. Jock co-piloted the Valiant prototype on its first flight with the legendary Mutt Summers from the then grass strip at Wisley in 1951. He had a fortunate escape ejecting from the prototype Valiant when it caught fire flying from Hurn on 16 January 1952.

Mike Lithgow was the One-Eleven Senior Project Pilot who co-piloted the prototype's maiden flight and captained her on her last fatal flight. Succeeding Jeffrey Quill as Chief Test Pilot of Vickers-Supermarine in 1948 he test flew the Attacker, made the prototype flights of the Swift and Scimitar and briefly held the World Speed Record in 1953. With the incorporation of Vickers-Supermarine into Vickers-Armstrongs he became Deputy Chief Test Pilot of the latter.

In *Mach One*, his autobiography published in 1954, Lithgow described his career; first as an RN pilot, flying from the *Ark Royal* with a Swordfish squadron to attack the *Bismark* and then his great fortune in being rescued by the aircraft carrier, HMS *Formidable*, in 1942 after twelve hours in the water. Interestingly, he also wrote of the need for fully powered controls rather than aerodynamically operated ones – which might have saved him and the One-Eleven test crew.

Brian Trubshaw was one of Britain's most famous test pilots who flew with the King's Flight and joined Vickers-Armstrongs in 1950. He was closely involved in the Valiant, Viscount and Vanguard and VC10 test programmes becoming Vickers-Armstrongs Chief Test Pilot in 1961.

His coolness in saving Britain's prototype VC-10 from disaster on 31 December 1963 won him the Derry and Richards Memorial Medal for 'outstanding test flying contributing to the advance of aviation' in 1965. Structural failure had been threatened when an elevator section broke loose and the aircraft shook 'as though the tail was shaking the dog'. Trubshaw could not read the instruments because of the violent motion, but broadcast to base the nature of the trouble in case he could not get back. He then managed to land the aircraft with only half the elevator control. He later described this manoeuvre as 'one of my trickier moments'. Three years earlier, Trubshaw had been awarded the same medal for his work on the Valiant jet bomber.

In 1964, he took over the management of the One-Eleven testing and made the first flight of the 500 series. In 1966, he became General Manager of Flight Operations for the Weybridge and Filton's Divisions and so was lead British pilot for Concorde. He made the maiden flight of the British prototype G-BSST in 1969 and led the programme to its successful conclusion in 1980. He retired in 1986 and died on 25 March 2001.

Dave Glaser joined the RAF in 1939 and served with 65 Squadron in the Battle of Britain. He graduated from the ETPS in 1949 and joined Vickers in 1953 where he did much of the Varsity, Viscount, Valiant and One-Eleven production testing. (Roy Radford commented that Dave's production testing was always to an exacting standard, airlines knew that when their airliner was delivered that it would be snag-free.) With the setting up of ROMBAC in 1979, he was appointed Flight Operations Manager and Test Pilot Instructor. He retired in 1983 and died in 2001.

Roy Radford joined the RAF in 1946, becoming a fighter pilot. He was an instructor at the Central Flying School and then an instructor on Valiants and Victors. He studied at the ETPS in 1957, winning the MacKenna Trophy. From 1960–64 he was with the transport and bomber test squadron at Boscombe Down, ultimately becoming senior pilot.

In 1964, he joined BAC, becoming the One-Eleven project pilot. He co-piloted the first flight of 'SYD as a 500 series, made the first flight of G-AVMH, first production 500, and led all the testing and subsequent development of the project including the first flight of 'SYD as a 475 and as a 670 series. On G-ASYD, Roy made 191 flights with it as a 400 series, 298 as a 500 and 413 as a 475/670 series; 802 flights altogether.

After his work on the One-Eleven he became a member of the Concorde team and took over from Trubshaw as BAe Commercial Aircraft Division Chief Test Pilot in 1981. Roy served in this post, test-flying the VC10 Tanker conversions until 1985; he then became Flight Operations Manager, retiring from BAe in 1989.

Peter Baker spent fifteen years with the RAF studying at the ETPS in 1953 and was also a tutor there in 1957. On leaving the RAF he joined Handley Page, mainly test flying Victors. While flying a Victor he had to use a tail parachute to recover from an uncontrollable spin – the bomber descending almost vertically as if hanging from the parachute which was later jettisoned allowing a safe return to base. He joined BAC in December 1963 and captained the maiden flight of G-ASYD in 1965. He later became one of BAC's Concorde test pilots and then Chief Test Pilot of the CAA (Civil Aviation Authority).

Johnnie Walker joined the RAF in 1948 and studied at the ETPS in 1954. In 1957, he was seconded to Fokker to help with Hunter testing, later testing the F-27 Friendship and Fokker-built F104 Starfighters. He joined BAC at Wisley in 1963 where he tested and trained customers on the BAC One-Eleven, graduating to the Concorde project in 1966. He did much work on the Concorde simulator, trained BA crews, overseas demonstrations with Trubshaw and testing in South Africa. He worked for various airlines between 1977 and 1989, when he was asked to test the Tay One-Eleven for Dee Howard, at San Antonio in Texas.

John Lewis served with the RAF from 1955–72 flying Canberras and piston trainers and graduating from the ETPS in 1967. John joined Rolls-Royce at Filton in 1972 flying the VFW 614 and many other types, becoming Chief Test Pilot in 1981. Subsequently he joined BAe Filton and was Chief Test Pilot from 1987–93 flying VC10 tankers and the adaptive control laws on One-Eleven G-ASYD. In 1990 he led the Tay One-Eleven test programme, making the first flight of the type and demonstrated it at Farnborough 1990. Chief Pilot of the Shuttleworth Trust from 1967–98, he has flown 13,800 hours on fixed wing, tilt wing, V/STOL and helicopters.

Appendix 9

Escape Hatches

Note provided by Chris King

The original forward escape hatches on the One-Eleven and the VC10 were of similar design concept. Essentially, a door held in place with explosive bolts replaced the freight door. On firing the bolts, levers on pre-tensioned torsion bars attached to the inside of the fuselage lowered the leading edge of the door into the airstream, which caused it to fly away. Any residual cabin pressure assisted the operation. There was a large duct, or trunking, fastened flush with the cabin floor and to the freight door surround for the crew to jump through. Within the duct was a spring-loaded blast shield that normally projected above the floor. It dropped down to project into the airflow on jettisoning the freight door. The function of the blast shield was to allow escapers to clear the fuselage and to progressively decelerate them to the speed of the airstream, rather than for the deceleration to be instantaneous. The duct and blast shield were of sheet metal skin, stringer and rib construction. The freight bays were sealed from the cabin, to be representative of production aircraft in this respect, so that associated flight and ground testing could be conducted. The escape drill was to depressurise the cabin before firing the escape hatch.

During the incident on the prototype VC10, G-ARTA, on 31 December 1963, the behaviour of the aircraft was rather alarming so the escape hatch was fired at full cabin differential pressure, around 8 p.s.i., in case the aircraft broke up before the crew could escape. Consequently, the duct in the freight bay and the cabin floor had to instantaneously withstand this differential pressure because the freight bays were not vented. This resulted in the escape chute being crushed and much of it tore out of the aircraft. Moreover, many areas of the cabin floor buckled, including the floor beams, which contained the flying control cable runs.

Following the G-ARTA incident, it was recognised that there could well be circumstances where there would be insufficient time to depressurise the cabin before needing to escape. To overcome these problems, all test One-Elevens with escape facilities, subsequent to G-ASHG, had beefed up escape chutes; i.e. G-ASJA, G-ASJC, G-ASJD and G-ASYD. (G-ASJB was scheduled to undertake performance and crew training, and therefore did not need escape facilities due to the low risk nature of testing, though she did have a rear escape hatch). Constructing the escape chute and the blast deflector from thick (approx. 1.5"), high density and multi-laminate plywood did this. Moreover, front and rear freight bays were adequately vented to the passenger cabin. Indeed Concorde's facilities were similar to the modified One-Eleven system.

A lever was added outboard of the co-pilot's seat which mechanically opened the pressurisation control valve to rapidly depressurise the cabin so the door in the rear pressure bulkhead could be opened to give access to the escape hatch in the rear ventral door.

Bibliography

Books & Publications

Aircraft Accident Report no. 1/92 G-BJRT, HMSO, 1992

Brian Trubshaw Test Pilot, Brian Trubshaw & Sally Edmondson, Sutton Publishing, 1998

The British Aircraft Corporation, Charles Gardner, Batsford, 1981

British Airways, Keith Gaskell, Airlife, 1999

Civil Aircraft Accident Report 219 G-ASHG, HMSO, 1965

Civil Aircraft Accident Report 222 G-ASJD, HMSO, 1965

Evolution of a Workhorse – the BAC One-Eleven, John Prothero Thomas – Lecture, 1985

Flying to the Sun, Geoffrey Cuthbert, Hodder & Stoughton, 1987

Fly Me, I'm Freddie, Roger Eglin & Berry Ritchie, Weidenfeld & Nicholson, 1980

Mach One, Mike Lithgow, Allan Wingate, 1954

Handling the Big Jets, D.P. Davies, CAA, 1979

Market Survey for the Tay One-Eleven, Andy Hofton, Cranfield Institute of Technology, 1986

Project Cancelled, Derek Wood, Tri-Service Press, 1990

Test Pilots, Don Middleton, Collins, 1985

Test of Character, Don Middleton, Airlife, 1995

The One-Eleven Story, Richard Church, Air-Britain, 1994

The Rolls-Royce Tay Engine and the BAC One-Eleven, Ken Goddard, Rolls-Royce Historical Trust, 2000

Testing Years, Roland Beamont, Ian Allan, 1980

Vapour Trails, ed. Mike Lithgow, Allan Wingate, 1956

Vickers Aircraft, C.F. Andrews & E.B. Morgan, Putman, 1988

Magazines

Aeroplane

Air International

Air Pictorial
Flight International

Interviews
Dave Glaser, former Test Pilot, BAC/BAe, 21/9/99
Roy Radford, former Chief Test Pilot, BAe Filton, 31/8/01
Chris King, former Senior Flight Test Observer, Chief Flight Test Engineer BAe Inc.
     4/11/01
Johnnie Walker former Test Pilot BAC/BAe, 4/11/01
John Prothero Thomas, former BAC Director of Marketing, 7/10/01
Ken Dyer, Commercial Manager, European Aviation, 2/11/01
John Lewis former Chief Test Pilot BAe Filton, 2/01/02
Heinz Vogel former Chief Aerodynamicist One-Eleven, 19/3/02
Peter Baker former Test Pilot, BAC/BAe, 28/3/02

Correspondence
Ken Goddard, former Rolls-Royce Tay Project Engineer
Bill Hurley, former Dee Howard Director of Flight Test and Certification

Archives
Aircraft Accidents Investigation Branch Reports: G-ASJB
Bournemouth Daily Echo Library 1963–1984
Brooklands Museum Photo Archives
Brooklands Museum Technical Archives
BAC/BAe publications 1961–1980
Dee Howard publications
The Times

Flights (on the flight deck courtesy of European Aviation)
European Aviation One-Eleven, G-AWYV: Hurn-Alicante-Hurn – 6/10/01
European Aviation One-Eleven, G-AZMF: Hurn-Turin-Hurn – 30/12/01

Index